GARDEN DESIGN

HISTORY · PRINCIPLES · ELEMENTS · PRACTICE

Introduction by John Brookes

William Lake Douglas
Susan R. Frey
Norman K. Johnson
Susan Littlefield
Michael Van Valkenburgh

With the Publication Board of the American Society of Landscape Architects

Principal Photographer: Derek Fell

A Fireside Book
Published by Simon & Schuster, Inc.
New York   London   Toronto   Sydney   Tokyo   Singapore

A FRIEDMAN GROUP BOOK

First Fireside Edition, 1987
Published by Simon & Schuster, Inc.
Simon & Schuster Building
Rockefeller Center
1230 Avenue of the Americas
New York, New York 10020

FIRESIDE and colophon are registered trademarks of
Simon & Schuster, Inc.

3 5 7 9 10 8 6 4

Library of Congress Cataloging in Publication Data
Main entry under title:
Garden design.
Bibliography: p.
Includes index.
1. Gardens—Design. I. Douglas, William Lake.
SB473.G288 1984   712'.6   84-1319

ISBN 0-671-47993-8
0-671-49592-5 Pbk.

GARDEN DESIGN
was prepared and produced by
Michael Friedman Publishing Group, Inc., 15 West 26th Street,
New York, New York 10010

Editor: Bill Logan
Art Director/Designer: Richard Boddy
Layouts: Katharine Wodell
Editorial Assistant: Mary Forsell
Photo Research: Nora Humphrey

Typeset by BPE Graphics, Inc.
Color separations by Hong Kong Scanner Craft Company Ltd.
Printed and bound in Hong Kong by Leefung-Asco Printers Ltd.

ABOUT THE AUTHORS

JOHN BROOKES is the author of numerous garden volumes, including *The Small Garden* and *The Garden Book*. He is a leading British garden designer.

WILLIAM LAKE DOUGLAS is a Harvard-educated landscape architect who writes regularly for *Landscape Architecture*.

DEREK FELL, the principal photographer, is a well-known garden photographer and writer whose gorgeous photos appear regularly in *Architectural Digest*.

SUSAN R. FREY is editor-in-chief of *Landscape Architecture* and *Garden Design* magazines.

NORMAN K. JOHNSON is founding editor of *Garden Design* magazine. He is also a prolific author and a practicing garden designer.

SUSAN LITTLEFIELD is a landscape architect employed by A.E. Bye. She has written numerous articles on gardens for major publications and is currently at work on a garden book for Stewart, Tabori & Chang.

MICHAEL VAN VALKENBURGH is a leading landscape architect who teaches at the Harvard Graduate School of Design.

CONTENTS

CONTENTS

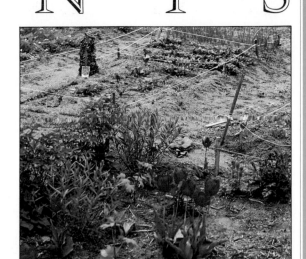

INTRODUCTION

Gardens are a reflection of the age in which they are created. The successful ones are a synthesis of the conditions of their time: their style is determined by function—whether medieval seclusion, seventeenth-century show, eighteenth-century contemplation, or nineteenth-century horticulture—and by the manner in which their functional form is realized. The style of a garden is then tempered by the way in which it is built, based on the materials available at the time. In earlier gardens the thought behind a garden's plan seems quite clear, for everyone knew their place in society and everyone knew what was expected of them by way of building. Indeed, before rapid transportation, you could *only* use local materials. So the gardens that were built seem very much "all of a piece" with the house that they served. With the mellowing of time these gardens have retained a quiet charm that is remarkable. It should also be remembered that it is only the best gardens that remain; dozens have perished. For gardening is actually a transitory art: The good ones remain because they worked; and like a well-tailored suit, they go on forever.

Gardening art in the latter part of the twentieth-century is much more cosmopolitan, but as in every other age it is a reflection of the social mores of the day. Our thought processes have been tempered by psychology, our taste molded by the media, and our ambitions broadened by travel.

We are hounded to keep fit, badgered to decorate, and coerced into filling every waking minute with climbing, camping, canoeing, skiing, or snorkeling in some part of the world other than home. And into this mishmash of divergent demands, we try to fit a working day. Somewhere along the line, when we do come to rest, we try to make a garden which, if well conceived, might help us to fulfill at least one or two of these pressing demands in a relaxed and pleasant fashion.

Alternatively, we dream up a garden to escape the rigors of our society. But in what style should it be? French, Italian, English, antibellum American? Since most people know little about garden style, the result is a little of each, contrived to fulfill our new-found interest in organic food too!

But you may also choose to design a garden for yourself, in a manner tailored to your own lifestyle in the latter part of the twentieth-century, realized in a material to suit your home and fitting into the harmony of your regional landscape. Do your *own* thing, in fact, not a pastiche of someone else's. Such a philosophy, however, presupposes that you are prepared to sit down and admit to yourself what you really *do* want and, tempering this with what you really *do* need, clear your mind of all sorts of preconceived romantic ideals. When you have a basic working form, you can then superimpose the less practical romantic ideals.

This book and its examples are intended to help you rationalize your thought processes and at the same time utilize your romantic ones. It goes on to help you realize your dream garden in a logical manner and interpret the planting of it according to your location.

The planting of the garden comes last, you will notice, after the structural bones have been laid down, their forms and shapes extending the design intention. New garden owners go wrong in buying their plants too early in the design process, for while plants give the bulk to a garden, they also give a third dimension to a two-dimensional plan. Seen in this light a garden is not unlike a huge piece of abstract sculpture where the voids or holes are balanced by their surround. In the garden you may feel comfortable when the bulky areas of planting hold the open spaces of grass or paving in balance. Too little bulk leaves you feeling exposed. The content of that bulk, which is the horticulturist's preoccupation, comes later in the design process.

There is an enormous new interest in garden history; and when styles can be recognized, gardens can be restored to their former glory. But society changes, and we are ourselves a part of future garden history. It would be satisfying to think that the gardens we create today would warrant comment as an expression of *their* time too.

The garden examples of which this book forms so much a part are case histories of classic and contemporary layouts, each evolved for a particular client in a particular place to extend a particular home. Study them carefully and then transpose any idea you like to your own situation. This way you will give a unique flavor to your own particular lot, and to paraphrase William Kent of the seventeenth century, you will become the genius of your own particular place.

JOHN BROOKES
West Sussex, England

CHAPTER ONE

A GARDEN PROGRESS

by William Lake Douglas

PROLOGUE • IN THE BEGINNING • ANCIENT EGYPT • GREECE
ROME • ISLAMIC INFLUENCES • ORIENTAL GARDEN ARTS
MEDIEVAL EUROPE • RENAISSANCE PROGRESS
THE FRENCH IDEA • THE ENGLISH LANDSCAPE GARDEN
OLD WORLD INFLUENCES IN THE NEW WORLD
NINETEENTH CENTURY ROMANTICISM
THE ENGLISH FLOWER GARDEN • THE TWENTIETH CENTURY

PROLOGUE

God Almighty first planted a Garden. And indeed it is the purest of human pleasures. It is the greatest refreshment to the spirits of man; without which buildings and palaces are but gross handyworks: and a man shall ever see that when ages grow to civility and elegancy, men come to build stately sooner than to garden finely; as if gardening were the greater perfection.

Sir Francis Bacon, "Of Gardens," 1620

The history of garden design is like a tapestry that covers every culture from early civilizations to the present time. The fabric is the product of many influences: natural features, religious beliefs, philosophical theories, scientific and technological advances, and the desire to improve one's immediate environment, making it more pleasant and productive and practical.

Throughout history, the components of gardens (plants that flower and bear fruit, shade for protection from the elements, water that cools the atmosphere and irrigates the land, man-made objects for delight and interest) remain constant, regardless of the geographical location of a garden or its cultural history. It is the great variety of natural phenomena (geography, climate, plant material, topography) and cultural influences (religion, architectural theories, functional determinants) that make gardens different. To study these differences is to follow the progress of garden design. To understand these differences is to gain an appreciation for how man has altered and been altered by—his physical surroundings.

Flowers for fragrance and beauty and fruit for the table are two of the most basic garden ingredients, and they can be combined to suit any number of settings and styles. A meadow of blue cornflowers, Centaurea cyanus, and a solitary apple tree are the elements of a simple, straightforward garden for an open, uncultivated-looking landscape.

IN THE BEGINNING

One third of the whole is city, one third is garden, and one third is field.

Description of the city-state Erech, in the Tigris-Euphrates basin, from the Epic of Gilgamesh c.2000 B.C.

I made gardens in the upper and in the lower town, with the earth's produce from the mountains and the countries round about, all the spices from the land of the Hittites, myrrh (which grows better in my gardens than in its native land), vines from the hills, fruits from every country; spices and Sirdu-trees I have planted for my subjects. Moreover, I have cut down and leveled mountain and field . . . so that plants may thrive there, and I have made a canal, one and a half hour's journey from the Chusur river have I brought water to flow in my canal. . . . I have set a pond in the garden . . . and in it I have planted reeds. . . . By the grace of the gods the gardens prospered, vines and fruit, Sirdu-wood and spices. They grew tall and flourished greatly, trees, and reeds also . . . palms, cypresses, and the fruits of trees.

Sennacherib, 705–681 B.C.

Tracing the roots of garden design leads to information from theological traditions and archeological sources. While references from the former are subject to interpretation, evidence from the latter is more specific.

The first garden most of us learn about is the Garden of Eden. As described in Genesis, it was a place with perpetually blooming trees and a constant, mild climate where "everything that is pleasant to the sight and good for food" grew. Specifics of the design of the Garden of Eden, as well as its exact location, have been a source of controversy for centuries. Named as the source of four rivers (the Pison, Gihon, Hiddekel [Tigris], and the Euphrates), the Garden of Eden is traditionally located in the area between the Tigris and Euphrates rivers. Rather than being concerned with the design or spatial organization of the Garden of Eden, early Christian interpretations were more concerned with the events in the garden (man's fall from grace and subsequent expulsion from the garden) and their consequences (woman's pain in childbirth and man's necessity for hard work to make the land productive). Medieval theologians postulated that expulsion from an earthly paradise was engineered by a merciful God to prepare man for an eternal paradise in heaven.

To the translators of the Old Testament, the words "garden," "park," and "paradise" were all synonymous. It is significant that in most ancient civilizations and religions, the life hereafter and the place of eternal happiness are depicted as gardens. In the ancient cultures, the basic ingredients of the earthly paradise are the same: plants that flower and fruit, shade that protects, and water that cools and irrigates.

Archeological evidence indicates that the first literate civilization—that of the Sumerians—developed in the basin of the Tigris and Euphrates rivers. Although the landscape surrounding these unpredictable rivers was harsh, by 3500 B.C. the Sumerians had developed a stable, orderly society based on agricultural production. Systems of canals drained the swamps and regulated water from the rivers, providing flood control, irrigation, and a means of trade and transport. By 2250 B.C. the Sumerian Empire was established. It was succeeded by Babylonia, with Babylon as its capital.

The legendary Hanging Gardens of Babylon, one of the Seven Wonders of the World, were built about 600 B.C. by King Nebuchadnezzar. Although no remains have been found, the Gardens' design was probably the combination of an agricultural method (growing plants on terraced hillsides) and an architectural monument (the temple tower or ziggurat). Composed of diminishing terraces built on a large platform, the ziggurat was a symbolic connection between heaven and earth. Greek accounts from the first century A.D. indicate that the Hanging Gardens were rectangular, but these accounts are inconclusive. Waterproofed terraces were supported by arches that held irrigation equipment, and hollow brick columns were filled with soil and planted with trees. From a distance, it appeared to be a green mountain.

Archeological evidence shows that a similar system was used on a smaller scale in some Mesopotamian cities. Rows of narrow pits set into rooftops were planted with a variety of specimen plants, forming gardens that were probably the world's first urban roof gardens. The plantings were associated with the cult of the god Tammuz, or Dummuzi, whose cult was later imported to Greece where similar gardens—known to have included flowering plants like the rose—were grown.

From the Assyrian civilization in northern Mesopotamia comes the concept of an enclosed park, developed for the amusement of the rulers and stocked with both animals and plants from distant lands. Small temples were built on existing hilltops or constructed mounds, the prototype perhaps for medieval garden mounts.

From the Sumerian and Assyrian civilizations there is evidence of the organization of the landscape and the development of technology to realize the garden designs. There was the beginning of an understanding of the environment, and practical efforts were made to mitigate adverse conditions. Outdoor spaces were important for both utilitarian reasons and social-ceremonial events.

Paradise depicted as a lush tropical jungle in an eighteenth-century rendition of Adam and Eve being driven from the Garden of Eden. Painted by an unknown Mexican artist. From the Philadelphia Museum of Art, Robert W. Lamborn Collection.

ANCIENT EGYPT

May I wander round my pool each day for evermore; may my soul sit on the branches of the grave garden I have prepared for myself; may I refresh each day under my sycamore.

Tomb inscription

Although there are no extant examples of ancient Egyptian gardens, more is known about them than about gardens in many other ancient civilizations. Wall paintings, hieroglyphics, and sculptural reliefs give a thorough understanding of how the ancient Egyptians successfully mitigated adverse effects of climate and topography and took advantage of positive environmental conditions.

The most detailed view of an ancient Egyptian garden comes from a wall painting found in Thebes. It represents the garden of a high official who served under Amenhotep III (1411–1372 B.C.), and its components indicate wealth and a refined sense of order. As in other Egyptian illustrations, front, back, side, and aerial views are all combined in one picture. Buried with its owner, the illustration depicts the pleasures of this world to ensure their continuance in the next life. Examination reveals a walled garden adjacent to a canal. Entry is gained through an imposing gatehouse into a bilaterally symmetrical space, with vineyards, orchards, water tanks, and garden pavilions. This residence, on axis with the gate, does not dominate the garden but is an integral part of the composition. Highly structured, the garden's design is primarily functional: High walls keep out desert winds and wild animals, the canal brings water for irrigation, the vines produce grapes for wine, the trees produce shade as well as fruit (dates, figs, pomegranates), and the water tanks hold both fish and ducks.

Another wall painting, from the Tomb of Minnakhte, in Thebes (c. 1475 B.C.) depicts a funeral scene in a garden and shows many of the same features: bilateral symmetry, alternating plantings of trees, a house with smaller structures in the garden, and a pool of water (where a boat bearing the owner's coffin lies at anchor).

Plant material in ancient Egypt provided inspiration for architectural detail as well as interior decoration. Columns are carved to represent papyrus and lotus plants; flowers are used to cover interior walls and floors.

In the Egyptian civilization, we see the beginning of important garden traditions: the use of axis for structure and order, the use of plants for specific functions (food, shade, decoration), and the knowledge that the natural environment can add drama and significance to a structure.

A temple garden at Thebes, as depicted in a tomb painting from the fifteenth century B.C., included vines trained on an arbor, palms, and a water garden. From the Egyptian Expedition of the Metropolitan Museum of Art.

GREECE

Their fruit never fails nor runs short, winter and summer alike, it comes at all seasons of the year, and there is never a time when the West Wind's breath is not assisting, here the bud, and here the ripening fruit; so that pear after pear, apple after apple, cluster on cluster of grapes, and fig upon fig are always coming to their perfections.

Homer, describing the garden of Alcinoüs, from The Odyssey

By the sixth century B.C., city-states had developed in Greece. They were linked with each other, as well as with other cultures in the ancient world, by commercial and maritime exchange. While the Greeks contributions to architecture, sculpture, science, and literature are unequaled in the ancient world, their traditions of garden design are little known.

The main reason for this is the paucity of existing records, but

The Dodoni theater illustrates the Greek genius for choosing dramatic sites for their buildings: the theater commands a panoramic view down a narrow valley, and its bowl-like form echoes the opening in the distant hills. The flat, fertile plain is reserved primarily for agriculture, just as it probably was in the days of the ancient Greeks.

Ruins at Delphi suggest a carefully organized sequence from exterior to interior space, articulated by changes in level and by passage through a colonnaded arcade.

Many scenes in nineteenth-century gardens were inspired by classical ruins like the ones at Delphi and by the relationship that the Greeks established between buildings and landscape.

there are two possible, additional explanations. First, the landscape of Greece, one of mountains and hills, with thin, rocky soil, is not particularly suited to extensive garden developments. Second, the Greeks' polytheistic religion assigned significance to all natural phenomena: To interfere with the pervading spirit of the natural surroundings—the *genius loci*—was to disturb the environment of the gods. For these reasons, their lasting contribution to design on the land lies in the dramatic siting of temples and shrines.

Greek temples, expressions of the logical search for perfection through geometry, took advantage of rather than dominated their sites. The location for temples and shrines corresponded to the domain of the deity honored, and there was often a special affinity between these structures and their sites, since stones were frequently carved directly from the site.

Gardens in ancient Greece were both domestic (courtyards with potted plants, small fruit orchards) and civic (public squares, academies). The courtyard gardens were often dedicated to the cult of Adonis, a kind of ritual gardening inherited from Mesopotamia. Plato appreciated that an ordered landscape was conducive

to education and is thought to have conducted classes in his own garden. The marketplace of Greek cities—the agora—became the center for public meetings and discussions. With the introduction of trees into these spaces, they became public parks.

An interest in natural science led to an appreciation for native wildflowers and the use of garlands for holidays and festivals. Theophrastus (c.372–c.287 B.C.) had an extensive garden and wrote a ten-volume history of plants. In the first century A.D., the physician Dioscorides, who traveled with the Roman armies, compiled an herbal, *De Materia Medica*, describing over 400 European plants, which remained an important source book well into the Middle Ages.

From the Greek civilization we get the tradition of using outdoor spaces for special functions (the public park, the sacred grove, the athletic field), the careful and logical placement of buildings in a site, the use of proportion in architecture, and the beginning of a scientific study of plants. These traditions strongly influenced the Romans when they adapted Greek customs to their own culture, leading to a rich and varied garden style.

ROME

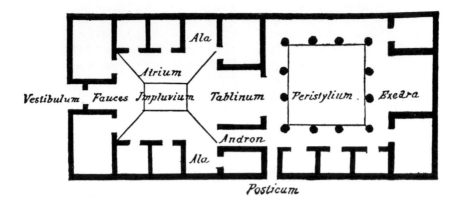

The greatest Part of the House is turn'd to the South and in the Summer from the sixth Hour, but in the Winter somewhat sooner, does as it were invite the Sun into a spacious well-proportioned Porticus. In which are several Parts; and an Atrium after the ancient manner. Before the Porticus is a Xystus cut in several Forms, and divided by Box; descending the Forms of Beasts fronting the opposite Box: On the Flat grows the soft and I almost said liquid Acanthus. This is surrounded by an Ambulatio, which is enclosed by Greens cut in various forms: after this is a Gestatio in the form of a Circus, which encloses the many shaped Box, and Dwarf-trees that are rendered so by Art: the Whole is fenced by a Wall, which is overcast and hid by several degrees of Box. From thence you have the View of a Meadow not less beautiful by Nature, than these the fore-mentioned Works of Art: then you see Fields, with many other Meadows and Shrubs.

Pliny the Younger to Apollinaris, Book V, Epistle VI, from The Villas of the Ancients Illustrated, *Robert Castell, 1728*

The civilization of ancient Rome began as an agricultural one. As trade expanded, cities and towns were consolidated under one political jurisdiction, and by 125 A.D. the Roman Empire extended from Spain on the west to the Persian Gulf and the Caspian Sea on the east; from Hadrian's Wall in England on the north to Egypt in the south. Rome's location in the center of the Mediterranean region permitted convenient communication, commercial trade, and military access to all parts of the empire.

Like other artistic expressions, the garden traditions of the Roman Empire were an amalgam of the cultures absorbed by its growth. This assimilation of customs spread throughout the Roman Empire styles and techniques from other cultures, while at the same time leaving a distinctly Roman impression in all parts of the Empire.

The climate of Italy, with sunny skies and Mediterranean breezes, encourages outdoor living. Greek traditions of domestic architecture (living spaces organized around a central courtyard) were adapted and improved by the Romans. By combining indoor

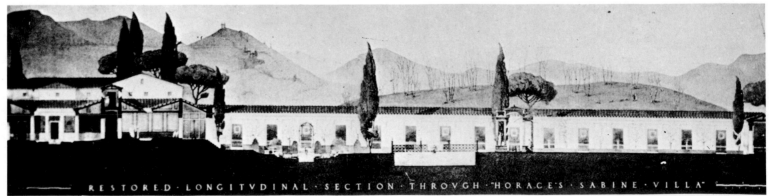

Top: *The plan of a Pompeiian house, showing the arrangement of rooms around central courtyards.* **Above:** *Horace's villa, built in the Sabine Hills between the third and fourth centuries* B.C., *framed the central axis of a formal garden.*

and outdoor spaces, the Romans were able to make their gardens logical extensions of their houses. Excavations in Pompeii and Herculaneum have revealed not only the design but also the content of these gardens. Courtyard gardens were a variety of shapes, filled with blooming and fragrant plants. Piped water systems fed fountains, jets, and pools, and basins held fish and collected rain water for irrigation. Bronze and marble statues of animals and mythological figures were frequent ornaments; paving was often executed in mosaics, depicting flowers, animals, or geometric patterns. Covered walkways or trellises with vines connected rooms and outdoor spaces. Inner walls were often painted with garden scenes or imaginary landscapes, thus eliminating the feeling of structural enclosure while increasing the conjunction of indoor and outdoor spaces. From these wall paintings, we can identify both plants and garden features.

With the emergence of a wealthy class, country villas became important as a means of escaping urban congestion. Pliny the Younger (c.62–113 A.D.) gives a detailed discussion of his villas (one for vacationing, one for farming) and describes gardening practices, principles of site planning, and the uses of plant material in great detail.

Another source of horticultural information of the period is Pliny the Elder's *Historia naturalis*. It gives a detailed discussion of what plants were grown in public and private gardens, and documents the common practice of clipping trees and shrubbery into fanciful shapes, a practice that emerged with renewed enthusiasm about 1500 years later.

In the Roman Empire, we see three important developments: Ornamental horticulture emerges as a separate pursuit, independent of functional agriculture; outdoor spaces are integrated with interior ones; and attention is given to the organization and maintenance of garden spaces purely for the pleasures they provide.

In Pompeii, the peristyle of the House of the Vettii was enclosed by a colonnade and the rooms of the surrounding house, but the ceiling was open to the air, creating a garden court where interior and exterior intermingle.

ISLAMIC INFLUENCE

In the garden is a small hillock, from which a stream of water. . . incessantly flows into the garden below. The four-fold field-plot of the garden is situated on this entrance. On the southwest part of this garden is a reservoir of water twenty feet [6 meters] square, which is wholly planted round with orange trees; there are likewise pomegranates. All around the piece of water the ground is quite covered with clover. This spot is the very eye of the beauty of the garden. At the time the orange becomes yellow the prospect is delightful.

The Emperor Babur's account of his garden Bagh-i-vafa (Garden of Fidelty), overlooking the Kabul River, Afghanistan, 1508

If the history of gardens were a giant tapestry, the influences from Islamic cultures would be a colorful thread that periodically emerges, disappears, and returns in a wide geographic area with slightly modified forms. Because the Islamic influence was widely distributed in a variety of climatic conditions and topographical situations—from Spain through the Near East into India—we see in these gardens the use of four basic elements (water, shade, color, and natural music) taking different expressions.

In much of the Islamic Empire, water was a precious commodity, and was therefore used sparingly, usually as a single jet or in a small linear channel faced with brightly colored tile. Shade was provided by trees, garden pavilions or tents, and covered passageways that connected indoor rooms with outdoor spaces. Colorful accents were provided by flowering plants and by the decorations of the architecture's exterior, which were geometric designs inlaid with colorful stones that sparkled in the sunlight. Music was provided by stationary musicians, splashing jets, caged birds, or mechanical instruments triggered by slight breezes. There were no statues in Islamic gardens (the Koran, like the Old Testament, forbids the making of graven images), yet there are references to trees made of gold, silver, and precious stones. In the garden of Tamerlane in Samarkand (late fourteenth and early fifteenth centuries) there was reportedly a 6-foot (1.8-meter) tree with leaves of silver and gold, and fruits of emeralds, rubies, diamonds, sapphires, and pearls.

Much of the information we have about Islamic gardens comes from the miniature paintings of the fifteenth and sixteenth centuries. As well as commemorating legends and activities of the rulers, they illustrate plant material, paving details, architectural features, and functions held in outdoor spaces. Another artistic expression inspired by Islamic garden traditions is the Persian carpet, which reflects the design of the garden and depicts the elements included: water, flowers, trees, and birds.

Islamic gardens generally preceded medieval European gardens, yet in Islamic gardens we see a sophistication and richness that does not occur in Europe until much later. The gardens of the Persian, Mogul, and Islamic empires share a religious heritage, intellectual philosophy, and environmental attitude that remain influential today. A direct line of influence runs from Persia and Islam, to Spain's Alhambra and Generalife, to the modern gardens of designers like Luis Barragán and Lawrence Halprin.

The Canal Garden of the Generalife in Granada makes the most of a limited water supply. Evergreens, vines, and flowers surround a long shallow pool rimmed with a double row of fine jets.

Above: *Brick channels run into a sunken pool at the Alhambra.* **Right:** *The source of the water is a grotto where horizontal troughs capture a rivulet before it spills into the channel below.*

ORIENTAL GARDEN ARTS

With its hills and pond this garden excelled in beauty many princely pleasure grounds. Here had been built up a number of hills...that look as if they had been formed by nature. Within these heights there were double peaks and curving ridges by the side of deep streams and valleys. There were plenty of tall, leafy trees which afforded protection against the rays of sun and moon, and hanging creepers which did not prevent the mist from creeping in. The paths ran zigzag up the hills and down the valleys.... The stony and curious water courses flowed in some places in winding bends and in other places straight on. Nature lovers were so captivated by this spot that they forgot to go home.

Description of a garden, Chang Lun, bequeathed to a monastery in return for a good place in heaven; from a Chronicle published in 547 A.D., Lo-Yang Chia Lang Chi

Eternity
And the pine trees on Tortoise Hill
Reflected in the clear waters
Of the palace pond

Thirteenth-century Japanese poem

Chinese garden traditions are rooted in an appreciation for the natural environment, emphasized by Confucius, Lao-tse, and Buddha, the founders of the three religions in China. Intimately connected with Chinese painting, the gardens of China were composed, like scroll paintings, as a series of views. It is from these paintings that we can gain an appreciation for Chinese gardens, because few historic examples remain today.

There were commercial links among ancient civilizations in the Mediterranean and China, but it was not until the return of Marco Polo (1295) that Western Europe became acquainted with the fantastic riches of the Orient. The characteristics of Chinese gardens that impressed European visitors were their scale (always intimate, whether the garden was actually large or small), their organization (never symmetrical but always natural), and their composition (always pictorial). Gardens always represented nature and included references to mountains, plants, and water. In both Chinese gardens and paintings, man is never dominant or supreme; rather he is a component—"one of ten thousand"—equal with other parts. Chinese philosophies taught that man would find his greatest pleasure in communion with nature and in

The temple garden at Ryoanji is a place for quiet meditation—a garden reduced to its most abstract essentials. Rocks set in moss and surrounded by swirls of raked sand have been compared to islands in the sea or mountain peaks above the mist.

contemplation of the many other elements of the natural world.

Chinese gardens were gardens of allusions. Components of the gardens—plants, water, bridges, structures, rocks—were arranged to suggest references and images from all aspects of Chinese cultural traditions. Garden-making involved not only an appreciation of nature but also the imagery of a poet and the perception of a painter. Cooperation among creative artists occurs periodically throughout the history of garden design, but only in China was the collaboration of poet, painter, and gardener the basis for fully realized artistic traditions that have lasted for centuries.

It was during the Ming Dynasty (1368–1644) that garden art of China achieved its highest development. Making gardens and cultivating flowers (one of the seven arts necessary to a man of culture) were seen as the way to align oneself with nature and thereby become immune from evil.

Cultivated, intelligent, and environmentally sensitive, the Chinese people derived profound pleasure from the simplest events in nature—the appearance of the full moon, the first peach blossom in spring, the fragrance of a peony—and Chinese gardens were designed to allow opportunities to experience these simple pleasures. Gardens were planned for every mood, occasion, and climatic condition, and they were used for intellectual meditation, environmental observation, and poetic contemplation.

Garden art was introduced into Japan by Buddhist monks from China. A collection of islands, Japan has always been a country with strong religious orientation, ingrained cultural traditions, and a deep respect for nature. Shinto, the primary religion, taught respect for the elements of the universe; early Japanese people worshiped environmental phenomena (the sun, rain, sea, earth, stones, mountains, etc.). All aspects of Japanese culture were strongly influenced by the Chinese, but a theoretical division occurs in the development of gardens.

The Japanese developed systems for garden design and affixed symbolic meanings to every component. Gardens were designed as a microcosm of everything in nature, and not, as in China, as small pieces of a larger composition. The *Sakuteiki,* written in the eleventh century, establishes strict rules for garden design. It discusses the movement of water, and describes ten different forms of waterfalls: linen-falling, thread falling, uneven falling, glide falling, straight falling, etc. Later writings address the qualities of stones (material, size, grouping and relationships, character, placement, etc.), the various categories of garden arrangement (the artificial hill garden *tsuki-yama;* the level garden, *hira-niwa;* and later, the tea garden, *cha-seki*), and the degree of refinement possible (elaborate, *shin;* intermediate, *gyo,* and simple, *so*). Within each category are further rules and basic features. The *shin/gyo/so* system covers components of the garden, as well as entire gardens. Four main garden styles developed: the dry rock, *kare-sansui;* the water garden, *sen-tei;* the literary men's garden, *bunjin-zukuri;* and the tea garden, *cha-niwa.*

In the dry rock garden, large rocks, gravel, and sand are symbolically arranged to represent water and land forms. No trees

Fruit trees and a walled garden in a Chinese rendition of the Land of the Immortals. Nelson-Atkins Museum of Art, Kansas City, MO.

or plants (other than mosses) are used. The abstract composition of this garden type (Ryoanji is the best example) is designed for meditation and contemplation. Water gardens vary in size and are designed to be appreciated from one view, or through a progression around and over the water. Details of rocks and plant placement are carefully resolved, to present compositional variety from different points of observation. The literary men's garden is simple, tranquil, and small. The tea garden is planned to serve as an entrance path for the tea ceremony and symbolically represents the virtues of restraint, politeness, sensibility, and modesty.

Even small spaces are given careful attention in Japan. A common technique of increasing the apparent size of a garden is *shakkei,* "borrowed scenery," which involves including views of distant landscapes into garden settings. The small-space garden evolved into today's *tsuboniwa,* or courtyard garden. In urban areas, these may be no larger than a vestibule, but they afford a taste of tranquillity in the midst of urban life.

From Japanese gardens we can learn to appreciate attention to detail: the placement of rocks, the pattern of shadows, the relationship of plants to each other, and the symbolic association of garden components. In Japanese gardens all objects—plants, rocks, sand, laterns, water—are appreciated for their intrinsic qualities as well as for the metaphorical association they carry—a forest, a mountain range, the ocean. Although it may not be immediately obvious to the casual observer, the position of all these components is governed by strict rules of composition.

It is a lack of understanding for this symbolic organization that makes Western imitations of Japanese gardens less than successful. An appreciation of this approach to garden design can add a great deal to a garden, and this metaphorical significance can enhance the basic elements of any garden.

MEDIEVAL EUROPE

This yard was large and railed all the alleys
And shadowed well with blossy boughs green
And benched new, and sanded all the ways,
In which she walketh arm and arm in between.
Chaucer, Troilus and Criseyde, c. 1385

This garden full of leaves and flowers
And craft of man's hand so curiously
Arrayed had this garden, truly,
That never was there garden of such prys
But if it were the very paradise.
The odor of flowers and the frech site
Would have made any heart for to light. . . .
So full was it of beauty with pleasance,
At after dinner gone they to dance,
And sing also. . . .
Chaucer, "The Franklin's Tale," c. 1386–1400

Though a life of retreat offers various joys,
None, I think, will compare with the time one employs
In the study of herbs, or in striving to gain
Some practical knowledge of nature's domain.
Get a garden! What kind you may get matters not.
**Abbot Walafrid Strabo,
of Ruchenau Abbey, Hortulus, ninth century**

The medieval period of garden history covers the centuries between the sack of Rome (A.D. 410) and the beginning of the Renaissance. The primary philosophical force of this period was Christianity. Through the establishment of the monastic orders in medieval Europe, beginning in the fifth century, civilization was preserved. The monasteries became centers of intellectual activity and the repositories of knowledge. They were also crucial for the development of gardening in the West.

Monasteries turned their backs on the hostile, barbaric world and were inwardly oriented until the later Middle Ages. Because they had to be self-sufficient, it was necessary to have a variety of garden endeavors: a physic garden for medicinal herbs, a kitchen garden for vegetables and cooking herbs, orchards and vineyards for fruit, and small ornamental beds to supply flowers for festivals and holy days.

The monastery's cloister, usually on the south side for the advantageous exposure to the sun, shows a relationship to Roman and Persian antecedents. Divided by two intersecting paths, the resulting quadrants held plants with both ornamental and religious significance. In the center would be a water feature: a well to drink from, a cistern for watering and bathing, or a tub holding fish for Lenten meals. The cloister garden was simple and quiet; vegetable and herb gardens, orchards, and vineyards were in a separate location.

The plan of Saint Gall in the twelfth century shows the spatial organization and functional relationships of the components of a monastic community, while clearly locating all its elements. Included are both garden sites and plant lists (perhaps foretelling twentieth-century landscape architectural practices), which are thought to be those that Emperor Charlemagne had decreed, (some three centuries earlier), should be grown in all towns in his kingdom. It is certain that plans and plant lists such as these were copied and recopied by monks as the information was carried by pilgrims and travelers to monasteries and also to the nascent castle gardens throughout Europe.

During the twelfth, thirteenth, and fourteenth centuries, as the danger of barbaric invasions lessened, gardens began to extend beyond the monastery and castle walls. Large areas were sometimes fenced and stocked as game preserves, repeating a Middle Eastern tradition. The Crusaders, returning from the Holy Land, brought back exotic plants (carnations, citrus fruits, tulips), fragrant spices, and the experience of exotic cultures. Some flowers still in cultivation—the Rosa Mundi (*Rosa gallica officinalis*), for example—may have been imported by the Crusaders.

These diverse influences led to the refinement of the simple cloister courtyard into the "paradise garden." As the orders of knighthood became important and the traditions of courtly love and chivalry developed, the medieval garden became the setting for many outdoor activities: eating, reading, telling stories, dancing and making music, playing games, and holding court.

The later Middle Ages also saw the rise of the home garden, the miscellaneous fenced-in enclosures surrounding the houses of common people. Though its purpose was largely utilitarian, the domestic pleasure, privacy, and intimate labor it gave make it an important predecessor of the modern private garden. Indeed, it reminds us that the root of the word "garden"—the Indo-European *gher*—meant farmyard, hedge, house, or enclosure.

From fifteenth-century miniature paintings, we can isolate specific garden features: lattice or wattle fencing, arbors for plants, ornamental shrubs and fruit trees, lawns planted with grasses and wild flowers, crenellated stone walls to enclose the garden, turf seats along the garden's edge, ornamental fountains, and the presence of birds and animals in the garden. The flowers illustrated held religious significance: The white lily represented the purity of Mary, the red rose indicated divine love, cherries represented the joys of heaven, strawberries represented the fruits of righteousness and its leaves the Trinity, and apples signified the fall of man and his redemption by Christ. The garden's enclosed organization (for which it was called the *hortus conclusus*) symbolized the Virgin Birth. Indeed, the garden could become a metaphor for the church and the Virgin Mary, as well as for paradise and the reward of the faithful.

The Middle Ages was—in garden design, as in the other arts—a period of intellectual consolidation rather than advancement, and an epoch of metaphorical images rather than metaphysical explanations. It set the stage for the architectural, commercial, scientific, and technological explosions that were to follow during the Renaissance.

Left: Quince trees and herbs used in the Middle Ages surround a central wellhead in the Bonnefont Cloister at the Cloisters branch of New York's Metropolitan Museum. The structure was brought from southwestern France and dates from the late-thirteenth or early-fourteenth century. In medieval gardens, portable wattle fences protected tender young plants from foraging animals. Below: Paradise as seen through the observant eyes of an early-fifteenth-century painter was a walled meadow with a fruit tree, flowers, and a water source. Strawberries, roses, lilies, columbines, daisies, and lilies-of-the-valley (Convallaria spp.) dot the flowery lawn; iris and hollyhocks are specially grown in a raised bed. Birds and beasts also populate the protected garden. The Garden of Eden, by the Oberrheinescher Meister, from the Städelsches Kunstinstitut, Frankfurt.

RENAISSANCE PROGRESS

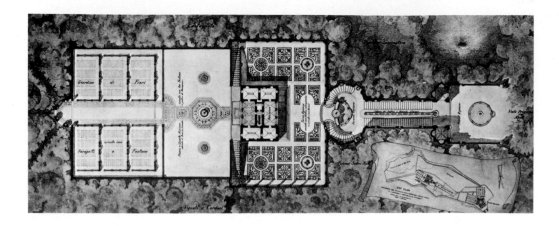

The charming garden was of wondrous beauty. On both sides of a pergola of vines, traversing the garden in the form of a cross, wide and shady, there ran to right and left two similar paths. They were long and wide and strewn with bright gravel. On the garden side, they were shut in, beyond where the pergola began, by hedges of thick yew. This yew reached breast-high, so that one could lean against it and get a wide view of all parts of the place.
Cardinal Bembo, late fifteenth century

The music of the organ, which is real music and a natural organ, though always playing the same thing, is effected by means of the water, which falls with great violence into a round arched cave and agitates the air that is there and forces it, in order to get out, to go through the pipes of the organ and supply it with wind. Another stream of water, driving a wheel with certain teeth on it, causes the organ keyboard to be struck in a certain order, so you hear an imitation of the sound of trumpets.
Montaigne, writing about Villa d'Este, sixteenth century

It was during the Italian Renaissance that the arts and the sciences together reached new heights. The reasons are varied and complex. The Crusades to the Near East and the exploration in the Far East had brought Europeans in contact with other lifestyles, made them want to live more comfortably, and gave them a desire to acquire exotic things. The growth of commerce and the accumulation of wealth made it possible for men of means to acquire large estates and to subsidize artisans to design, build, and decorate them. Relative political stability led to the growth of city-states, which reinforced the power of the wealthy and ensured continued artistic growth and commercial prosperity.

This rebirth of civilization started in Italy and subsequently spread throughout Europe, taking with it the Italians' love of theatrics and amusements, their orderly approach—based on beauty as well as on function—to design, and their technical expertise that made unusual effects and elaborate garden features possible.

During the Italian Renaissance, the concept of the universal man—*uomo universale*—led to an interest in all areas of intellectual pursuit and artistic endeavor. The educated man was expected to be conversant in the arts (painting, sculpture, music, architecture, garden design), the sciences (botany, astronomy, mathematics, engineering), and the letters (classical literature, prose, poetry).

Since medieval scholars had deduced that the Garden of Eden probably still existed somewhere on earth, New World explorations in the fifteenth and sixteenth centuries endeavored to find it. By the mid-sixteenth century, however, much of the earth had been explored and the Garden of Eden had not been found. Renaissance theologians and scientists decided that since the Garden of Eden could not be located, it could instead be recreated by gathering in one place all the evidence of God's handiwork. It was in this academic atmosphere that modern science began. The great botanical gardens of Europe (in Padua, 1545; Leyden, 1587; Oxford, 1621; Paris, 1626; and Uppsala, 1657) developed as a result of this scientific interest in botany and horticulture. These gardens were places for study rather than social events or utilitarian production. Unlike other gardens of the Renaissance, their significance to garden design lies not in their design (usually geometric, representing traditional thoughts about the organization of the universe) or their use of space (they were collections of plants); instead, these gardens are important because they collected plants from all over the world, promoted the scientific study and development of horticulture, and fostered the idea that by understanding plants, one could understand the universe.

The most pragmatic approach to spatial organization was ex-

Left: *The Villino Farnese, a casino above the Villa Caprarola, with fountains, stairs, pavilions, and parterres arranged in a bilaterally symmetrical plan.* **Above:** *At the Villa Lante, water marks the garden's central axis, starting as a trickle in a shady grotto and tumbling downhill through a series of troughs, canals, and fountains before coming to rest in four pools on a sunny parterre.*

pressed in the writings of the fifteenth-century architect Leone Battista Alberti, which reiterated techniques of site design defined centuries before by Pliny. Palladio (1508–1580) used Platonic geometry to determine a system for harmonic proportions that extended from interior spaces through structural expression into the organization of the landscape. The Renaissance mind sought perfection based on order, reason, and geometry.

The growth of commercial centers in Venice, Genoa, and Florence led to efforts by the wealthy to establish villas in the countryside, much as the wealthy had done centuries before during the Roman Empire. It is in the design of these villas—a term that includes the structures as well as the settings—that we see the essence of the Renaissance contributions to garden design: the system of spatial organization, the unity of design elements, and the richness of detail.

The landscape of Italy, for the most part, is hilly, and therefore sites for villas were often steep. To make these sites useful, terraces were constructed along the hillsides. These terraces were sometimes great engineering feats and produced outdoor spaces that were usually small, contained, and sequentially arranged. Later, we see this ordering system expanded to include decorative ramps and ceremonial staircases as the means of connecting exterior spaces. With loggias and windows, structures opened into the garden and took advantage of views into the countryside. In

addition to providing views, hillside sites made it possible for designers to manipulate streams and rivers to create complicated fountains, often with spectacular effects, run by natural water pressure.

The small compartments in gardens of the Italian Renaissance lent themselves to various treatments. Some were secluded and private (the *giardino segreto*), retaining the spirit of the medieval *hortus conclusis*. Others were groves of trees (*boscetti* or *bosco*), which provided shade from the heat of the afternoon. The space devoted to settings for outdoor plays and festivals bespeaks an interest in theatrics. A revival of interest in topiary led to the occurrence of clipped hedges and fanciful animal shapes in shubbery. Altogether, the Renaissance garden was geometrically organized, with allegorical references and intricate detail.

The components of these gardens, as in others throughout history, were simple: indigenous evergreen shrubs and trees, stone walls and buildings, sculpture, and water features. The wide variety we see in gardens of this period results from the individual tastes of the owners, the personalities of the sites, and the specific skills of the designers.

In these gardens is the merger of geometric form with natural setting: the supreme blend of architecture with landscape. From these gardens we can gain a renewed appreciation of what happens when large concepts are brought to a small site.

THE FRENCH IDEA

The gardens at Vaux-le-Vicomte consist of flat terraces and sloped ramps of manicured grass, trimmed evergreens, broad gravel paths, water, and statuary grouped around a central axis. Probably the greatest single creation of le Nôtre, Vaux was a disaster for Nicolas Fouquet, its owner. Le Nôtre played masterfully with changes of grade on a lavish scale; Fouquet evoked Louis XIV's ire with his garden and was soon in prison.

It tires me inexpressibly when I find every garden laid out in straight lines, some in four squares, others in nine or in six, and nothing different anywhere.

Jacques Boyceau, Traité de Jardinage selon les raison de la nature et de l'art, 1638

...work with the space with the other laborers, learning well to cultivate the earth, to bend, straighten, and bind the wood for the works of relief: to trace upon the ground his designs...to plant and clip the parterres...and several other particulars which comprise the embellishments of the gardens of pleasure.

Jacques Boyceau, on the education of a gardener

In the mid-fifteenth century, France emerged as a unified nation, and, by the end of that century, French armies under Charles VIII had invaded Italy. Although their military success was brief, the French became acquainted with the products of the Italian Renaissance and returned to France with Italian inclinations.

Charles VIII imported Italian artisans to redecorate his castle and grounds at Amboise. His successor, Louis XII, established court at Blois, and employed an Italian gardener to create an elaborate, three-terraced garden. From a contemporary engraving, it is obvious that this garden had many of the elements of a garden of the Italian Renaissance: parterre gardens, walkways covered with trellises, and the use of sculpture and fountains.

The landscape of France (in the areas where the court was centered) was different from that of Italy; consequently transplanting Italian garden ideas into France was not always successful. Nevertheless, Italian influences joined with political stability to cause a major development in design theory: Gardens could expand beyond castle walls and into the countryside, incorporating the surrounding landscape.

The most complete restoration of a sixteenth-century French garden design is found at Villandry, in the Loire Valley. The garden is on three terraces, and its features were inspired by the garden engravings of Androuet du Cerceau: vine-covered arbors, clipped trees, an orchard and vineyard, four parterre gardens bordered with clipped box (representing *l'amour tendre, l'amour tragique, l'amour volage, l'amour folie*), gravel walks, and a *potager* (vegetable and herb beds).

During the reign of Francis I (1515–1547), the arts of Italy and the ancient worlds became models for French architecture, gardens, and art. Books with woodcuts and engravings illustrating "la bonne manière italienne" were widely circulated in France. Francis I brought to his court at Fontainebleau a retinue of Italian artisans (including Leonardo da Vinci, Benvenuto Cellini, Andrea del Sarto, and Rosso) and soon the works of Italian architects (Vignola and Alberti, both influenced by Vitruvius) and artists became primary sources for French design. It was during this period that young French artists began pilgrimages to Rome to study the remains of classical culture, establishing a tradition that has remained well into the present century.

Inspired by Italian theatrical festivals, artists, playwrights, musicians, and architects were brought to Fontainebleau to create lavish spectacles. As the events grew more complicated in scale, larger spaces were required. The design of gardens in sixteenth-century France as well as the location of architectural features (canals and ponds, fountains, terraces, sculpture, and walks) reflected the desire to provide settings for these theatrical events. Architectural fantasies (grottos, pavilions, hermitages) were a necessary part of theatrical imagery and were included regularly in garden designs.

Italian influences on French gardens continue throughout the sixteenth and seventeenth centuries. It is not until Le Nôtre's design for Vaux-le-Vicomte (1661), which coincides with the beginning of the reign of Louis XIV, that garden design in France discovered a style of its own. Created for Nicolas Fouquet, the *Surintendant des Finances* for Louis XIV, Vaux-le-Vicomte is the brilliant collaboration of garden designer Le Nôtre, architect Le Vau, and artist LeBrun. It represents the beginning of a garden tradition that is a high point in the history of garden design and is one of the best examples of the unity of architecture, decorative arts, gardens, and site.

The house itself is a masterful combination of geometrical shapes and architectural composition. Situated in a highly structured setting, the chateau is balanced with a progression of architectural elements (gates, buildings, steps, ramps) and landscape features (terraces of clipped grass and crushed gravel, sculpture, reflecting pools and fountains; shaped shrubbery, dense woods). The entire development, from the approach through the house into the garden to the adjacent forest, reflects a well-organized composition that successfully combines its components.

The concept of unifying structure with setting can be traced to Italian origins. The realization of this concept at Vaux is derived from a physical environment, political climate, architectural theories, and socioeconomic conditions that are completely French.

Vaux paved the way for Versailles, which, because of its scale, is the quintessential example of French garden design. Versailles derives more from Vaux than just an enlargement of scale. Louis XIV was enraged by the ostentatious festival Fouquet hosted at Vaux (it lasted for days, and included lavish banquets, a comedy written by Molière, music by Lully, fireworks, and hundreds of guests). Shortly thereafter Louis imprisoned Fouquet, and commissioned Le Nôtre, Le Vau, and LeBrun to remodel the modest hunting lodge at Versailles built by Louis's father. Ultimately the development included almost 15,000 acres. Le Nôtre spent six years on the plans, and the rest of his life making minor changes and seasonal alterations based on the collaborative relationship he enjoyed with his client.

The gardens are laid out on an east-west axis emanating from the palace facade. The termination for this grand axis was the distance it ran, the implication being that, like the sun's rays shining on the earth, the influence of "Le Roi Soleil" extended *ad infinitum*.

The gardens were composed of large elements and grand gestures: Water was used in long pools, reflecting the sun, sky, and clouds; fountains were as effective when playing as when not, because they were designed first as sculptures; broad walks were framed by clipped hedges and dense growths of trees; the science of optics was effectively used to direct attention, either to lengthen or shorten apparent distances.

Throughout Versailles, in the palace as well as the garden, all elements are placed in their order of relationship *avec le soleil ou sa personnification*. Decorative motifs throughout reflect the image of the sun, and like their Italian precedents, indicate that the garden was viewed as an opportunity to exploit and expand on the iconographical self-image of the owner.

Versailles, which took over 50 years to build, is important because of its grand scale and overall concept, as well as for what it did to theories of garden design. Its influence has spread throughout Europe to Russia, America, and even China.

Several of Vaux-le-Vicomte's parterres are embroidered with intricate patterns of clipped box or woody low-growing herbs, offset by a ground of richly colored gravels.

THE ENGLISH LANDSCAPE GARDEN

*First follow Nature and your judgement frame
By her just standard, which is still the same:
Unerring Nature, still divinely bright
One clear, unchang'd, and universal light,
Life, force, and beauty, must to all impart,
At once the source, and end, and test of Art.
That Art is best which most resembles her,
And still presides, yet never does appear.*

Alexander Pope

When under the guidance of Le Nôtre and his disciples, the taste for nature in landscape gardening was totally banished or concealed by the work of art. Now, in defining the shape of land or water, we take nature for our model, and the highest perfection of landscape gardening is to imitate nature so judiciously that the influence of art shall never be detected.

Humphrey Repton

Stourhead, created by Henry Hoare in the early eighteenth century, presents a series of garden scenes fit for a romantic painter. Here, a temple in the classical style nestled midway up a gently rising slope at the foot of a towering evergreen commands a view of a lake and the surrounding landscape.

In the eighteenth century, England produced a major new development in garden history. From Roman times to the present, the English have had a love of the landscape, an appreciation for gardens, an inclination for plant collecting, and a tradition of horticultural scholarship. These qualities, influenced by literary, artistic, architectural, philosophical, and economic developments, combined in the early 1700s to revolutionize garden design.

Few examples of English gardens prior to this period exist today. From engravings and manuscripts, however, it is known that Tudor, Elizabethan, and Jacobean gardens contained elements from medieval gardens and contemporary developments in Renaissance Italy. Intricately patterned knot gardens and geometrically shaped topiary display evidence of Italian influences, transferred through France and Holland. Usually constructed within a rectangle or square, knot gardens were composed of patterns made with shorn evergreen hedges and filled with either fragrant herbs and blooming flowers (a "closed knot") or brick dust, crushed stone, sand, or grass (an "open knot"). Designs were taken from geometric patterns or heraldic designs. Topiary, a necessary feature in these gardens, could take the shape of animals and men, or geometric shapes such as cubes, globes, or pyramids. Mazes, composed of sheared evergreen hedges that were often "fram'd to a man's height," were also commonly used. These features remained popular throughout the sixteenth and seventeenth centuries until their excessive use became the target for the satirical essays of Alexander Pope and Joseph Addison in the early eighteenth century.

French influences became important in architecture, art, and garden design in the last half of the seventeenth century, upon the return to England of Charles II from exile in France. Medieval references and Italian designs (mazes, knot gardens, small garden rooms) were erased by grandiose schemes reminiscent of Versailles. Enormous estates were assembled; modest country houses were sometimes enlarged but frequently demolished to make way for monumental houses constructed by the wealthy, titled landowners. Since the model for these developments was Versailles, extensive gardens were necessary embellishments. Gardens in late seventeenth-century and early eighteenth-century England were highly structured, with symmetrical parts, axial vistas into the countryside, and parterre beds close to the house.

The eighteenth century was a golden—or at least silver—age for the arts in England, particularly for garden design. Throughout this period, such designers as Charles Bridgeman, William Kent, "Capability" Brown, Sir William Chambers, and Humphrey Repton encouraged their clients to rid their grounds of axes and vistas, rectangular beds, and clipped hedges, replacing them with winding paths, irregular lakes, and picturesque groupings of trees. Gardens of this period, inspired by the landscape paintings of seventeenth-century artists Salvator Rosa, Claude Lorrain, and

The lake at Stourhead, framed by mixed masses of evergreen and deciduous trees and shrubs. Plants with different forms, colors, textures, and sizes were intermingled in an effort to create a more natural looking composition.

Nicolas Poussin, reflected the clients' wealth, social status, knowledge of mythology, and their appreciation of classic art and architecture. The English landscape garden revolutionized the countryside on a grand scale. Indeed, when "Capability" Brown was asked to design a garden in Ireland, he is supposed to have responded, "I have not finished England yet." And the modern writer Ian McHarg went as far as to call the resulting English landscape "the greatest creation of perception and art in the Western world."

Plant-collecting expeditions produced horticultural introductions into England from the Orient, the Americas, Africa, and the Indies. Conservatories and orangeries, where these exotics could be grown, studied, and appreciated, were common features in eighteenth-century gardens. This interest in horticulture—which by the nineteenth century made greenhouses (or "stoves") a necessary part of every garden and led to a mania for different colors, patterns, textures, and plant combinations—is ironically the reason that interest waned, by the early nineteenth century, in the elaborate and studied styles of gardening popularized by Kent and Brown.

The legacy of this period—born from an appreciation of nature and as a reaction against formality and structure—is the philosophy that "all nature is a garden" and that the most appropriate design for a garden is one that appears as if it had always been there. This philosophy found acceptance in the late eighteenth century with the French, who were anxious to rid their country of all evidence of previous monarchy. It was championed in the writings of Girardin and Rousseau, whose advocacy of a return to nature and the nobility of the savage found expression in gardens in France and Germany.

It is curious that as gardens became more natural and informal, the geometry of previous landscapes was transposed into city planning throughout Europe and America. It would not be until the middle and late nineteenth century that the informal, romantic notions of late eighteenth-century English gardens would find their way into civic and residential planning.

OLD WORLD INFLUENCES IN THE NEW WORLD

A parterre garden at Colonial Williamsburg, formally laid out in materials that will carry the geometric pattern through the winter months. Box-edged beds with ivy and aucuba surround a central topiary; dogwoods add a flush of color in spring and fall.

No occupation is so delightful to me as the culture of the earth, and no culture comparable to that of the garden. I am still devoted to the garden. But though an old man, I am but a young gardener.
Thomas Jefferson

As did other aspects of material culture in colonial America, garden designs reflected the heritage, traditions, and plant material of the immigrants who settled here. The first gardens of early settlers were planted with seeds and cuttings carefully nurtured through the long transatlantic journey. As colonists became better acquainted with the New World and its native inhabitants, gardening techniques adjusted to fit local conditions and plant selections expanded to include native species.

Early settlements reflected contemporary European ideas about town planning and military fortifications; agricultural efforts reflected a desire to tame the wilderness. Food crops were planted in painstakingly cleared fields; medicinal plants and kitchen herbs were grown in small plots close to domestic structures, much as they had been in medieval home gardens. Living conditions were not easy, and it was only in the mid-eighteenth century that the colonial settlements had matured enough to allow the development of decorative, rather than purely functional, gardens.

As prosperous English settlers came to the middle colonies, both domestic architecture and gardens began to reflect the symmetry and structure of the old manor houses of Great Britain. With the influx of Dutch settlers into the colonies of New York and Pennsylvania came skilled gardeners and plantsmen with agricultural expertise and an appreciation for ornamental horticulture. The early settlers of the southern colonies took advantage of the rich land and the lengthy growing season to establish an agrarian society that lasted well into the mid-nineteenth century. The expression of this society was the plantation, a self-contained agricultural community organized very much like the rural villa of Pliny and the Palladian villas of the Italian Renaissance.

Garden influences from England became predominant as economic and cultural ties joined the Colonies with Great Britain. The best example of this English influence can be found in Williamsburg. Although often criticized for being unrealistically perfect in its restoration, this development nevertheless is important because of the archeological and technological research into colonial material life it has generated, and the interest in preservation of our architectural heritage it inaugurated. Gardens in Williamsburg show evidence of seventeenth-century English styles (arrangements are formal, controlled, and highly structured) and Dutch horticultural traditions (simple topiary and clipped hedges; extensive use of bulbs, exotic plants, and ornamental flowers).

Colonial developments in other parts of North America reflect regional influences from other European sources. New Orleans was a colony that began in the early eighteenth century, settled by both French and Spanish settlers. Gardens are shown in early maps as being rectangular, often bordered with hedges. These designs probably were intended not to accurately represent what existed but to promote to potential settlers back in France a certain level of civilization. Just as the architecture of settlements in the Gulf region resembles structures in Italy and southern France, garden traditions reflect Mediterranean influences. As cities grew, patios, with adjacent galleries and paved terraces, became inwardly oriented spaces that provided relief from the congestion of urban living, protection from the climate, and a source of sensuous pleasure.

Many of the political, economic, and philosophical leaders of colonial America were experienced farmers. The meticulous records kept by both George Washington and Thomas Jefferson provide a phenomenal insight into garden practices of this era.

For his home at Mt. Vernon, Washington displayed a skillful sense of design and a comprehensive knowledge of plant materials. It is known that he sent to England in 1758 for a copy of Batty Langley's *New Principles of Gardening* (1728), the standard English reference of the day on garden design. Washington successfully combined the informality popularized by Langley and the formality of Palladian proportions in the organization of features necessary for a self-sufficient plantation. Included were orchards, a bowling green, vegetable beds, flower gardens, a framed vista to the Potomac, groves of trees, an orangerie, and an area for horticultural experimentation.

Thomas Jefferson, unlike Washington, had the opportunity to travel in Italy, France, Germany, and England, and to visit many of the important gardens in those countries. His architecture displays an understanding of Palladian organization, and the grounds at Monticello reflect an appreciation for eighteenth-century styles of garden design. Jefferson's garden notebook, kept from 1766 to 1824, is a comprehensive record of plants, horticultural techniques, and garden practices. Jefferson's place in American horticulture corresponds with his place in American politics, architecture, and letters. More than any other figure, Jefferson brought America into the nineteenth century as a nation influenced by European traditions, yet independent enough to set its own course.

By the end of the eighteenth century, horticultural explorers had introduced new plants from South America, Africa, and the Orient into American gardens. Commercial nurseries were well established, and naturalists such as John Bartram of Philadelphia, John Custis of Williamsburg, and Peter Collinson of London exchanged horticultural information and plant specimens.

In the seventeenth century, garden expressions in America were purely functional. By the beginning of the nineteenth century, transplanted European traditions, local environmental conditions, and native ingenuity had combined to produce styles that were derived from European traditions but defined by the independent, imaginative, and industrious character of a new nation with unlimited resources.

Thomas Jefferson assiduously collected a wide variety of trees, flowering plants, and vegetables for his gardens at Monticello from acquaintances and nurserymen in America and Europe.

NINETEENTH CENTURY ROMANTICISM

The development of the Beautiful is the end and aim of Landscape Gardening, as it is of all other fine arts. The ancients sought to attain this by a studied and elegant regularity of design in their gardens; the moderns, by the creation or improvement of grounds which, though of limited extent, exhibit a highly graceful or picturesque epitome of natural beauty.

Andrew Jackson Downing, Treatise on the Theory and Practice of Landscape Gardening, Adapted to North America, 1841

Prior to the nineteenth century, major movements in garden history seem to be limited to developments in particular countries: sixteenth-century Italy, seventeenth-century France, eighteenth-century England. With the nineteenth century, all this changed. As the social revolutions of the late eighteenth century brought changes in economic and political structures, and the Industrial Revolution brought new developments in science and technology throughout the Western world, garden design in America and Europe became increasingly romantic in concept, eclectic in character, and complicated in detail.

In England, the writings and work of Humphrey Repton (*Observations on the Theory and Practice of Landscape Gardening,* 1803) and J. C. Loudon led to the reappearance of flowers in the English garden and the development of the "gardenesque" philosophy of

The fanciful house at Sezincote, planned and planted with a distinct taste for the exotic. Greenhouses harbored tender tropical plants.

design. Fueled by the general Victorian taste for eclecticism, this philosophy proposed using plants in as many combinations as possible. Beds were packed with fanciful patterns of low-growing, colorful, and exotic plants, creating a carpet-like effect. The love of plants led to the development of botanical collections in public and private gardens. These gardens provided opportunities to study new and exotic plants from all over the world. They were exercises in the composition of different textures, colors, and shapes, and expressions of the philosophy that realistic imitations of nature (as practiced by designers of the eighteenth century) were inherently deceptive and therefore bad. The technology of cast-iron architecture allowed the building of glass structures that housed palm trees and exotic flora from tropical regions.

The second major philosophy of the nineteenth century gave rise to the "romantic landscape," popularized by the writings of Sir Walter Scott in England and Rousseau in France. Based on intellectual rather than horticultural concerns, this approach suggested man's subservience to nature and gave rise to such picturesque details as rustic Gothic architecture and landscape structures fashioned from trees.

In America the fascination with the picturesque was popularized by the writing of Andrew Jackson Downing (1815–1852) and the architecture of Alexander Jackson Davis. Downing, a horticulturist, was a prolific writer influenced by the works of Repton and Loudon. His *Treatise on the Theory and Practice of Landscape Gardening, Adapted to North America* (originally published in 1841) was the most important book in American garden design in the nineteenth century. Downing edited the *Horticulturist,* a widely distributed periodical, from its founding in 1846 until his premature death in 1852. His definitive work on fruit culture, *The Fruits and Fruit Trees of America* as well as his *Treatise,* remained in print until the century's end. They were both widely read and extraordinarily influential. Downing's *Treatise* gave basic rules for designing gardens to complement the Italianate, Gothic, and Tudor revival architecture of his colleague Davis, and he defined two approaches to garden design: the "graceful school," composed of curving lines, sloping land forms, and rounded plant shapes; and the "picturesque school," with bold plant forms, irregular landscapes, wild growths, and rustic ornaments. Downing's work is important for many reasons: He proposed a unity of overall concept, a relationship between structures and grounds, and a variety of elements to carry out the overall scheme. His suggestions were both general in concept and specific in detail, and his writings were consumed by America's growing middle class, a group who seized upon Downing's philosophies as the final authority for social acceptance.

An allée of majestic live oaks, Quercus virginiana, their branches draped with a hanging epiphyte called Spanish moss, lines the approach to the plantation house at Magnolia Gardens outside of Charleston, South Carolina.

Two painters' gardens. **Opposite page, top left:** *Monet's garden at Giverny with water lilies, weeping willow, dark-leaved beech, and a pastel-colored footbridge creating patterns on the water's surface.* **Bottom left:** *Peonies, delphinium, poppies, and valerian line a path at Giverny, and roses spill over towers and arches in beds alongside.* **Bottom right:** *Masses of red and yellow flowers bring hot color to a cooler part of the garden.* **This page, top right:** *Frederick Church's estate at Olana, set on the banks of the Hudson River, reflects his interest in topography, trees, and open sky—the elements that he liked to paint.* **Bottom right:** *Beneath a canopy of mature trees, dogwoods bring spring to Olana.*

Following Downing in American garden history is Frederick Law Olmsted, generally acknowledged as the "father of landscape architecture" in America. Olmsted, who had studied scientific farming and had met Downing, was the driving force behind the social reform movement in the second half of the nineteenth century that recognized the value of open spaces. His work (which included plans for urban parks, institutions, college campuses, state and national parks, resource management, and estates, and is represented across the entire country) displayed an understanding of the environment, an appreciation for human needs, and an ability to manipulate both land forms and vegetation.

Throughout the nineteenth century, American domestic gardens were the products of local stylistic traditions, specific environmental conditions, and, occasionally, trained designers. Prior to the Civil War, itinerant artisans, craftsmen, plant salesmen, and gardeners wandered throughout America, selling their goods and bartering their services. This led to dissemination of horticultural information and plant material and the introduction of new styles of gardening in remote rural areas.

There are several examples of gardens in the South reputedly designed and planted by French or English "landscape artists." Extensive gardens, like elaborate interior furnishings, were a sign of affluence, prosperity, and social importance, and although they did occur in all regions of America at this time, by far the most common gardens, regardless of region, were modest combinations of functional requirements and ornamental interests, influenced strongly by the writings of Downing.

As America became more industrialized and urbanized in the years following the Civil War, gardens followed European traditions and became more stylistically eclectic and horticulturally complicated. Gardens were cluttered with statues, structures, parterres, benches, geometrical flower beds, fountains, and ornamental fences. Downing's two philosophies remained important, yet their expressions changed, reflecting new affluence and tastes in architecture and design. As the nineteenth century closed in America, industrial magnates began to look to Europe—particularly to Ancient Rome, Renaissance Italy, Tudor England, and seventeenth-century France—for architectural inspirations to express their newly acquired wealth, social status, and culture appropriately.

THE ENGLISH FLOWER GARDEN

Christopher Lloyd's border at Great Dixter—whose house and garden were originally redesigned by Sir Edwin Lutyens—is an extraordinary combination of herbaceous plants and shrubs, with spikes of white kniphofia, dark-leaved cannas and cotinus, alliums, and osteospermum spilling over a stone path.

Above: *Red roses, zinnias, begonias, petunias, and nicotiana in a border at Barrington Court.* ***Right:*** *Vita Sackville-West's white garden at Sissinghurst, with calla lilies and roses, is most exquisite at dusk when white flowers begin to release their scent. It is clear why it holds a place among the finest English flower gardens.*

I hold that the best purpose of a garden is to give delight and to give refreshment of mind, to soothe, to refine and to lift up the heart in a spirit of praise and thankfulness.
Gertrude Jekyll, Color Schemes for the Flower Garden, 1908

By the nineteenth century's end in England, the divergent garden philosophies expressed by horticultural eclecticism and the Romantics had been both consolidated and criticized in the writings of William Robinson (*The English Flower Garden,* 1883). He succeeded in blending plants in naturalistic yet carefully planned schemes. Discarding the eclectic "carpet bedding" techniques of garden design, Robinson used instead plantings of hardy perennials, which flourished in the mild English climate and provided a continuous parade of colorful blooms and textural combinations over a long period of time. For Robinson, each plant could be appreciated for the seasonal effects of height, color, leaf texture, size, and fragrance, as well as for flower.

Robinson's ideas about garden design gained a wider audience through the work and writings of his famous contemporary, Gertrude Jekyll. Her work, which is currently enjoying a renewed popularity, demonstrates a thorough understanding of horticulture, an appreciation for what plants can do, and a skillful eye for proportion and design. Much of her work was done in collaboration with Sir Edwin Lutyens, whose buildings demonstrate a skillful assimilation of historic references and provide an appropriate setting for Jekyll's combinations of plant colors, forms, and textures. Jekyll is important also because of her techniques of using color in the garden. Few developments can match her "white garden" or "pink garden" schemes. Having impaired vision, Jekyll is reported to have planned her gardens by composing blurs of colors, much as the impressionist painters composed their canvases. (Indeed, she was herself a painter.) Many gardens enjoyed today in England are influenced by her work and writings, including Vita Sackville-West's astounding gardens at Sissinghurst in Kent.

Jekyll's influence spread to America through the work of early twentieth-century landscape architects whose work consisted mainly of estate commissions, notably those of Beatrix Jones Farrand. For many in England and America, Jekyll was the ultimate garden designer. Her work—with its innovative uses of color, texture, and form; its details; and its intimate scale—is representative of the best in the history of garden design.

THE TWENTIETH CENTURY

At Longwood Gardens, created between 1906 and 1954, a waterside pavilion with grape-enveloped columns and a filigreed dome provides a breezy spot to look from and a picturesque scene to look at. The broad steps at the water's edge invite sitting.

Landscaping is not a complex and difficult art to be practiced only by high priests. It is logical, down-to-earth, and aimed at making your plot of ground produce exactly what you want and need from it.

Thomas D. Church, Gardens Are for People, 1955

The words beauty, inspiration, spellbinding, sortilege, enchantment and also serenity, silence, intimacy, and astonishment, have disappeared in alarming numbers from architectural publications. All of these have found a loving welcome in my soul, and if I am far from having done them full justice in my work, not for that have they ceased to be my lighthouse.

Luis Barragán

Garden design in the twentieth century is an aggregate of historical references and styles, economic and social influences, and changing attitudes about architecture and environmental quality. During the first three decades of the century in America, the profession of landscape architecture was defined by the career of its nineteenth-century founder, Frederick Law Olmsted. Although the profession assumed a leading role in designing public parks, replanning cities, and designing residential neighborhoods, most professional activity was devoted to making gardens for large estates. Known as the "Country Place Era," this period reflected

the inspiration of European architectural and garden traditions, and provided designers with opportunities to transpose both Romantic notions and historical details of design, content, and planting into American gardens. Estates were usually extensive. Away from the house, grounds were planned, either additively or subtractively, to be irregular, assymmetrical, and informal. Close to the house, more formally planned garden rooms were sited. Sequentially organized, they provided a variety of both function and effect. The design vocabularly was defined by geometry, symmetry, and axis, and included perennial borders, rose gardens, sculpture and water features, and garden structures. These gardens reflected an attention to classical details and a knowledge of European design traditions. Much of this professional activity was curtailed by the economic effects of the Great Depression of the 1930s.

It was a reaction against the Beaux Arts philosophies of the Country Place Era and the lifestyle it represented that led to the development of the "California School," the single most important influence on American garden design of this century. While studying landscape architecture at Harvard's Graduate School of Design in the late 1930s, James Rose, Dan Kiley, and Garrett Eckbo rebelled against the formal concepts, the inherent insensitivity to

Above: *Clipped hedges and cropped grass surround a lily pool in one of the garden rooms at Filoli, south of San Francisco. The design dates from the teens of this century. Pots of pink petunias add a colorful vertical accent.* **Right:** *A pebbled path lined with bricks and cobblestones runs beneath an avenue of purple-leaved* Prunus blireiana *at Dumbarton Oaks. Beatrix Farrand, designer.*

unique site conditions, and the predictable solutions that the Beaux Arts philosophies produced. Concurrent with this academically oriented rejection was the professional work of garden designer Thomas Church on the West Coast. Throughout the decades of the 1940s, 1950s, and 1960s, the work of these men had a significant effect on landscape architecture in general and residential garden design in particular. These gardens are noted for their sensitivity to the site, their use of materials, their functional arrangements, and their providing solutions to the specific requirements of the client.

The prosperity that followed World War II enabled many Americans to buy the houses, automobiles, and appliances rapidly being produced by advanced technology. There was an exodus from cities to suburban neighborhoods and an eager acceptance of modern design and industrial technology. Architecture of the post-war period proposed the mingling of indoor living areas with outdoor spaces, and advanced technology promised relief from the drudgery of household activities, thereby increasing recreational and leisure time. Gardens, influenced by the philosophy of the California School and the writings of both Eckbo (*Landscape for Living*, 1950) and Church (*Gardens Are for People*, 1955) were designed to enable these things to happen.

Common features included patios, terraces, swimming pools, garden structures for outdoor living, play spaces for children, and "service" areas for the equipment required by self-maintenance. Residential lots were small (generally a half acre); few people could afford large estates or the staff to maintain them. Plants were used to reinforce functional concepts of the design (hedges for privacy, ground covers for low maintenance, trees for shading

A dark pool with a narrow concrete rim filled with lilies, lotus, and iris at Pepsico's headquarters in New York. Day lilies bask in the sun at the foot of a retaining wall; clumps of perennials line the bank above. Russel Page, designer.

outdoor living spaces, annuals for seasonal color, and exotic plants for accents and design emphasis) and were combined to exploit textures, colors, and forms. The main idea of these gardens was to provide enjoyable spaces for outdoor social and recreational activities. The guiding principles were convenience, low maintenance, and function.

A parallel development took place in Europe and Great Britain, after World War II. The Continent led the way in modern gardening. Many areas, particularly in Germany, had been devastated by the war, so there was a pressing need for new building and a virtual *tabula rasa* to work with. Garden plots were typically smaller, and technological advances tended to make the garden smoother and less cluttered. The mechanical lawn mower, for example, made an extensive lawn more possible and indicated smooth, sweeping lines rather than irregular ones. Improved weed-killers and chemical fertilizers, together with easier availability of select plant species, also contributed to the streamlining of the garden.

The Festival of Britain, in 1951, brought Continental gardening ideas to England. It also popularized new garden styles from the United States, particularly the clean, functional lines of Thomas Church's California gardens. A third influence was the new Scandinavian garden, made to harmonize with the architecture of builders like Alvar Aalto and Eero Saarinen.

The result of all these influences was a simplification of the garden space, making it more practical and useful for the postwar middle class. The garden became an extension of the house: a place for relaxation, play, even outdoor dining.

Another approach to garden design in the twentieth century can be found in the work of Mexican architect/landscape architect Luis

Outside a villa in northern Italy, turf steps with stone risers climb a bank between stepped beds with mounds of juniper, lavender, clumps of violets, and patches of red-flowering impatiens and wax begonias. The lush planting shows the influence of British flower gardening on the design of twentieth-century gardens. Henry Cocker, designer.

Barragán and Brazilian landscape architect Roberto Burle Marx. Each is obviously a product of his environment, and the work of both displays an approach to design derived from modernist artistic traditions (abstraction, cubism, and color theory), an appreciation for the local environment, and European design traditions. Barragán's work combines architecture with environment through his dynamic uses of color and shape. Burle Marx is known for his fantastic combinations of exotic plant forms, colors, and textures, and for his bold, painterly approach to large-scale spaces with plants native to Brazilian jungles.

The social upheavals of the 1960s and 1970s made a direct change in the profession of landscape architecture, with indirect influences on garden design. Environmental awareness, growing from nineteenth-century Romantic appreciation for the land, focused attention on the pernicious effects of a consumer-oriented society on natural systems, the sprawl of unlimited development, and the environmental dangers of industrial pollution. It propelled the profession into a position of political importance. The movement to "return to nature" has given a renewed interest in preserving and even creating gardens and landscapes with native plants, and an interest in self-sufficiency has increased general interest in growing fruits and vegetables.

It is difficult, in the final years of the century, to predict where garden design will go from here. There are, however, a few indications: Historical references are again becoming sources of design inspiration in both architecture and landscape architecture, and increased population and diminishing natural resources will influence what and how our gardens are designed.

Above: *In a Thomas Church garden, junipers, bergenia, ivy, and silvery mats of stachys along a path, framed by a wisteria-draped pergola.* **Right:** *Church's backyard garden in San Francisco is packed with architectural and horticultural details—latticework, topiary, tree ferns, palms, rhododendrons, and agapanthus.*

CHAPTER TWO

DISCOVERING YOUR STYLE

by Norman K. Johnson

A MATTER OF STYLE
THE PARTERRE
THE OUTDOOR ROOM
THE COUNTRY COTTAGE
THE ORIENTAL STYLE
THE WILD GARDEN

A MATTER OF STYLE

Throughout the course of history, the garden has been a place where man and nature coexist. Unlike a work of architecture, which defends us from extremes of climate and the world at large, a garden depends on sun and rain and seasonal progressions for its richness and life. And just as gardens cannot be divorced from their location, garden styles are also bonded to a certain time and place that provide their inspiration. How, then, can a style endure beyond its time, and how do "foreign" styles survive outside their native lands?

Style is largely a matter of dealing with common situations; what makes a style appropriate to its original situation will often be found in other places or will recur with time. The Renaissance Italian villa, for example, developed an intimate relationship between its house and setting—so much so that "villa" implies not just a structure or a garden but an integrated environment where architecture and landscape cannot be separated. Villas also responded to specific social needs.

Typically, a villa was a self-contained community of farmers, craftsmen, and tradesmen; their families; and the household of a noble or powerful churchman who owned the villa. Thus, the villa is similar to the French chateau, the English country manor, and the plantation communities of the American South. The modern "California" style is also related to the villa. Although this style is largely applied to private, single-family residences, its merging of house and garden was inspired by the organic nature of the villa, which in turn drew inspiration from ancient Roman and Persian gardens and from the Moorish gardens of northern Africa and Spain.

Indeed, the history of gardening is a chronology of borrowing and adapting styles to better suit new situations. The French chateau, for example, is an adaptation of the villa to the broadly horizontal landscape of France; the English "flower"

Left: *Broad grass paths, dogwoods, azaleas, and rhododendrons are the bones of this bright and inviting garden in Connecticut. Masses of forget-me-nots, alyssum, and spring-flowering bulbs carpet the ground with color.* **Above:** *An ellipse of tulips and English daisies,* Bellis perennis, *planted around the gnarled trunk of an old tree. Clean lines, clipped hedges, and prim upright flowers combine to make a tidy-looking garden, all without the use of obtrusive architectural elements.*

gardens—such as those at Sissinghurst, Hidcote Manor, and those designed by Gertrude Jekyll and Edwin Lutyens—are formalized renditions of the country cottage dooryard. So it has been with gardens of almost every nation and time. A style is borrowed and then tailored to specific needs; with time, these adaptations may become a new, distinctive style, with its own unique characteristics and particular intents.

THE PARTERRE

Patterns on the Ground

The parterre garden is one of the oldest and most versatile of garden styles. As the name implies—its etymological meaning is "along the ground"—parterres are characterized by patterns on the garden's surface. Although parterres may contain tall plants or be enclosed with fences or other structures, parterres most directly address and emphasize the ground plane.

The term parterre is frequently applied to gardens that have formal, geometric characters, such as Medieval knot gardens and the elaborate parterres de broderie of seventeenth-century French gardens. In a more generic sense, however, one may think of a parterre as any garden that focuses attention on the formal pattern of its layout. Thus, parterre gardens are largely two-dimensional; their richness comes from the arrangement of horizontal elements such as walkways, planting beds, lawns, reflecting pools, and terraces. The "parterreness" of a garden may also be as narrowly focused as the design of a paving or a formal planting of roses, or as encompassing as the layout of the garden's total plan.

Of all the garden styles, the parterre is most easily related to the garden plan on paper. When the lines of a design drawing are translated to the ground, the resulting pattern creates an immediate sense of order and spatial definition. Consequently, a parterre may be the first step in any garden design as well as an independent garden style.

As an intermediate phase, the parterre form is very useful to the makers of new gardens because it ensures good "bones"—the framework that must underlie the structure of all gardens. As one waits for hedges and shade trees to mature, for example, the layout of walkways, lawns, and planting beds gives unity and harmony to juvenile plants that may otherwise seem disparate and insubstantial. The quick effect that parterres offer can also be seen as a legacy to future gardeners. Many young professionals are frequently relocated in the course of their employment, and the parterre satisfies their immediate short-term garden needs while establishing a structure that may be more fully developed by future owners.

For all of its advantages in interim solutions, the parterre garden's greatest value lies in permanence. Unlike a garden in which plants provide the basic structure, the parterre's form is frequently defined with pavings—walkways, terraces, and edgings—which are more durable than plants for shaping space. Plants, of course, are not excluded from the parterre garden; they merely take a lesser role in terms of overall design. Because they are most often grown in beds, the parterre garden's plantings also reinforce its pattern by enlivening its order with color and texture.

Permanence of form, however, is not the parterre's only value. The parterre style endures because it is both logical and highly versatile. By offering an orderly arrangement of garden spaces, the parterre style may be applied to many garden needs.

Parterres are the obvious solution to a level site where changes of grade are either impossible or inappropriate. These gardens also lend themselves to difficult environments, especially those places where soil or climatic factors complicate the making and maintaining of a garden. The low profile of parterre gardens, for example, is ideally suited to those areas of strong or drying winds that may inhibit or

distort the growth of trees and larger shrubs or colder climates where extensive snow accumulations may destroy the form of plants. A parterre of container plants or elevated beds, on the other hand, is a practical solution to shallow, rocky, or infertile soils, and for gardens where the water table is quite near the surface.

In dimension, the parterre is equally adaptable. Parterres may be as small as a postage-stamp-size lawn surrounded with beds of flowers, or as grandiose as the reconstructed *potager* at Villandry, which covers several acres. Unless one has the benefit of an extensive garden staff, however, large parterres are best designed as simple patterns of water, lawn, or paving, since highly detailed patterns will be lost when viewed from a distance.

As a viewing garden, of course, the parterre is a classic. The pattern of walkways, open lawns, and ornamental sheets of water that are typical of the gardens surrounding most French chateaus creates a most effective prospect. Thus, parterre gardens are most successful when their patterns may be seen in "plan." From the upper stories of a house, an elevated terrace, or a hillside, the parterre spreads a carpet-like design across the garden.

Most of us, of course, prefer to live within our gardens, not just view them from afar. Properly designed, however, the modern parterre allows for both passive viewing and inhabitation: It lives as well as it looks.

Although it is typically a high-maintenance garden style, the parterre counters this concern with elegant design. The overall simplicity and orderly arrangement of the parterre garden's spaces is dignified, gracious, and livable; these qualities are reaffirmed by the parterre's enduring success as a garden style.

Left: *Billowy lines of boxwood in a formal maze. When mazes were popular they were typically accompanied by a garden feature called a mount, which offered a bird's-eye view of the intricate hedges.* **Above:** *A knot garden tied in herbs creates a low, readily visible pattern. Herbs are the ideal plants for knots, as their leaves tend to be more ornamental than their flowers, with different textures in silvers, blue-grays, and greens; and they respond to handling by releasing their pungent fragrances.*

Flower beds between the house and the front gate provide a colorful welcome. Here, roses and annuals surround a pair of circular beds, where standards bring blossoms to eye level.

Front Garden Geometries

The appearance of any residence is always enhanced with proper garden planting; by calling attention to the ground plan, the parterre complements rather than camouflages the verticality of a house. Because as the parterre garden is composed of horizontal planes, this style is also useful when designing driveways, visitor parking spaces, and entrance walks. A simple, functional arrangement of garden pavings amplifies the sense of order that is so essential to arrival gardens.

The simplest of parterre patterns applied to the front garden is the walk passing through an area of lawn. Although this may be adequate for traffic, it offers little in the way of garden character. This most basic plan can be greatly improved when walkways are enriched with detailed paving patterns. Rarely is an entrance walk sufficiently wide for comfort when two people are walking together. But when an existing walk is widened with bands of brick, stone, or other contrasting paving, both the function and appearance of that walkway is improved. When secondary walks of similar design are added to connect with drives or visitor parking spaces, the resulting pattern may become the framework for a formally gardened space.

Perimeter walks around a lawn are another way of giving shape to garden spaces. The portion of such walks that parallels the house, for example, may lead from a driveway to the front door, and beyond, to a gateway giving access to the private garden. The space between the walk and house also becomes a well-defined planting bed. Similarly, a walk that parallels the street creates another space that may be planted with ground covers or low-growing plants to give a subtle separation between public and private areas. Walks that parallel the property line provide an equally effective demarcation between adjacent gardens; because the lawn within these walks is

Rectangles of trimmed boxwood punctuated by irregularly shaped standards bring sculpture into a small city garden. The hedges are evergreen, which is an important consideration for a space that is used in every season. In spring panicles of lavender wisteria cover the surrounding wall, introducing ephemeral color and fragrance to the entry court.

At Colonial Williamsburg a simple plan kept strong with clean lines and a limited number of elements. A sweep of yellow chrysanthemums frames a lawn and a well-proportioned garden bench. Rusty-colored mums nearby blend with the brick paths, leaving the brighter flowers to call attention to the more important part of the space.

framed with paving, even that typical garden surfacing takes on new dimension.

For all of its advantages in durability, however, lawn grass is not the only plant that may be used for lawns. Flexibility in planting is especially important in areas of heavy shade, where turf may be difficult if not impossible to maintain. English ivy, periwinkle *(Vinca minor),* myrtle, and pachysandra are all suitable for shady garden plantings, as is mondo grass *(Ophiopogon japonicus).* Mondo grass, however, is not a plant for colder climates, just as pachysandra may not thrive in very hot or humid regions. In sunny locations, chamomile and thyme, both of which have fragrant foliage, make desirable alternatives. (Chamomile needs a frost-free climate.) These low-growing herbs also offer the bonus of flowers, delightful for the color they provide.

Sometimes it is possible to concentrate driveways, walks, and parking in a single expanse of paving. Indeed, a motor court may be the logical solution for small entrance gardens or a practical enhancement to larger properties. Set into the center of a planted surface, and directly

before the house, a motor court can also be a handsome garden feature, especially when it is framed with planting beds, small shrubs, or low walls. The plaza-like appearance of motor courts, however, demands elegant paving. A well-compacted surfacing of gravel is both simple and attractive; when it is divided with slightly concave bands of brick, concrete, or stone, these channels will also be useful for directing surface water to drainage inlets. In areas of heavy traffic or frequent rains, both of which complicate the maintenance of gravel courts, a more durable surfacing of asphalt, concrete, brick, or stone may be required. Such pavings also offer an expanded range of pattern possibilities to enrich the garden's surface.

The plaza-like character of paved parterres need not be restricted to areas of vehicular circulation. A large expanse of paving adjacent to front doors, for example, provides a very pleasant area for greetings and good-byes. Such an area can be especially effective with contemporary homes that are constructed on concrete slab foundations. Since there is so little change of grade between interior

and exterior, a parterre entrance court can both emphasize and soften the transition.

A similar effect can be achieved around older homes with partially raised basements. Although steps and landings may provide convenient access to the house, they may not be sufficiently large for several guests. Thus, a parterre landing at the foot of entrance steps affords a gracious, outdoor entrance hall where guests feel welcomed before they reach the door.

The all-paved entrance garden is another possible variation of the parterre style. Organic materials such as pine needles, shredded bark, wood chips, or tanbark may be used in various combinations to create a soft effect within a formal frame. Combined with paths of gravel, stone, or brick, the patterns can become even more complex. Hard-paved entrance gardens, on the other hand, are more strictly formal. But whether it be a field of gravel interspersed with small plantations of herbs or flowers or a geometric medallion rendered in various colors and textures of stone or brick, such pavings take full advantage of the permanence and pattern of the parterre style.

Back-Garden Symmetries

Flowers, herbs, and vegetables interplanted around a strawberry patch, with a narrow path leading up to it, present a formal and relaxed look.

Because it is essentially a formal garden style, the parterre may at first seem out of place in private, backyard gardens. Where the street-front garden amplifies the parterre's visual qualities, however, the backyard takes advantage of its versatility for organizing space.

Many of the activities that take place in a garden require a level, open site: terraces for outdoor living, dining, and entertaining; lawns for play; formal pools and swimming pools, tennis courts, and child space for organized recreation; service and storage areas; and planting beds for everything from flowers to vegetables. Accommodating various conflicting needs often complicates decisions on placement.

Since the parterre is an arrangement of garden elements to create a practical and unified effect, the first item to consider in planning is circulation. The paths that link a garden's parts define its spaces and enhance the pleasure of moving from place to place.

Rather than moving through the center of a garden, walks may be located at its edges; this is especially effective in smaller gardens. Because these walks give definition to the garden's boundaries, they reinforce the sense of space within the garden proper. By offering two connections to the garden as a whole, perimeter walkways also give a choice of routes within the garden, which further enhances its apparent size.

A centered, principal walkway, on the other hand, does not necessarily make a garden seem smaller, but it focuses attention on its total length. In a spacious backyard, this focus can be a benefit. Natural perspective will enhance the garden's depth. In a smaller garden or a backyard that is wider than it is long, a central walkway can be used to emphasize the horizontal dimension by subdividing the garden into equal parts. To counteract the shortening effect of perspective, however, such walks should be quite broad; if they narrow slightly as they move into the distance, the resulting forced perspective will increase the sense of depth as well.

Formal pools and swimming pools are equally valuable in a parterre plan. Too often swimming pools are thought of only as recreational features. Because of their size and usually geometric forms, however, they can also be used to organize garden space in parterre styles. The length of any rectangular pool may be aligned with a garden's central axis to create a very formal appearance; if that pool is set into a lawn, with just a narrow band of paving around its edges, its formality and ornamental character will be further enhanced.

Because they are nondirectional, round pools emphasize neither the length nor depth of garden spaces but focus attention toward their center. Oval pools create a similar effect. By eliminating corners, these pools enhance a garden's sense of space by drawing the eye's attention around their edges. Square pools are also self-focusing, especially when they are set into an expanse of paving that repeats the grid-like pattern of this most basic geometric form.

Aside from the overall arrangement of the garden plan, the principles of the parterre may also be applied to individual garden features. Terraces, for example, may be designed in outline to create a pattern of edges and in detail to create a paving. Then there is the pattern of features that fit into or sit upon that surface—furnishings, ornaments, barbecues, planting pockets, and containers. This pattern-on-pattern quality may also be observed in planting beds, lawns, water features, and even the shadows cast by trees and passing clouds.

Paving patterns afford an unlimited richness of parterre expression because of the possibilities within a single material or combinations of surfacings. Brick, stone, wood, gravel, concrete, asphalt, tiles, metal, terazzo, and sand are just a few of the materials that can be used to pave a terrace, garden walk, or other surfacing. One of the most delightful variations on this theme, however, is the planted pavement. Through the introduction of planting pockets into a paving, hard surfaces take on the lively quality of change. Creeping herbs, perennials, bulbs, and smaller shrubs can all be tucked into the cracks and crevices within a paved expanse; as these plants come into bloom or fade with winter's chill, they interject the element of spontaneity into what might otherwise seem static garden spaces.

The specimen lawn is another effective means of turning the familiar into something unexpected. Because lawn grass is so commonplace, we often fail to see its beauty. When a smallish piece of turf is framed with plants or paving, however, it is no longer a neutral background but the point of focus. And because it is so simple, it is a nearly perfect *tour de force* of basic parterre thinking.

A mixture of red and yellow tulips, forget-me-nots, and purple violas fills beds with bright spring color on a terrace outside a contemporary house. Purple-leaved Japanese maples and plants espaliered against walls carry the garden up to eye level. William H. Frederick Jr., designer.

Edible Horticulture

The vegetable garden at Monticello, set on the brow of a hill, with squash, onions, and beans growing on sapling teepees, savory to accompany the beans, and sunflowers. The garden is being restored with vegetables listed in Jefferson's Plant Books.

The earliest parterre gardens were designed, not for appearance, but for practicality. The cloistered gardens of medieval castles and monasteries provided a source of plants for "meat" and medicine that was safe from enemies and animals alike. Due to the limited space within these walled retreats, these gardens had to be designed for maximum efficiency of space and productivity. Thus, these gardens were most often arranged in geometric patterns that conformed to their architectural enclosures.

Today, we also plant our gardens of utility near our homes—if not for safety,

then for convenience. Gardens planted to produce vegetables, herbs, and flowers for cutting also need full sun. Once, these gardens were hidden in corners. Today, they are becoming ornamental gardens in their own right.

Kitchen gardens, such as the one designed by George Washington at Mount Vernon, are both secluded and attractive. Entering this garden is like crossing the boundaries into a cultivated Eden. The garden is divided into small parterres, each with its own geometry; brick walks and tidy plots of lush green foliage lay a formal pattern on brown earth. Different

plants provide contrasting foliage textures.

Several considerations recommend a formal plan. Most vegetable gardens need long rows for plants like peas and beans, and shorter rows for things such as cucumbers and eggplant. The parterre gardens of Old Salem, a restored Moravian community in Winston-Salem, North Carolina, offer a solution. There, square garden plots are planted in striking chevron patterns; as the diagonal rows naturally vary in length, this allows the gardener to match decorative row lengths with the useful quantities of plants desired.

The current trend in vegetable gardening is to maximize garden space by minimizing the number of walks within a garden. Instead of having a path between each row, many gardeners plant several rows of vegetables between walkways, and grow such plants as lettuce in beds 3 to 4 feet (1 to 1⅓ meters) wide. Because a grid-type layout provides numerous plots of soil, one may plant in blocks and rows, depending on the crop. The width of individual beds, however, should not exceed the distance one can comfortably reach from the beds' edges.

With a little thought for the inherent beauty of vegetable plants, one can make a striking scene. Border the blue-green leaves of broccoli, for example with bright green-leaf lettuce for a doubly attractive and productive planting. Low-growing, finely textured plants like carrots and parsley may also be used to border coarsely textured vegetables such as cabbages and squash.

One of the nicest aspects of the vegetable garden is that it grows so quickly, which can be a solace as one waits for slower-growing ornamental plants to mature. Yet, because the vegetable garden is so frequently bare—the sign of a successful harvest—the overall appearance of the garden must depend on the design of its beds and walkways. Thus, a handsome layout is essential for bare spots to fit into the pattern and to give a hint of future bounty.

Herb gardens may also appear aimlessly planted unless beds have strong patterns and plants are diligently tended. Unlike ornamental plants, most herbs were not collected from the wild for beauty, but as sources of flavorings, medicines, and dyes. Herbs do not always have the best of forms or the showiest of flowers, so pattern is doubly important, and the plants should be closely spaced.

Herb gardens have typically been formal, if only due to their demands for full sun and regular maintenance. Despite their irregular habits of growth, most herbs have compact shapes or tend to form low mats of finely textured foliage. Lower growing herbs are often used as edgings

An herb garden in a stepped wall features stachys, artemisia, sorrel, and basil.

Herbs grown in ornamental knots in the garden at Filoli in Woodside, California.

Masses of purple-flowered chives in the vegetable garden of artist Robert Dash give a wild garden effect.

Roses, lilies, and achillea share quarters with squash, beans, lettuces, and onions.

for those with upright or weeping habits. The various foliage colors of herbs also lend themselves to striking combinations. Gray foliages, for example, may be used to frame a planting of bright green herbs or brilliant flowers, such as Bee Balm (*Monarda didyma*). Shrub-forming herbs like rosemary and lavender may also be planted as hedges; as one walks along adjacent paths, and brushes past these plants, their fragrant oils are released to fill the garden with sweetness.

Medieval herb gardens frequently took the form of elaborate embroidery patterns. Known as herb knots, these gardens were composed of sheared herb hedges arranged to form a pattern resembling interwoven rope. Strands of different colors were achieved with foliages of varying shades of gray or green. Germander and lavender were popular combinations, as were the gray and green forms of santolina. The beds formed by these loops of hedges were filled with pebbles or crushed brick for added color. For more diversity, however, these areas could be planted with low-growing herbs such as creeping thyme, lady's mantle, chamomile, or lamium—all of which also offer a display of flowers.

THE OUTDOOR ROOM

A change in level helps define a garden room with standard wisteria, globes of boxwood, English daisies, and iris around a sundial.

At Hever Castle, yew hedges outline a sunken garden, offsetting silver and gray plants, shrub roses, lavender, salvia, and geraniums.

Formality in Three Dimensions

Where the parterre garden lays a pattern on the ground, the outdoor room projects a pattern upward. Edges rise above the ground as fences, walls, or hedges; terraces become compartments, and walkways corridors. Overhead, these spaces may be open to the sky, canopied with trees, or ceilinged with a structure to contain the space entirely. Within, these outdoor chambers are furnished, much like indoor rooms, for dining, entertaining, relaxing, working, or playing. The outdoor room is as much architecture as it is garden.

Courtyards, of course, are the most familiar and oldest type of outdoor room. The homes of ancient Greece and Rome, for example, were frequently designed around a central open space, as were medieval castles and the palaces of Moorish Spain. During the fourteenth-century, however, the outdoor room "escaped" the courtyard. The Renaissance Italian villa was encompassed by its garden—a series of enclosed compartments used much like an annex to interior living spaces. Even so, the villa was a house within a garden.

The modern outdoor room eliminates this separation and forms a total living space where house and garden merge. In the early 1900s, architects began designing homes for a growing middle class. As the houses and plots tended to be modest, these houses also emphasized connections with the outdoors to maximize their sense of space. Walls were made of glass to open vistas to the garden, and doors of sliding glass made that connection physical. Also, the advent of the concrete slab foundation made it possible to extend the floor plan of a house into the garden as a terrace.

Because it is the most architectural of garden styles, the outdoor room is best described in house-like terms. As with rooms inside a house, these garden counterparts have walls, floors, ceilings, doors, and furnishings. Sometimes these are structural elements, or they may be adaptations of the gardening palette.

The character of the space depends largely on the form of enclosure. Walls and fences, for example, give a formal, highly architectural effect, as do tall clipped hedges. An untrimmed hedge, on the other hand, creates a softer, less precise effect. Lines of trees may also frame the edges of an outdoor room, much as a colonnade defines the limits of a porch. The spacing between trees, however, should be equal to ensure consistency along the room's perimeter.

The height of enclosure is also important, for this determines the proportions of an outdoor room. Generally, the higher its frame, the smaller a garden will appear. This doesn't mean, however, that a smallish garden room should have low walls. Indeed, the opposite approach is often more successful. When a restricted outdoor space is framed with lofty edgings, it seems more intimate, and more exciting because of the contrast. Similarly, large rooms appear quite grand when they are framed with tall enclosures. An elegant compromise is a stepped room, with low boundaries flanked by higher ones. A sunken garden with a low wall, flanked by a perimeter walk above it and a high wall or hedge as the outermost frame, gives a pleasant, enfolding effect. On a smaller scale, a patio that repeats the house's material in low walls can have taller hedges behind, closing all but a selected view.

Because it is enclosed, the outdoor room also creates a sheltered microclimate. By blocking winter winds and "trapping" the sun, it may extend the gardening season by several weeks. This advantage, coupled with the privacy the garden room affords, is of special value to city gardeners and those who live in colder climates. The order and convenience of the outdoor room, however, make this style appropriate to any situation where gardens are inhabited on a daily basis.

Much of the enjoyment, of course, depends on how the garden room is furnished. If one has the luxury of several outdoor rooms, each may be designed to have a unique character and a specific purpose. Rooms adjacent to the house, for example, may be paved and furnished for outdoor dining and entertaining, while other spaces may be used as flower gardens, playgrounds, or storage areas. This separation of uses also offers the advantage of closing off certain portions of the garden—to small children, pets, or casual visitors.

Even single garden rooms, however, can provide a diversity of uses. Just as interior designers zone a family living room for many needs, so the well-planned garden room can serve a multi-purpose role. For maximum flexibility, the center of a garden room may be completely paved, with planting beds restricted to the edges of the space. This arrangement also makes a small room seem larger.

If space is not a problem, the floor plan of a garden room may be more varied. Even so, a formal pattern is advised, as it will reinforce the orderly, architectural effect. A central lawn, for example, may be framed with walks and plantings; terraces may be designed much like area rugs to organize the garden's furnishings.

Most garden rooms benefit from some degree of overhead enclosure. In hot and sunny climates, a light but open arbor will give shade and still permit cool breezes to pass through, as will retractable canopies and louvered awnings. In areas of frequent, heavy rains, this covering may be a roof, so that the room may be enjoyed regardless of the weather.

Although shade trees may not offer shelter from the rain, they do provide a pleasant sense of spatial definition. Whether it be the lofty ceilings of tall-growing trees or the intimate canopy of smaller ornamentals, trees are natural architecture. Their trunks appear as columns and their branches form a roof. And when these trees are planted in a geometric pattern, the effect is even more pronounced.

Generally, the trees for outdoor rooms should be deciduous, to reinforce the microclimate these sheltered spaces make. During the summer they shade and cool the living space; as they lose their leaves in autumn, sunlight may penetrate and warm the garden room in winter. Flowering or fragrant trees, of course, are always welcome, as their color and perfume will be just overhead.

A central pool set in a stone-edged panel of grass. Evergreen shrubs articulate the cross-axes, and trimmed hedges give architectural definition to a perennial garden.

Between House and Garden

*B*ecause it is a hybrid style—a blend of house and garden—the outdoor room includes all sorts of open air compartments. Atriums, courtyards, porches, breezeways, balconies, and loggias belong as much to garden-makers as they do to architects. Thus, when one is making plans for a new residence, the outdoor room should be included in the process of design.

Of these house-related spaces, court-yards form the strongest link between a house and garden. They are also the most versatile of outdoor rooms. Generically, a courtyard is a room without a ceiling. More specifically, however, courtyards are enclosed with walls; at least one of these is a house facade, with doors or windows to give access to the garden space. Many times, of course, a courtyard is enclosed completely by a house. The courts of Latin architecture, for example, form the central feature of a home. Because it is connected to all major indoor rooms, such a court will often serve as the main hallway of a house and as an outdoor living room.

Enclosed but roofless courtyards—patios—are very energy-efficient. They bring air and light into the center of a house and provide a form of natural air conditioning. As most patios are paved, their surfaces collect and store the heat of sunlight during winter and enhance the flow of air in summer. By causing updrafts of warm air, the patio draws cool air through the indoor rooms. In drier climates, patios are often furnished with fountains; aside from the cooling effect of the sound, fountains increase humidity, lowering temperatures.

A glass-roofed atrium adapts these benefits to cooler climates. Like a courtyard's, the central placement of an atrium increases the flow of air throughout a house in summer and maximizes the heat of the winter sun. In warm weather vents within

Left: *A massive tree takes center stage in a house built around an open atrium, the canopy spreading high above the tiled roof. Evergreen ground cover skirts the earth below, and bromeliads attached to the trunk provide a splash of color.* **Above:** *A festive striped awning and pots full of annuals soften the edge between a raised porch and the garden beyond. Red and pink geraniums flank the stairs alongside a pair of New Zealand flax, Phormium tenax, and white petunias line the foot of the wall below. Pots of petunias, fuschias, and tuberous begonias perch on top, creating a colorful screen that encloses the porch without disrupting the flow between house and garden.*

the skylight should be opened to exhaust hot air and draw cool air into the space. When these vents are closed, however, the atrium becomes a solar stove. Atriums with retractable covers allow these rooms to be opened to the sky or closed.

Courtyards and atriums, of course, must be designed in concert with the planning of a house. The owners of existing homes, however, may enjoy the benefits these rooms provide by attaching courtyards to a house's outer walls. Indeed, this is an ideal way of gaining extra living space with minimal expense—especially if courtyards can be set into an ell, or between a house and detached garage or other structure. Existing hedges, fences, or walls

also simplify the process of transforming outdoor spaces into courtyards. But even if one must construct three sides of the enclosure, a courtyard is still less expensive than enclosing indoor space.

Porches are an alternative way to structure the transitional space between house and garden. They may be attached to one side of a house, or wrapped around a residence to form a gallery; they may be narrow, hall-like spaces, or wide enough for a true room. A porch provides a covered extension of indoor space.

Porches are most often found in warm and humid climates, where burning sun or frequent rains make coverings essential. In arid regions, porches are most often

Opposite page, top left: An interior window box with freesias and pansies offers an early breath of spring. *Top right:* Baskets of hanging geraniums repeated in the planting beds below. *Bottom left:* Tender oleander, lantana, and citrus in pots. *Bottom right:* Astilbe, delphiniums, and achillea bring summer into Robert Dash's Sagaponack (Long Island) living room.

This page: A wisteria-covered arbor at Dumbarton Oaks, constructed from a sixteenth-century design, with pool and bench, opening onto a sunny terrace.

placed on south and west exposures to shade house walls and windows from the heat and glare of sunlight. This placement also takes advantage of prevailing summer breezes. North-facing porches, on the other hand, create a reservoir of cooler air that can be drawn into the house by natural convection.

Where summers are hot and humid, houses are quite frequently surrounded with porches to insulate their walls from sun and rain. These porches also tend to be elevated above the ground to protect them from excessive moisture; many are also screened against mosquitos and other insects.

Aside from moderating the climate, of course, a porch provides a pleasant outdoor living space. As they are protected from the weather, porches may be furnished with comfortable, cushioned chairs, dining tables, and even rugs. Removable glazings convert the porch into a sun room during winter.

Loggias are like porches, in that they connect directly to a house and open to the garden. In a loggia, however, the garden connection is purely visual, for loggias are cantilevered porches—covered balconies that extend beyond an upper floor. Although they are less common than open balconies, loggias have the added advantage of being roofed. Thus, they may be used much like a porch for modifying indoor climate and extending living spaces to the outdoors. If they are sufficiently wide, of course, loggias may also form the covering for a ground level terrace or serve as a canopy over an entrance.

The City Garden

When it comes to outdoor living, city gardens offer both advantages and problems. Most city gardens are rather small, and the nearness of adjacent buildings also makes them warmer than suburban counterparts. Pollution, compacted or tired soils, and the lack of privacy are common problems. Also, city gardens tend to be leftover spaces—narrow yards or service courts between a house and alley, street-front setbacks, balconies, and rooftops. Yet, with practical design, most any room outside is a potential garden room.

Sun exposures, soil types, existing plants, and privacy should all be studied prior to making plans. Access is also important—both in terms of daily living and construction time. Does the garden, for example, open onto an alley (through which plants and other materials may be delivered to the site), or is the only access through the house? Utilities connections, views, and security must be considered.

Typically, one thinks of a city garden as a courtyard—a walled enclosure at the back of a town house. Yet the street side of a house may also have potential as an outdoor living space. If a house is set back from the sidewalk, for example, that area may be enclosed with walls to make a garden room. This is a special asset for houses on the north side of a street.

Courtyards with southern exposures take full advantage of prevailing, cooling summer breezes and the warmth of the winter sun. As these courts are also sheltered from the winter wind, they form passive solar collectors by trapping heat within their walls and pavings. If these courts are shaded with deciduous trees or with climbers trained on an arbor or trellis, they also modify the summer climate.

Courtyards that are set against the north side of a house, of course, will be much cooler all year long. While this is an advantage in summer, the northern orientation need not be a winter liability. Light-colored pavings will temper winter's chill

A straightforward plan with paving and rectangular pools complemented by a rich palette of plants in a London garden—pots of palm, fuschias, and nicotiana mixed in with silvery Dusty Miller surrounded by a Japanese maple, fatshedera, and climbers. John Vellam, designer.

Two columnar evergreens tower above an enclosed garden in Charleston, South Carolina, with beds of azaleas, mahonia, podocarpus, and geraniums. Robert Chesnut, designer.

Paired stepping-stones and neat wood edges highlight a water garden. Brophy, designer.

by absorbing heat from sunlight. Interior walls should also be designed to maximize solar gain. This is best accomplished by using tall masonry walls that have been painted white, gray, or another light color. Masonry retains heat better than wood or metal; light colors make a courtyard brighter and more cheerful.

Because most urban gardens are framed, and often overlooked, by adjacent houses, privacy is a prime consideration. Thus, it may be necessary to screen or even cover portions of the garden to reduce its open, "fishbowl" character.

While trees provide the simplest solution to this problem, many city gardens have compacted or infertile soils that retard their growth. Also, if a courtyard is surrounded by tall buildings, it may be too shady for most trees. Even those that thrive in shade, however, may compound the problem by excluding sunlight from the space below them. In such cases, roofs provide a practical alternative.

A roof, of course, need not be solid to give privacy. Indeed, complete enclosure makes small gardens claustrophobic; they also cut off light and reduce air circulation. An open arbor, latticework, or wire-trained vines, on the other hand, provide a light and airy cover. Although these structures may not block out views entirely, they define a garden's upper edges; this, in turn, directs attention inward and minimizes the importance of space outside the garden.

Because they are so architectural, city gardens often are hard-edged, geometric spaces. Consequently, plants are an important element for softening walls and pavings, and for achieving seasonal diversity. A large expanse of wall, for example, may be given interest by planting it with vines or espaliered trees. Lattices or trellises may also be attached to walls to add architectural detailing and to provide support for plants.

Planting beds enrich and organize the floor plan of a garden, but to overcome the difficulties of urban soils, it may be necessary to replace existing soil or to make raised planting beds. Elevated planters also improve drainage and prevent the accumulation of mineral salts, as do container plantings.

Potted plants are an especially effective means of adding seasonal color to a garden; as they are portable, they may be moved indoors during winter or rearranged periodically to give variety. Permanent container plants, of course, should be selected for interest in several seasons and for hardiness.

If vegetables are grown in city gardens, it is essential to replace existing soil or to plant in raised beds or containers. City soils frequently contain dangerous concentrations of toxic metals; plants such as cabbage, broccoli, and greens absorb these metals and store them in their foliage. Automobile exhausts and smoke from nearby industries may also deposit dangerous chemicals on plants or into the soil through rainfall. Thus, vegetables should be watered frequently to prevent accumulations in their roots, and leaves should be washed throughout the growing season to minimize absorption of pollutants.

The Roof Garden

When ground-level space is not available, many urban gardeners turn to balconies and rooftops for their outdoor space. Even a narrow ledge outside a window may become a garden. These "sky gardens" also take advantage of the views across a city.

Although window sills and balconies may not be large enough to serve as living space, they still may be designed for active gardening. Planters set outside a window or along the edges of a balcony give a living framework to the home. Climbing vines may be encouraged to surround a window or trained along a railing. These plants, of course, should be selected for drought tolerance, since the comparatively high winds on urban balconies and roofs will tend to dry them out.

Larger spaces, on the other hand, offer real opportunities for outdoor living. Depending on their size and convenience of access, these spaces may be designed and furnished for outdoor dining, entertaining, or growing plants. Due to their exposed conditions, of course, these gardens must be planned for frequent maintenance—especially watering—and protection from wind and sun. Also, structural stability should be assured before installing furnishings, pavings, or plant containers.

As with all city gardens, large balconies and rooftops are artificial environments. Yet the absence of natural amenities need not exclude the city dweller from the joys of garden living. Indeed, the presence of an outdoor room may be most valued in a city because it does much more than just extend a house into the outdoors. Urban garden rooms create an integral relationship between a house, its occupants, and their environment.

A simple line of ivy and red geraniums provides summer and winter color without disrupting the river view from this spectacular New York terrace.

Top: Small containers filled with annuals or vegetables and herbs bring summer to a city roof; and being portable, they can travel with the sun (and with the tenant, once a lease expires). Lightweight tables and chairs can be moved indoors and out, as necessary. **Above:** Trees provide rooftop privacy and protection from sun and wind. This garden is a shady bower in summertime with a green Japanese maple, yew, rhododendron, wisteria, and ivy. Geraniums add color.

The Garden of Rooms

Just as courtyards and patios project a house into its garden, so too may the pattern of a house extend to garden planning. The modern garden of rooms applies the principles of architecture—spatial volume, privacy, convenience, and order—to the total site. Thus, there is an equity and unity of space within both house and garden rooms.

One of the finest gardens of rooms is to be found at Sissinghurst Castle in Kent. There, the house and garden are so thoroughly combined, it is impossible to separate architecture from garden planning, and horticulture from design. Indeed, the "house" at Sissinghurst is sited throughout the garden. Four separate buildings—two cottages, a tower, and a long, barn-like structure—are related with a series of outdoor compartments, garden walks, and open corridors.

A garden of rooms divides a site into a number of related living spaces; some of these are covered while others are left open. Because the garden of rooms takes full advantage of a site, its planning should begin at the lot line. Ideally, the entire property is framed with fences, walls, or hedges to create an envelope of private, outdoor space. Many zoning codes, of course, do not allow a street-front space to be enclosed with permanent structures or hedges above a certain height. Trees, however, tend to be excluded from these limitations. Thus, a front yard may be framed with "aerial" hedges—closely planted trees that can be pruned to form a formal box of foliage just above eye level.

Small, ornamental trees may also be used to make a more informal screen; these may be combined with shrubs to seal the space between their trunks.

Within these lot-line frameworks, garden spaces are designed to suit the needs and inclinations of the gardener. If a house sits near the center of the garden, for example, outdoor rooms may be attached to each facade to totally surround the house with outdoor compartments.

This arrangement is especially useful in suburban settings where side areas are too often overlooked as garden space. Side gardens also offer promise as private living space. Depending on the arrangement of interior rooms, they may be used as quiet courtyards off a bath or bedroom, library, or dining room.

In the back garden, space may be organized to serve different needs. Areas adjacent to the house, for example, may be designed as outdoor living rooms; other spaces may be used as playgrounds, vegetable or flower gardens, or for storage. Although each outdoor room should form a self-contained enclosure, rooms should be connected to sequence space as one moves through the garden. They should also be arranged to form a logical, but varied and stimulating, progression of uses and characters.

A small dining court, for example, may open to a spacious flower garden so that its color and fragrance may be enjoyed during meals. A swimming pool enclosure, on the other hand, may be attached to a smaller, shaded space, for contrast. Long, narrow corridors also serve as counterpoints to the more open character of the garden's rooms and provide connections throughout the garden.

The structures that separate compartments should also be designed for maximum variety. One side of a hedge, for example, may be clipped to make a formal space, while the reverse side may be left untrimmed. Similarly, walls and fences may be painted, stained, or espaliered with plants or vines to give additional richness to their surfaces.

Overhead structures—arbors, gazebos,

Even without a wall, the separation between these two garden rooms is clear; the lower grade, richer plant palette, and paved floor of the sunken garden contrast distinctly with the open lawn above. In addition, the small scale and raised banks of the sunken garden demand special handling, for every plant is plainly visible. The design differentiates between the two rooms without dividing them. Valerie Stevenson, designer.

Paving and a change in elevation help define this outdoor seating area, and the limbs of an adjacent tree provide a canopy overhead, further enhancing the sense of enclosure. The bank is higher, wider, and more protective where it meets the terrace.

and pergolas—also have their place in the garden of rooms. An arbor may be designed as an extension of the roofline of a residence, with posts and beams to match the construction of the house. Freestanding arbors, on the other hand, may be constructed of rustic timbers, finished lumber, concrete, brick, or stone; worked metal arbors offer the advantage of being sculptural elements as well as garden spaces. Arbors of contemporary design may be painted bright colors to accent or contrast with a garden's color scheme, while the intricate geometries or naturalis-

tic patterns of Victorian wrought iron give a softer and a more romantic character.

Gazebos and pergolas are rooms within rooms. Typically, gazebos are designed as architectural ornaments to organize a view or terminate an axis. Pergolas are more versatile. They may be used to enclose one side of a rose garden or other formal, sunny space, as well as to create an outdoor corridor. Placed between two rooms, pergolas give subtle separation between compartments without excluding views or breezes; when they are planted with flowering vines, pergolas further en-

rich the garden with shade and color.

The interconnections within a garden of rooms should also emphasize connections with indoor space. The placement of doors and windows should maximize the views from house to garden. A central walkway or corridor, for example, may continue the alignment of a hallway out into the garden. Sculpture, fountains, and garden doors should also be located to serve as focal points for garden rooms and window views. Plants with unique characters or seasonal value are equally effective in directing attention outdoors.

THE COUNTRY COTTAGE

Kaleidoscopic Horticulture

The rural gardeners of England, Europe, and America have always been more concerned with growing plants for color and diversity than for formal effect. Yet these unpretentious gardens have inspired elegant design: Hidcote Manor, Sissinghurst, and Great Dixter in England; the painterly garden of Claude Monet at Giverny in France; and the "country-place era" gardens of early twentieth-century America. Today, the cottage garden is enjoying a renaissance at the same time as it is being made practical.

Bounty is the key word in the cottage style. Although plant selection is some-times limited to a particular type of plant, such as natives, perennials, or even a specific type of perennial such as daylilies or herbs, the hallmark of the cottage garden is the full range of plants it can draw from. Trees, shrubs, vines, ground covers, annuals, biennials, perennials, herbs, and vegetables all find their place.

For this reason, the cottage garden tends to be a testing ground for horticultural experimentation. New selections and introductions join the ranks of well-established garden favorites and rarities. Yet because such testing calls for close attention to plant requirements and an understanding of horticultural procedures, the cottage gardener must be both adventurous and willing to learn, as ready to cope with failures as to enjoy success.

Thus, the cottage style is useful to beginning gardeners. By starting with "sure" things that have been proven over many years, the novice gardener gains the confidence to try out something new. Gradually, the plant collection grows, as do the gardener's expertise and understanding.

With this growing skill, the cottage gardener frequently begins to specialize in certain types of plants; with time, the garden slowly starts to focus on a theme. This may be a simple preference for certain colors or for plants that flower in a particular season. Often, however, the cottage gardener will build a definite collection of specific types of plants: hostas, roses, dahlias, minor bulbs, for example, or plants that require similar growing conditions, such as alpines and shade-loving plants.

Even so, there is a need to organize the cottage garden so that its abundance may be best enjoyed. Gertrude Jekyll, the turn-

Opposite page: Shade gardens hardly need be monochromatic, particularly in spring. Azaleas, primulas, ajuga, violets, and phlox bring a burst of color to the Connecticut woods. **Above left:** *Forget-me-nots, alyssum, violets, and azaleas line a path in the same garden.* **Above center:** *Vita Sackville West's cottage garden at Sissinghurst with full beds of astrantia, pink and white lilies, and ferns planted arm-in-arm. Banking taller flowers toward the back of the beds reinforces the sense of enclosure.* **Above right:** *Tulips, forget-me-nots, and special moisture-loving plants find comfortable footing around a stone-edged woodland pool.*

of-the-century gardener and author—and the most respected authority on the cottage garden—was "strongly of the opinion" that possessing a collection of plants does not a garden make. "This does not constitute a picture," she said, "and it seems to me that the duty we owe to our gardens . . . is so to use the plants that they shall form beautiful pictures." Indeed, the romantic, pictorial quality of cottage gardens is their greatest value and the main source of their delight.

Too often, however, cottage gardens are planted with total disregard for color harmonies. Sometimes, of course, this may produce a pleasant hodgepodge; especially if colors, plant heights, and flowering seasons are freely mixed to form a paisley or calico effect. But even the most informal of gardens will benefit from some degree of order in planting. Taller plants,

for example, are best located behind low-growing flowers so that both may be enjoyed to maximum advantage. Such a hierarchy also simplifies the process of weeding and grooming plants.

Cottage garden plants may also be arranged along a color theme that blends or contrasts hues. The single-color garden is an especially effective means of organizing flowering plants. "It is amusing," wrote Vita Sackville-West, the author who created the garden at Sissinghurst Castle in Kent, "to make one-colour gardens. . . . For my own part, I am trying to make a grey, green, and white garden." This "amusement," of course, resulted in Sissinghurst's White Garden, perhaps the most famous cottage garden in the world—and one of the most extensive.

Obviously, the country cottage garden is not a low-maintenance garden. The

care and tending of such gardens, however, is largely their purpose. Maintenance can be reduced if plants are grown according to their appropriate horticultural requirements. Vigorous plants or those that tend to be invasive, for example, may be planted in containers or planting beds surrounded with paving. An underground barrier, such as a galvanized tub from which the bottom has been removed, may also be used to contain aggressive plants. Delicate or tender plants, on the other hand, may all be grown together in an easily accessible location to guarantee that they receive the frequent attention they require. In dry climates, an irrigation system will simplify the process of watering the garden during droughts; plants that prefer very moist conditions may also be set out in pots with solid bottoms to better ensure an evenly moist environment.

Beds and Borders

Order within the cottage garden is influenced by the horticultural requirements of its plants; soil conditions and sun exposure are the limiting considerations in both plant selection and overall design. The ideal garden, of course, affords a full range of conditions: sun and shade, moist and well-drained planting areas, sweet and acid soils. While it may not be possible to meet all these requirements, with careful planning the cottage garden can provide a wide range of conditions.

Since most flowering plants prefer a sunny, open spot, the cottage garden should, whenever possible, restrict the size and number of its trees. While there is no lack of plants that thrive in shade, their selection is more limited than full-sun-loving plants. With a densely wooded garden, however, it may be necessary to remove some trees to offer more warmth and light for optimum plant diversity.

Garden soils are, of course, the most important aspect of any successful planting. The great majority of garden plants prefer a light, well-drained soil that is rich in organic matter. Thus, heavy soils may require the addition of sand, perlite, or vermiculite; thin or shallow soils benefit from compost, leaf mold, and other moisture-retaining materials. The acidity or alkalinity of garden soils may also need to be adjusted to achieve a balanced soil chemistry. Although very acid soils are easily "sweetened" with the addition of agricultural lime, alkaline soils are more difficult to adjust because of the concentrations of soil salts that inhibit plant growth. Mildly alkaline soils may be amended by adding acid fertilizers, gypsum, or soil sulfur, but very alkaline conditions may necessitate the removal and replacement of garden soils to achieve a healthy growing medium. Still, there is a surprising variety of plants that will grow in chalky soil.

The need for proper soil preparation cannot be overemphasized, because once planting has begun it is very difficult to amend soils without disturbing existing plants. Consequently, the planning of a cottage garden should begin with the preparation of its planting spaces.

Generally, the planting areas within a cottage garden are composed of beds and borders. A "bed" is loosely defined

as any area in which plants are grown. More frequently, however, a planting bed is surrounded with lawn or paving, and is thus accessible from all sides. A border, on the other hand, is set against a wall, hedge, or fence. Each of these planting spaces offers certain advantages and liabilities to the overall design.

Since they can be seen from every side, planting beds must be designed in-the-round. They do, however, offer the advantage of easy access for tending, and their open character also ensures exposure to sun and healthy circulation of air within the planting.

Beds set into terraces or framed with walks tend to give a better effect than those surrounded with lawn, because the former look less arbitrary or accidental. Lawn beds also interrupt the continuity of the garden's open spaces, which can lead to a generally confused appearance in the garden's plan. Lawn beds present a particular problem when several smallish beds are scattered throughout a lawn. A single, massive bed, on the other hand, may seem too dominant and out of scale with its surroundings. On the other hand, if beds are designed with flowing curves or as formal elements within an open lawn, they can provide an effective means of organizing space. Prior to cultivation of these beds, it is a good idea to test the pattern by laying it out with a garden hose or with a series of stakes and string connectors. A light dusting of flour or sand may also be used to plan the shape of garden beds. Such approximations, of course, will not account for the color and texture of flowers and plants, but they will be useful in determining shape and size.

It is the border, however, that is the cottage garden's glory. Whether it be a planting of shrubs, perennials, or a combination of these plants, the garden border makes the best of cottage planting and design.

As foundation plantings, borders are the perfect choice: They give ornament to house walls, which in turn provide a backdrop for the border. Even borders placed away from architecture benefit from backgrounds. Walls and hedges are most effective enhancements to a border because they give a solid, vertical surface against which to view the plant display. Fences may also be used behind a border; the darker and more solid the structure of the fence, the better the effect. If such backgrounds seem too formal, one may plant

Left: The mixed, polychrome border looks best when drifts of each plant are used. *Above:* A "hot" border featuring different hues of one species, the long-flowering Helianthemum cistus. *Right top:* The purple of spring-blooming lily turf gives way to orange Chrysanthemums in the fall *(bottom).*

Pink, purple, and white petunias and marigolds surround a stand of delphinium in a sunny garden. Annuals can be useful in determining effective juxtapositions of color, texture, and height for a flower garden that ultimately will be planted with perennials. In themselves, they make a cheerful scene.

the border against an irregular hedge of evergreen shrubs. The interplay of forms between such plantings and the border is quite attractive. Large, upright shrubs, for example, may be interspersed with lower, spreading plants to give a very informal, undulating top edge to the screen; shrubs of various depths may also be interspersed to create pockets between the background plants, and these pockets can be filled with border materials.

Shrubbery borders themselves are very popular; if they are designed as combinations of evergreen and deciduous flowering shrubs, such plantings will have pictorial interest throughout the year. Shrub borders may be fronted with a flower border or merely used alone. A combination of shrubs and flowers, however, will increase the garden's richness of plant types.

The most classic border, of course, is that composed of flowers, especially perennials. As a garden element, the perennial border is a fairly recent innovation, developed as a means of bringing order to the horticultural chaos of late-Victorian gardens. The English garden writer William Robinson expressed profound dislike for the highly contrived and wasteful mania for ''carpet beds'' so popular in the mid-1800s—elaborate plantings, mainly of exotics and annuals. In their place he recommended a more ''natural'' garden of wild plants and perennials. What Robinson started, however, Jekyll perfected; due in part to her more diplomatic style of writing, she succeeded in converting the British to her way of thinking.

The perfect perennial border stays in bloom from earliest spring through frost. In such borders, something is always beginning to bloom as something else is fading.

Because even the longest-blooming perennials do not stay in flower for more than a month to six weeks, however, the real border invariably falls short of constant bloom. Consequently, perennial borders are best designed for specific seasonal interest. By choosing plants that flower within closely overlapping time frames, the gardener enjoys six to eight weeks of continual bloom; then the border fades. As one border declines, however, another may start moving toward its own perfection, followed by yet other borders in their

seasons. This does represent a compromise, but on the whole, it is a successful and satisfying approach for achieving consistency and fullness in the cottage garden.

Aside from choosing plants that flower simultaneously or in series, the gardener must define the characteristics those plantings should possess, such as color theme. Single-color borders are the easiest to design because they guarantee a unified effect. But singleness of color theme does not mean that every plant must be of the same color quality. Dark and light shades will blend agreeably, as will their pastels; in combination, these various shades of color give a very rich effect.

As one adds more color, the chances for disharmony increase. Two-color borders are usually more unified than three- or four-color combinations, until one reaches a blending of all colors. One often-successful principle is to plant "hot" or "cool" borders, mixing only colors that come from the warm or cool end of the visible spectrum.

Panchromatic borders are delightful, because they make no pretense of precious sophistication. Thus, they are well suited to the character of country cottage gardens. The only goals one needs to keep in mind when planning multi-colored borders is horticultural compatability and evenness of effect. Plants should be allowed sufficient room to reach their maximum size, and each color of flower should be evenly distributed throughout the border. All-color borders also benefit from generous amounts of white flowers and gray foli-

ages to "neutralize" colors that tend to clash.

Because the planning of perennial borders requires a well-developed awareness of plant varieties, even the simplest of borders is a challenge to beginning designers. The use of familiar and time-tested perennials—such as garden phlox, yarrow, bearded iris, daylilies, chrysanthemums, peonies, and columbines—helps to build one's confidence for trying lesser-known selections.

Because the design of a perennial border requires the coordination of so many variables—color, flowering season, and plant forms and heights, as well as horticultural needs—the beginning gardener may sometimes do well to approximate the planting effects of a border with annuals. This will make it possible to try out color combinations prior to planting the border with permanent plants. Annuals are also less expensive than are perennials and may be grown from seed. Thus, color combinations can be perfected with these temporary plants; the effect can then be translated to appropriate perennials.

Flower arrangements offer a similar opportunity to test color combinations for the garden. Many cut flowers have characteristics similar to those of perennials. The tall spikes of gladiolus, for example, may be used to *simulate* foxgloves, veronica, delphenium, or any tall, slender flower; florist chrysanthemums and daisies closely resemble their garden counterparts. Then there are perennials that also serve as cutting flowers—iris, liatris, baby's breath, kniphofia, chrysanthemums, and shasta daisies. They provide an excellent and inexpensive opportunity to test the garden's plantings in a vase. Such arrangements also help remind one that the border can be a source of flowers for the home.

Celosia doesn't suit everyone's taste, and it certainly isn't for timid gardeners—but it can make a striking addition to a flower border. Here red, white, yellow, and salmon-colored Celosia 'Fancy Plumes' appear with brightly colored marigolds and zinnias.

Roses at Lyndhurst Castle, arranged with the classic elements that contribute to a rose garden's success: a dark background, a sculptural feature (this one includes a place to sit and enjoy sight and scent), and roses in profusion with a variety of forms and heights.

Themes and Variations

Sometimes, a gardener's favorite plants may be so dominant in the design as to become the garden's theme. For the connoisseur of roses, narcissi, or ferns, for example, the garden's purpose becomes to grow the most or best of possible selections. Other gardeners may come to specialize in plants that are indigenous to a specific region, say natives or alpines.

There are also "literary" themes, limited to plants mentioned in the Bible or the works of William Shakespeare, and art-related themes, such as the garden inspired by the "Hunt of the Unicorn" tapestries at the Cloisters Museum in New York City. Whatever the source of inspiration, theme gardens offer a distinctive principle for organizing both the garden and its plant collection.

The rose is perhaps the most familiar of garden themes; even though roses may be grown in many situations, there is something to be said for giving them a garden of their own. When roses are grouped in a single bed or garden space, maintenance will be simpler. Roses also tend to be "antisocial." Because they are heavy feeders, roses need to be kept separate from other garden plants that may compete for nutrients and moisture. Overcrowding also encourages the development of fungal diseases.

The best recommendation for a rose garden, however, is purely aesthetic. When they are in bloom, massed roses are spectacular. Their perfume is also more enjoyable because it is concentrated. To take full advantage of these treats, one should, whenever possible, place rose gardens near outdoor living spaces—and if this isn't practical, then one should, as Mohammed to the mountain, take measures to go to the rose.

A central arbor or gazebo makes an ideal focus for a formal rose plantation; if these structures are garlanded with climbing types to offer shade, the effect is truly romantic. When roses are grown in a border, a covered seat within a niche or recess in the planting—or set along a walkway opposite the border—will provide a cool retreat for viewing the display.

Where roses lend themselves to rather formal treatments, other plant collections may be better suited to casual effects. Extensive plantings of iris, daylilies, chrysanthemums, and peonies, for example, are ideally suited to informal, curving layouts. Since these plants prefer full sun, they may be planted in sweeping masses to paint the garden with broad strokes of color. Such plantings may also be arranged according to color gradations—from light to dark, or the reverse—to give a spectrum effect along a bed or border. This is especially effective when the alignment of plantings parallels the garden's principal line of view. Because cool colors recede and warm colors advance visually, a planting that progresses from vivid foreground colors to soft pastels will help increase the apparent depth of smaller garden spaces. When the more brilliant colors are planted farther from the viewer, on the other hand, the opposite effect occurs. If plantings are arranged across the garden's line of sight, dark colors should be placed behind more delicately colored flowers to keep the latter from being overpowered.

Collections of shade-loving plants are often most effective when arranged very informally. Unlike the woodland garden, however, the cottage shade garden does not attempt to duplicate a truly natural effect. Rather, it takes advantage of cool and moist locations to display a particular group of plants. Collections of shade-

In a border designed to create a brilliant spring display, a collection of tulips is planted in bold blocks of reds and yellows; their variety is neatly incorporated in the simple scheme and the strong sweeping line of the curved bed.

Chrysanthemums bring the tawny colors of fall to a perennial garden—a last burst of bloom after summer flowers have faded and an effective way to take advantage of the interesting tones and textures of the perennial plants' foliage.

Left: *Mats of pink and yellow flowers, clumps of gray-green dianthus and the round leaves of viola, and mounds of dwarf evergreens interwoven in a garden in northern New Jersey.* **Right:** *A collection of lychnis and calluna lines a stepped gravel path in the heath and heather section of the Van Dusen Botanic Gardens in Vancouver, British Columbia.*

loving plants usually develop in response to natural conditions; most shade gardens begin with many types of plants, until the gardener becomes familiar with the richness possible within a certain plant group. Ferns, hostas, and hellebores, for example, offer hundreds of species and hybrids; a garden devoted to these plants has a most effective means of turning a limitation to advantage. Although hostas and hellebores have attractive flowers and many ferns produce handsome sori (the fern's equivalent of flowers), these are basically foliage plants. Thus, such collections should be designed to blend or contrast

A palette of dusty roses, grays, yellows, and blues was selected for an English garden that features heaths and heathers. Sculptural evergreens structure the beds, adding height and mass to the low-growing ericaceous plants. Adrian Bloom, designer.

variations of leaf size, shape, and color.

While almost any group of plants may be developed into a collection, there is one theme that may be used to underscore all gardens. Whether it be for a heady sweetness or a subtle perfume, fragrant plants add another sensory dimension. The most familiar sources of scent are flowering plants. Many garden plants, however, also have fragrant foliages; a few, such as lavender and carnations, double the effect with scented blooms *and* leaves. There are other fragrances that must be discovered, such as the mellow sweetness of mint and the tart, refreshing spice of rosemary, whose delicate and lovely perfume is released only when the leaves are crushed.

Containers in the Garden

The classic pot and the classic pot plant: terra cotta and geranium.

It is perhaps a little odd to talk about containers in the context of the cottage garden, since one of their best uses is to feature plantings that are not hardy enough to remain outside all year. It was, after all, the Victorian greenhouse—that most elaborate excuse for container gardening—that Robinson and Jekyll disliked. But since the modern use of containers is typically more modest—and since their most prominent effect is to add color to the flower garden or allow a flower garden where none was possible before—we may admit them to this chapter.

Often, plants are grown in pots because they are not suited to the garden proper. This may be a matter of hardiness, as with tender tropicals that are moved indoors for winter, or it may be a specific horticultural requirement, such as the need for alkaline soil or constricted roots. Thus, containers extend the gardener's palette.

Portability is also an advantage. Plants may be moved to sun or shade as necessary, or stored away from sight when out of season. Container-grown flowers are often started in the garden and brought indoors when they are at peak bloom; potted annuals bring color to decks, terraces, and other spaces where in-ground planting is not possible.

Placing a plant in a container makes it instantly important, by setting it apart. Just as framing reinforces the appearance of a print or painting, potting emphasizes the character of a plant. Although plants with handsome flowers, foliage, or branching patterns are most often thought of as container subjects, even common plants seem special when grown in a pot.

Proportions are especially important in matching plant to container. While large containers may be filled with either tall or spreading plants, a larger plant will always call for a substantial planter—to accommodate its roots, of course, and to assure a visually pleasing mass beneath that plant. A 3-gallon planter may, indeed, support a 3-foot (910 mm) shrub or even taller tree, but it will look too small. Also, such a planter may not be sufficiently heavy to anchor the plant securely in strong breezes.

Container plants are often used to complement an architectural feature, like an entrance, or as focal elements to terminate or organize a view. In either case, the scale of both the plant and planter should be in proportion to their setting. Small container plants, for example, may seem insignificant or accidental when used adjacent to a house or in an open garden. A very large container, however, rarely seems too large or out of scale in any setting. Massive jardinieres, tree boxes, or metal urns, with equally impressive trees or shrubs, provide a dramatic contrast to small courtyards, entrances, and terraces, as well as help to fill larger spaces.

Container plants may also "substitute" for architecture. A series of large potted shrubs may enclose a porch or deck, much like an open balustrade; a pair of trees or upright shrubs may define a gateway at the intersection of a walk or terrace. Container-grown trees may also form a canopy for garden living spaces. Four Italian lemon pots—huge terra cotta containers used for growing citrus trees—French tree boxes, or other large-scale planters, for example, may be arranged to form an open square; that room-like space may then be furnished for outdoor dining or conversation, or as a setting for a fountain or piece of sculpture.

One of the most common uses of container plants, of course, is for seasonal color. In an all-green courtyard, in a small

Arrangements of mixed pots can be attractive, but for a spot in a small garden, the simplicity of this stand is striking. Three tiers of primulas—pink with just a few purple, each in a terra cotta pot—have a clean, uncluttered look. The stand makes it possible to rearrange color groupings easily.

city garden, or in colder climates where the growing season is short, the use of potted flowers add color and variety to garden settings. To maximize this value, and to minimize expense, many gardeners depend on the vast array of seed-grown annuals. Although these plants do grow quickly, they rarely flower in the early spring. Thus, to fill this void, annuals may be started indoors in containers and brought into the garden for early-season color.

Container-grown bulbs are an especially easy means of gaining springtime color. As these bulbs are sold in autumn, the gardener may plant a few bulb pots every two to four weeks to assure that early spring will have its flowers. Cro-

cuses, freesias, tulips, and daffodils may also be forced into bloom by bringing pots of bulbs indoors, where they will quickly develop flowers for late winter color and fragrance for the house. Best of all, most bulbs can be recycled in the garden for repeated color over many years. Containers of summer-blooming flowers may also be started, to fill the awkward time between early season flowers and summertime abundance.

Almost any plant can be grown in a container if it is given sufficient soil and water and proper light. Larger plants, of course, will not attain their maximum size, but rather will take on an interesting contorted and dwarfed appearance. Plants that have naturally erratic habits of growth

will seem even more attractive when grown in pots. For maximum effectiveness, of course, these plants should be displayed where their forms and characters may be enjoyed: on a table, a low platform, or the railing of a porch or terrace. One or two of these will have the greatest impact.

When it comes to using mixed plants in one container, however, restraint is less important. In a very large container, for example, one may mix all sorts of flowering plants to give the effect of a living flower arrangement. Individual pots of flowers, shrubs, and trees may also be grouped together to form a collage. Clustering potted plants will also simplify watering, feeding, and grooming.

Containers provide an ideal opportunity to give favorite plants center stage or to sample a new variety before introducing it in garden beds. Here Begonia 'Glamour Rose,' Browallia 'Blue Bells,' Geranium 'Flash Fire,' and Coleus 'Fiji Red' provide mounds of bright portable color in a walled garden.

At its best, trough gardening elevates the practice of growing in containers to a fine art, for it invites special collections of alpines and miniature plants arranged with a keen eye to nuances of form, scale, and texture, as well to more practical cultural requirements.

Orchids and epiphytic plants need a well-ventilated soilless medium that can be messy to water; they look undistinguished when out of blossom. Thus, where climate allows, they are ideal subjects for growing in or attached to trees. A cluster of pots makes an effective display.

THE ORIENTAL STYLE

Subtle Balances

The gardens of Japan and China possess a subtle beauty that is both enigmatic and profoundly simple. To the Western eye, these gardens seem exotic, mysterious, and captivating, because they are so different. Even though many Westerners have traveled in the East and almost everyone has access to its gardens through photographs, books, and magazines, the Oriental garden continues to perplex and to delight.

This fascination is largely due to cultural conditioning. In the West, we tend to think of gardens as a means of organizing and enhancing daily life through practical design. The Oriental garden, on the other hand, tends to be a place of tranquil, even passive, pleasures; where Western gardens are outward-focused and gregarious, the gardens of the East usually look inward; or if they look outward, bring the surrounding landscape into the garden. They are largely designed for personal meditation and contemplation.

This is not to say that Western gardens are insensitive to nature or that Oriental gardens are more sympathetic to nature's order. Their approaches to nature, however, are quite different. The Western garden has a pragmatic naturalism that attempts to minimize disruption by fully understanding the "mechanics" of environment; the Oriental garden conceptualizes nature and interprets it, abstractly and artificially. The stones, plants, and water features of Oriental gardens presume not to reproduce but to symbolize the harmonies of natural design.

Whether it be the patterns of raked

sand, stones, or moss of a Buddhist temple garden, or the quiet intimacy of a tea garden, these gardens instill a sense of peace in visitors. If one is willing to borrow and interpret elements from these gardens, rather than copy their arrangement without accepting their philosophies, the Oriental style can be a valid garden form in the West. One must, of course, respect their spirit to avoid the gimmickry that characterizes many so-called Oriental gardens. It is silly to expect that many Westerners will contemplate the universe while gazing at a stone. The beauty of that stone, however, and its placement in a garden may enhance our appreciation of natural forms.

The Oriental style is frequently described in terms of calculated informality. Elements are so well suited to the total composition that the garden seems almost accidental. Yet the arch of a maple tree across a path, a tuft of fern against a stone, or the placement of a lantern on the far side of a pool are quite deliberate. Indeed, each garden element is carefully designed to call attention to itself and to enhance some other feature.

The maple tree across the path, for example, is usually planted so that it is seen against a background of contrasting foliage texture. This emphasizes the leaves and branching of the tree, and builds a layering of space that increases the garden's apparent depth. More often than not, such trees or other features are also placed at the turning of a path to reinforce the change of direction. As one continues along the path, however, some other feature, such as a bench or bridge, becomes a visual destination from which one looks back across the garden.

Such reciprocal elements are integral to Oriental gardens. Foreground objects invariably become part of the background as one passes through the garden. This is more than just a matter of distance, however. By allowing features to be studied close at hand and then as part of a larger scene, the Oriental garden builds a subtle harmony between its parts and whole. These gardens tend to have a limited number of features but many points of view.

The minimalism that characterizes Japanese design in particular is often attributed to the crowded conditions of Far Eastern cities and the relatively small areas of land available. Simplicity and restraint, however, are also related to the Oriental philosophies and symbolism. Distilling a house, a vase, or a garden to its essential elements stimulates imagination. The mind fills in details that may only be suggested. Thus, a single tree, stone, or basin of water may represent a forest, a mountain, or the ocean.

For Westerners, the sparseness of Oriental design appeals to our preferences for order and practicality. The simple, almost Spartan spaces of an Oriental garden lend themselves to a diversity of uses. A surfacing of river pebbles, for example, may be used as a driveway, a terrace, or a logical solution for spaces with dense shade or saturated soils. The limited use of plants and ornaments is also economical. By emphasizing the characteristics of a single tree or a small plantation of shrubs, minimalism gives the appearance of order with the least amount of effort.

Even so, minimalism should not be mistaken for absolute simplicity. While Oriental gardens tend to be uncomplicated in their layout, they are rich in detail. Pavings, for example, frequently combine irregular stone blocks with cut stone, gravel, brick, and tile, yet such patterning is rarely used for only decoration. An intricate paving pattern or a change in surface materials, for example, is frequently used to call attention to a nearby plant. Detail pavings also encourage one to pause; while one studies the pattern, the sound of water or the wind in pine trees slowly becomes apparent.

Oriental garden plants are also chosen with much care. Although evergreens play an important role, these are always combined with deciduous materials that flower, produce colorful fruit, or take on autumn color. The Japanese cherry, for example, is a favorite because it offers year-round beauty: springtime flowers, deep green summer shade, and yellow

Left: *Flowers are used sparingly in Oriental gardens, in favor of combinations of greens. Here, fallen maple leaves pattern a bed of ferns and moss.* **Above:** *Raked sand and rocks are less ephemeral garden elements— and the Japanese combine them in abstract dry landscapes that encourage passive contemplation rather than garden activities.*

leaves in fall; in the winter, its irregular form of trunks and branches weave an intricate calligraphy of line and pattern.

Flowering plants are an important, if sparingly used, feature in Oriental gardens. Each season has its signature bloom; rarely do two flowers appear at once. Because each flower is so important, most have vivid colors to create dramatic impact. Most are fragrant as well.

Whether it be a garden in the purest and most formal manner, such as a temple garden, or a very free adaptation, the Oriental style creates a placid, painterly effect. Each feature "speaks" its part; collectively, their voices blend in simple harmony.

In the Oriental Manner

When designing an Oriental-style garden, it is useful to forget temporarily about details—lanterns, water basins, gateways, moon bridges, and the like. These are merely elements within *some* Oriental gardens. Also, one should not assume that all Japanese gardens have stones or that every Chinese garden is a courtyard. It is also advisable not to rely too strongly on particular examples of Japanese or Chinese gardens. The most familiar Oriental designs—the raked sand garden in the monastery of Ryoanji in Japan and the gardens of the Forbidden City in Beijing—were not designed as ordinary residences. Thus, they are no more representative of everyday design than is Versailles of a typical French home.

Due to the small size of typical Oriental homes, however, the garden is rarely a place for active recreation. These gardens tend to offer passive pleasures: viewing, strolling, and quietly entertaining friends. Oriental gardens are closely related to the house and the activities of daily life. Indeed, most Japanese houses combine walls and doors to form a sliding partition so that the garden may be fully enjoyed in pleasant weather from indoors.

Because sliding glass doors and fixed-glass walls afford a similar effect, the Oriental style fits well in modern homes. The overall simplicity of contemporary architecture is also sympathetic to the understated character of Oriental gardens. With older homes, the Oriental style may be best applied to quiet garden corners. Since harmony is so essential to these gardens, a very formal residence may have to limit Oriental features to a separate garden space.

The Oriental quality of any garden is largely established by its plantings. Although tall shade trees, and especially pines that whisper in the breeze, provide a useful starting point for a design, it is the use of smaller trees that best evokes an Oriental character. The nursery trade provides a wealth of ornamental trees that may be used in Oriental gardens: Japanese maples, cherries, plums, apricots, and flowering crabs. Many occidental trees are also very "Oriental" in their characters; the irregular, sculptural forms of the native American redbud, dogwood, and sourwood are particularly suitable to Oriental effects, as are European hawthorns, willows, and bamboo.

Typically, small trees are used as single specimens or in small, informal groves. Also, the ground beneath these trees is usually left open or simply carpeted with mulch, moss, or ferns. To achieve the assymmetrical balance so familiar to Oriental design, small trees are often planted off center in a bed of low-growing shrubs or ground cover. These plantings should, of course, be of a kind; if they flower, they should not bloom in season with the tree to ensure that each may be enjoyed completely in its time.

Trees with weeping forms are frequently located near a water source, such as a naturalistic spring or a cascade, to mimic the effect of flowing water. Weeping trees are also used to complement the edges of a pool, and at the garden's borders to create the effect of distant mountain ranges. When trees are planted near water, however, they should be given a "companion"—a horizontal-branched shrub or a flat stone—to keep them from appearing too outstanding and isolated.

Spring brings the blossoms of flowering trees and shrubs to the landscape garden at the Shugaku-in villa in Kyoto.

Left: A garden composed almost entirely in greens with rocks, pine, cotoneaster, Japanese maples, and a blue-green cedar, Cedrus atlantica 'Glauca,' that seems to recede into the distance. Makoto Hagiwara, designer. **Above:** *A pebbled beach is a landscape in miniature within a Japanese-inspired garden planted with Hinoki cypress, junipers, azaleas, and bamboos. The high wall gives a Western sense of enclosure. Alex Rota, designer.*

Boundary plantings are especially important to Oriental gardens. To emphasize the garden's separation from the larger world, these plantings should be dense and rather tall. Evergreens or mixed hedges are especially effective for this purpose. Rather than forming a regular hedge, however, these plantings should form an undulating screen. Also, each plant must be allowed sufficient room to develop its full form and character. Flowering evergreens such as camellias, rhododendrons, nandina, and azaleas may be included in these border plantings, but their flowering seasons should be carefully considered to produce an orderly progression of bloom.

The paths and walks of Oriental gardens are, perhaps, their most important non-plant feature, because they sequence the garden experience. Usually, these walks will follow a meandering route, with frequent jogs and detours to avoid a plant or stone—which, of course, is purposely located to deflect the walk's alignment.

Indeed, each segment of a path should focus on some feature, such as a tree, shrub, or ornament, to draw the visitor along the way. Whenever possible, natural pavings are preferred; these surfacings should also be in harmony with their immediate surroundings. A walkway through a grove of trees and ground cover, for example, may be paved with bark or mulch to emphasize the woodland quality of the adjacent plantings. Walks in open areas may be composed of stone, gravel, brick, or even precast concrete pavers laid in narrow, linear bands to encourage a faster pace.

Paths along the edges of streams or pools, on the other hand, should have an undulating pattern to echo the ripples of the water's surface. River pebbles are especially effective along a stream, while large, flat stones, which call to mind the mirror-like quality of still water, may pave a poolside walk. Stepping-stones are best reserved for crossing open water, since each stone affords the opportunity to pause and gaze into the water's depths.

Ornaments within the Oriental garden may take many forms: natural rocks, small pieces of sculpture, or the weathered stucco of a wall. Utilitarian features such as lanterns, water basins, benches, and garden structures also add an ornamental quality to Oriental gardens. Stones and boulders, however, are the most familiar decoration for this garden style. Although stones have religious meaning in many Japanese gardens, they are best used simply as sculpture in the interpreted Oriental style. As ornaments, these stones should be selected for their inherent aesthetic interests of form or surface patterns, and they should be placed to focus or counterpoint a view. A large, irregular boulder, for example, may be set into the garden's boundary plantings to contrast with the evenness of evergreen foliages, while a large, flat stone may serve as a bench or viewing platform.

Lanterns should be placed so that they will illuminate a step or the intersection of a walk, or where they will cast shadow patterns on the surface of a pool or paving. Even if lanterns are never set with lights, they should be placed at logical locations where illumination would be required; otherwise, they will appear arbitrary and pointless.

Pines, azaleas, and red-leaved Japanese maples frame the view of a lakeside pavilion. The stiff, spiky needles and bright flowers provide a vivid foreground, which makes the scenery beyond seem more distant than it actually is.

Borrowed Landscape

The "borrowing" of landscape—taking advantage of those views that lie beyond a garden—has found interpretation in most every garden style. It was, however, the Chinese who first defined the principles of borrowed landscape and the Japanese who exalted them.

Due to the rugged and often mountainous terrain that typifies much of China, landscape vistas often form a natural backdrop for a garden. To emphasize the wildness of that background, Chinese garden designers frequently arranged elaborate, artificial mounds of earth, stone, and irregularly shaped trees as features of a

valley garden. As these miniature landscapes (many of which were quite extensive, but minute in comparison to real mountains) could be studied close at hand, they provided the garden visitor with vicarious access to that distant, wild terrain. Mountain scenes were also painted on scrolls so that one might enjoy, through art, natures grandeur.

In time, these scrolls were carried to Japan; although many Japanese gardeners never traveled beyond their sacred islands, these landscape paintings had a profound impact on their garden-making methods. Rather than using landscape merely as a symbol inside the garden, the Japanese developed a technique for incorporating distant vistas into their gardens.

These methods were first applied to gardens that had natural vistas; the most

beautiful section of that view would often form the focus of the garden's plan. Other portions of the scenery, however, would be concealed with walls, fences, and tall trees to amplify the favored view. The general arrangement of that distant scene would then be interpreted in the foreground to create a single, unified perspective from garden to far horizon.

When mountains were not part of the garden's backdrop, the Japanese designer still applied the principles of borrowed landscape to the situation at hand. A handsome tree, the spire of a pagoda, or the roofline of a neighboring garden pavilion would be singled out by carefully arranging groups of trees to frame the view or by placing a window in the garden's surrounding fence or wall. Hedges, fences, and walls can be used for the same purpose and to the same ends.

If one is so fortunate as to have a splendid natural garden background, this asset should be maximized. This is most easily accomplished through planting. By removing a few trees to open a corridor through a woodland, for example, distant landscape features become an integral part of the garden's plan. In open settings, the planting of vertical trees or horizontal masses of shrubs may also be used to organize the view. An uninterrupted grass slope can serve the same purpose.

Intervening "interruptions" such as the roofline of a neighboring house or power lines along the garden's edge should, if possible, be excluded from the view. This can be done by planting large shrubs in the foreground to contain the view with foliage or by planting horizontally

Left: *Fruit trees and lavender make a decorative but uncluttered foreground for a mountain view.* **Below left:** *Columnar evergreens and palms frame the valley that surrounds San Simeon in California.* **Above:** *Stone and raked sand against a wooded background. Alex Rota, designer.*

branched trees in the middle ground to camouflage taller intrusions to the scene. Evergreen plants, of course, will give a year-round horticultural framework to borrowed scenery.

On more level sites, or in a suburban situation, the borrowing of landscape is more difficult, but worth the necessary effort. The tall growing trees of adjoining gardens, for example, may be used as more than just a background for a garden. Although it may not be possible to include the entire tree within the borrowed view, its canopy or upper branches certainly deserve attention. By focusing on a tree that offers seasonal flowers or handsome autumn foliage and by placing plants with similar characteristics in the foreground, the entire composition takes on large-scale unity.

Plants as Art

Two plants are featured at the entry to an Oriental-style home: an evergreen bonsai set on a stone base and a knotted tree trunk played against the abstract architectural elements.

Of all the values to be found in Oriental gardens, it is their plants to which the West is most indebted. The Orient provides us with some of our finest landscape plants, as evidenced by the countless species names ending in *asiatica, chinensis, japonica,* and *sinensis.* The use of plants as accent specimens, ground covers, and container subjects also traces its origins to Oriental gardens. One of the greatest debts we owe the Orient, however, is the treatment of plants as works of art.

While Western gardeners were busily pruning boxwood into columns, cubes, and pyramids, their Oriental counterparts wrote poems to commemorate the beauty of a cherry tree and the contorted elegance of mulberry and pine. These same gardeners also extolled the beauty of the plum, the lotus, peony, bamboo, and rhododendron; they tended bonsai that were passed down through generations; and they pruned azaleas and other shrubs in smooth, natural lines.

The veneration of plant forms for artistic merit is now expressed in almost every culture's gardening; while we rarely wax poetic on the subtleties of pines, we value their irregular forms or stately, slender trunks as elements of composition and for their inherent value as living works of art.

Bonsai is the most familiar plant. These dwarfed, container-grown plants are also the most difficult of gardening arts to perfect. True bonsai may be "in training" for several decades; during this time, limbs and roots are regularly pruned to restrict the plant's size. Although the form of some bonsai is purposely contorted, others are allowed to assume their natural shapes to produce a miniature version of their garden counterparts. Depending on the plant and the training, some bonsai are only a few inches high, while others may be 3 or 4 feet (910 or 1200 mm) tall.

Once a bonsai artist has achieved the desired effect, training gives way to maintenance; with proper care bonsai may live for centuries. Thus, bonsai is not a quick-effect procedure but an artistic endeavor that usually extends beyond the lifespan of the person who begins the training process. For this reason, bonsai are revered as living legacies.

Anytime a tree or shrub is placed in a container, however, it becomes a type of bonsai. The plant will naturally grow more slowly and will remain much smaller than its garden-grown equivalent. Placed near a front door, at each corner of a terrace, or where they terminate an axis, container plants may also serve as architectural features. A line of potted trees, for example, may take the place of a balustrade along a porch or terrace; if plants and containers are carefully matched, they lend a handsome unity as well. The quantities of container plants, of course, should be limited to maximize their impact.

In-ground specimen plants should also be located where they can be appreciated. Specimen trees, for example, may be planted in the center of a lawn so that their growth will not be hampered by surrounding plants or near an entrance so that they can be regularly enjoyed. Specimen shrubs should also be set off by planting them in an open space, against a simple background such as a wall or fence, in ground cover, or to either side of a main door or window. Locations should be suitable to the plant's soil and light requirements and to its ultimate size.

Topiary—the art of shaping plants to alter their natural form—is an ancient means of using plants as art. Oriental gardeners frequently restrict the size and shape of plants through pruning to symbolize mountains and other natural features. The use of geometric plant forms, however, is largely a Western practice. Yet, topiary has a certain charm that cannot be denied. Dense, slow-growing evergreens such as box and yew have long been shaped into spheres, cubes, and obelisks for formal garden accents, or as fanciful, exotic works of living sculpture. Such creations should, of course, be used with some restraint to keep the garden from becoming a gallery of curiosities.

A colony of smoothly sheared shrubs at the Shugaku-in, interrupted only occasionally by a patch of grass, rocks, or a heavily pruned tree.

THE WILD GARDEN

Nature Exalted

Unlike their Oriental counterpart, where nature is abstracted, the wild or woodland garden celebrates the genius of the place—of nature's forms unchanged. Consequently, these gardens are both modest and romantic in their attitudes, for rather than improving nature, the wild garden accentuates nature.

Typically, we think of wild gardens in terms of native plants, but they may also contain "near" natives, which are indigenous to nearby regions of similar soil, climate, and habitat, and even exotics, which are imported from distant areas or foreign lands. Non-native plants, however, should be included only when they harmonize with local landscape.

There is much to recommend the exclusive use of natives. Because of natural selection, native plants are less vulnerable to damage by disease or insects than are exotic plants; they also tend to be more tolerant of drought, excessive moisture, and extremes of heat and cold. More important, however, natives most completely express the character of a region. They are right, both in terms of horticulture and aesthetics, because they truly belong in these most natural of gardens.

Wild gardens are also characterized by a paradoxical appearance of spontaneity. Indeed, they should appear as though they were not planned. This does not mean, of course, that one does not make changes. Pathways may be added to encourage exploration; stepping-stones and bridges may cross streams; and benches, shelters, and ornaments may be located to direct attention toward a pleasant view. One may also build a weir to make a garden pool, and steeply sloping hillsides may be subtly molded to create more planting space.

Because the purpose of a wild garden is first to preserve existing features and then to make additions that enhance their character, however, additions should be carefully designed for minimal disruption of the naturalistic theme. They should also be simple; if possible, the garden elements should be made from natural materials such as wood or stone. Bark or wood chips, for example, are well-suited surfacings for the wild garden's paths; undressed logs or native stones are appropriately rustic materials for garden structures. If natural materials are unavailable or insufficiently durable, pressure-treated lumber, concrete, or metal afford acceptable alternatives. Although these may be stained or painted to minimize their presence, the natural process of weathering may be preferable.

On the whole, it is better to do a little later than too much too soon. Nature is self-regulating; as one becomes familiar with the system, one understands the value of restraint. When laying a garden path, for example, it is advisable first to approximate its routing—by raking away leaf litter in a woodland or by mowing paths through the tall grasses of a meadow—before any final surfacing is installed. This allows one to assess the rightness of the route before the final surfacing is installed and to make adjustments before it is too late to save that patch of wild orchids. A similar evaluation should precede the cutting of trees or the removal of any plant that is not identified; most wild garden treasures go through periods when they are not especially conspicuous. The labeling of plants is also recommended to avoid possible inadvertent damage during periods of dormancy or when a plant is out of season.

Although patience and restraint are important to the planning of any garden, they are critical to the wild garden. Once established, however, wild gardens can be self-maintaining. Plants are rarely pruned or trimmed, except to remove diseased or damaged branches, and "volunteer" plants (which elsewhere are considered weeds) may be retained as part of the garden plan. Indeed, the management of a wild garden is largely a matter of not doing. Fallen leaves need not be raked because they form a protective and soil-enriching mulch, and faded flowers may be left in place so that their seeds will ripen and be scattered to form

future plants. Benign neglect is, however, no excuse for total inattention. Some degree of grooming and tending is necessary to keep the garden healthy, and it also provides a pleasant excuse for leisurely walks in the garden.

Ease of maintenance, of course, may be a relative advantage, but wild gardens can satisfy the full range of gardening personalities—those who want the least demanding garden possible and those who find real pleasure in daily chores. The difference depends on the degree to which one wishes to be "bothered." A simple garden of mostly natives, for example, may need little effort to maintain in optimum condition, while gardens of rare or delicate plants will need intensive care.

Opposite page, left: Springtime in a woodland garden would hardly be complete without primulas. Center: Starry blue chionodoxa, or glory-of-the-snow, colonized in shallow pockets of soil around the roots of a massive beech tree. Right: The pasqueflower, Anemone pulsatilla, is a spectacular addition to a woodland or rockery, and the fuzzy fruit is as striking as the flowers. Here it grows with select blue companions—phlox, muscari, and the pea-like flowers of vetch. Above: Yellow lady's slippers, Cypripedium calceolus var. pubescens, thrive at a wood's edge.

The Woodland Garden

Masses of shade-tolerant azaleas, among the showiest plants for the woodland, blanket a wooded hillside with brilliant spring color.

Developing a woodland garden is largely a matter of underplanting. Brambles and random undergrowth should be removed to make more room for smaller trees and shrubs; overcrowded trees may also be thinned to enhance the natural forms of the remaining trees. Once the forest canopy is set in order, however, the woodland gardener must plan and plant the woodland floor.

Because woodland soils tend to be rich in humus, they are ideally suited to the growing of perennials and shallow-rooted plants that thrive in shade. The acidity, texture, and moisture content of woodland soils also provides a congenial environment for a wide range of bulbs, shrubs, and ornamental trees. (Specific selections, of course, must be determined by hardiness and horticultural suitability to individual situations.) Thus, woodland plants may be arranged by height to give a layering of foliage from ground to sky.

Low-growing plants, for example, may be used in drifts or islands to carpet the garden with foliage; mid- to large-size shrubs lift attention upward. Next come understory trees, which spread a leafy canopy just above eye level. The presence or addition of smaller trees to lofty woodlands also increases, through contrast, the apparent height and scale of the canopy trees that form the garden's ceiling.

The horizontal plane can be equally rich if plants are carefully arranged to give a sense of depth or to contain the views within a woodland. If plants with open forms, for example, are backdropped with denser foliages, the resulting "transparency" will make a smallish woodland seem much larger. This technique is also effective in flat woods, which tend to look too open. The sense of space in level woodlands is also enchanced when portions of the garden are concealed from view. By screening certain garden areas, the woods take on the mystery of things to be discovered.

Evergreens are particularly useful for shaping space in a deciduous forest garden. Shrubs, for example, separate the woodland into rooms; evergreen trees outline vistas through the garden, define its borders, and screen objectionable views. Evergreens also carry the woodland garden through the winter, offsetting the browns and grays that typify this season. Similarly, a forest of evergreens benefits from the addition of deciduous plants, especially plants that flower, take on autumn color, or have conspicuous winter fruit.

Because large existing trees are so important to a woodland garden, every effort must be made to save them when a wooded site becomes a woodland home. This involves more than merely saving trees from the chain saw. When excavations must be made for house foundations, driveways, or septic fields, some disturbance usually occurs; typically, this damage results from root compaction by vehicles or heavy materials.

To avoid root compaction, workmen should not be allowed to operate heavy equipment or to park outside areas that will be covered by the house or paving. Piles of excavated soil should not be stored beneath large trees, because this will impair the roots' ability to gather moisture and nutrients. (Mature trees are particularly susceptible to this sort of damage because they have grown beyond the period of active root development. Consequently, if roots are damaged even slightly, trees may suffer permanent injury.) Plants should also be protected from damage like broken branches and scarred trunks; this is most effectively done with temporary fences to restrict construction activities to the smallest area possible.

Care should also be taken to avoid siltation of waterways and the disruption of natural drainage patterns. Although most residential construction is not so protracted as to warrant extensive erosion control, it is best to minimize soil loss by using barricades or temporary berms. Bales of hay, for example, may be placed at the top of a steep slope to minimize the amount of soil washed downhill; during periods of heavy rain, a temporary swale and berm may also be required to prevent downslope erosion.

Opposite page, top left: *Pink primulas are delicate companions for black jack-in-the-pulpits* (Arisaema triphyllum) *in this half-wild woodland garden.* ***Top right:*** *A sea of Spanish bluebells,* Endymion hispanicus, *provides ground cover.* ***Bottom left:*** *Green horsetail,* Equisetum hyemale, *makes a billowy ground cover beneath Japanese primroses and wood hyacinths.* ***Bottom right:*** *Narcissus, phlox, ajuga, and violets bloom while spring sunshine warms the floor of a woodland garden.*

This page, top: At Great Dixter, circular steps designed by Sir Edwin Lutyens lead to a mown path through a meadow of yellow and white wildflowers. **Bottom:** *Gaillardia and coreopsis fill a field with summer color. Coreopsis is an excellent choice for meadow gardens because even the annual varieties are prolific self-seeders.* **Opposite page:** *A drift of pink and white* Primula japonica *winds its way through an open landscape, miming a stream. To establish a colony of flowers, choose plants adapted to the niche that you have. Primulas like moisture, so low places are suitable; most coreopsis need full sun and are tolerant of dry soils.*

Meadow and Water

Meadows tend to be more durable than forests: They are better suited to the harsh conditions of full sun and poor soils. Left untended, of course, a meadow or prairie may become a juvenile woodland if there are nearby trees to provide a source of seeds. The permanent meadow, however, can also be an exciting and distinctive natural garden in its own right.

Unlike the woodland with its inward focus, the meadow garden is a place of sweeping vistas; even in areas of rolling hills, a wide expanse of meadow can take on panoramic grandeur. This diversity of topography—hilltops, slopes, and valleys—also gives variety to the garden's planting palette. The brows of hills, for example, lend themselves to plants that need a good drainage; south-facing slopes are suitable for plants that thrive in heat and have brightly colored flowers to reflect the sun. Northern slopes, on the other hand, may be planted in dark colors or pastels to intensify the subtle shadings of their more protected and thus less brilliantly lighted situation.

Valleys offer the occasion to grow moisture-loving plants; if plants are selected for the darkness of their foliages or flowers, this will also make those valleys seem much deeper. Bright blue flowers or plants with gray or silver foliage also give the appearance of water, even when planted in dry depressions.

Level fields and meadows tend to be less varied in both their plantings and appearance than rolling countryside; they can also be monotonous if there is no structure to diversify their views. Consequently, level meadows require more complex planting schemes to enhance their interest.

If there is any elevation to provide a vantage point, a broad expanse of level ground may be designed in sweeping patterns of color and texture, perhaps like the abstract patterns of modernist paintings. (Curiously, profuse wild fields of flowers can give this effect.) Plants may either be contrasted to create sharp definitions, or they may be subtle variations on a theme. Because there is such richness and diversity in grasses, one could even design an all-green meadow that ranges from palest silver gray through celadon, citron, and verdigris to deepest emerald.

If the open garden must be viewed from eye level, it still is possible to make a richly varied planting. Progressively taller plants, for example, could be arranged to give the effect of receding layers, or very tall

Opposite page: Sculptural lotus leaves, pods, and shell-pink flowers seem larger than life surrounded by the finer textures of bamboo, cyperus, and a weeping willow in this rustic, pond setting. **Above:** *A stand of cyperus thrives with its feet in the water at Cypress Gardens in Florida. The cascade brightens the scene by reflecting light.* **Below:** *Primula alchemilla, and spiky clumps of iris border a stream at Burford House in England. The large leaves in the background are* Gunnera manicata, *a moisture-loving plant that grows to a height of 12 to 14 feet (3.65 to 4.26 meters) by summer's end. Big succulent plants suit water gardens, for their form reflects the lushness of the riparian environment.*

plants could be used both to frame the foreground and to punctuate the background, creating the illusion of undulation.

Paths can also be mown across a meadow to direct both views and access to the garden's distant edges. It can be very pleasant to explore these avenues; if these paths become narrower as one moves toward the garden's center, the forced perspective can make even a small grassland appear extensive.

Because of the numbers of plants required for even smallish meadows, these gardens are best established by seeding. Nowadays, seed mixtures are available featuring different combinations of grass and flowers for all types of soil. Since most grassland plants achieve their full maturity within a single season or no more than a few years, meadow and wildflower gardens also offer the advantages of quick effect. And once established, they require very little maintenance. A periodic mowing between flowering seasons, however, tends to improve the meadow garden's vigor, and ensures the continuation of hardy annuals by scattering their seeds. Specific plant selections, of course, should be determined by their horticultural appropriateness and their similarities of propagation and maintenance. Of course, because meadow plants tend to "migrate" over time, highly invasive plants will not be suitable for complex planting schemes.

Wetland gardens are very specialized environments, as are bogs and marshes. Depending on the amount of water present throughout the year, a wetland may vary from a moist meadow to swamp. Consequently, these gardens are sensitive and difficult to design. If moisture levels can be maintained at constant or at least predictably fluctuating levels, one can select suitable plants. Highly variable moisture levels, however, severely restrict the types of plant that can be grown. In such cases, the services of a biologist, botanist, or horticulturist will be a necessary but well-rewarded expense. Without such advice, there is a risk that fully one half of the plants will not survive the extremes of drought and flooding.

Dune and Desert

The seashore is, perhaps, the most popular location for summer or vacation homes. For this reason, waterfronts are also one of the most heavily abused of natural situations. Essentially, the seashore is a series of parallel and highly varied environmental zones. Although the beach and primary dunes are too delicate for any sort of artificial development, the "trough" or valley behind primary and secondary dunes is usually stable and suitable for houses and gardens.

Seashore gardens are subjected to the constant winds and salt spray of the ocean, so it is advisable to limit plant selection to natives and plants that tolerate high concentrations of salt. Because of fluctuating levels of groundwater, seashore garden plants should also be drought-resistant and deeply rooted, qualities that also permit them to survive those periods when gardeners are absent.

Frequently, windbreaks will be needed in the seashore garden to minimize blowing sand and create protected planting pockets. Coarsely textured evergreen shrubs are usually best because they offer year-round protection and their roots help stabilize sandy soils. Durable ground covers stabilize the landward side of dunes.

The structures of a seashore garden—arbors, decks, and boardwalks—are best constructed of wood and galvanized metal; these materials best resist the corroding effects of salt spray. These structures should also be sufficiently open to permit free circulation of air and water; whenever possible, they should be elevated above ground level to maintain the natural drainage patterns of surface water.

Because the landward side of beachfront houses offers more protection from ocean winds, these areas can usually be planted with a wider range of materials. Depending on climate and orientation, these spaces may be developed as morning or afternoon retreats; with houses of more than one story, it may be possible to grow small trees, which will provide a shady alternative to the seafront exposure. Often, of course, there will be large existing trees, especially in the troughs of secondary dunes, that should always be retained to maximize areas of shade and wind protection.

Desert gardens tend to be similar to seashore gardens, in that they are places of poor soil and high-velocity wind. The temperature variations are more extreme for desert gardens than for those along the coast, both seasonally and in day-to-night fluctuations. Also, where the seashore tends to have an evenly high humidity, desert moisture levels vary from extreme drought to brief but violent periods of heavy rain.

Because they are so well adapted to harsh conditions, desert plants are commonly assumed to be extremely rugged. Although they are quite tolerant of their natural conditions, desert plants are not indestructible—quite the contrary is true. Desert plants exist in a tenuous balance; even minor changes in soil moisture can be disastrous. An increase in water levels, such as the runoff from a paved driveway or a roof, may stimulate a temporary and abnormally rapid rate of foliage growth that, once moisture levels return to normal, the plant's roots may not be able to support. The reverse is true when moisture levels are reduced. If the flow of surface water is redirected by the grading for a house site, for example, the reduction in soil moisture may be fatal to surrounding plants. For this reason, desert houses should be elevated whenever possible, and pavings should be severely restricted or of a porous nature, to maintain the soil's capacity to absorb water.

Despite these restrictions, the desert is rich in plant life. Most desert vegetation tends to have a very slow rate of growth; because of their extremely deep root systems, which take advantage of subsurface water, these plants are also difficult to transplant. Thus, the preservation of existing plants is the foremost consideration in the desert garden.

Ideally, desert gardens should be

Opposite page, top: *Rock and pine are rugged materials for a dry landscape, for they endure with little assistance from man. To appreciate them as garden features requires a frame of mind not unlike that which appreciates the* karesansui *(dry gardens) of Japan.* **Bottom:** *A seaside garden with yarrow, red poppies, and silvery artemisia.* **This page:** *Impatiens, blue-green hostas, and a raised bank lined with marigolds and wax and tuberous begonias make even a dry garden look lush.*

Opposite page, top left: Creating a garden with cactus and succulents is an exercise in playing unusual forms, textures, and subtle colors against one another. Here, a varied collection of startlingly shaped cacti. **Top right:** *Sculptural barrel cacti, planted in masses, make an otherworldly scene.* **Bottom left:** *Opuntia, or prickly-pear, growing in a beachfront garden.* **Bottom right:** *Cactus and succulents can be effectively incorporated in mixed plantings, but they require careful placement, for their spectacular forms can dominate a composition.* **This page:** *Clumps of yucca and opuntia set with rocks in a gravel bed, each plant given enough room to breathe and be admired. This Mediterranean garden is suitable for many semi-arid climates. Its sparseness gives an Oriental feel.*

planted exclusively with natives. As desert communities—whether Mediterranean or Sonoran—become increasingly popular as winter or retirement homes, local nurseries have responded to this increased demand with an equally abundant supply of desert plants, so there are ample sources for native materials. Of course, these nurseries also carry many non-natives and exotics that are well adapted to arid conditions.

Shade and wind protection are equally important in the arid garden, for both sun and wind accelerate the process of evaporation. Shade trees, however, are rare, so it is usually necessary to construct both arbors and windbreaks to help moderate the climate. As with the seashore garden, desert garden structures should have an open design and should be elevated to allow the circulation of air and water. Barrier fences may also be required to discourage foraging by desert animals, a particular problem with deer, which feed on almost any plant without too many thorns, and with rabbits

Because the desert garden tends to be open, walls and fences may also be used to create a visual foreground for the panorama of distant mountains and far horizons. The columns of arbors and free-standing gateways also help to frame the vistas of the desert landscape.

A SENSE OF PLACE

by Susan R. Frey

INTRODUCTION

One way to approach a garden plan is to think of the styles that most appeal to you, but they themselves developed in response to the sense of place. Land forms suggest the ways in which they can be transformed into satisfying gardens, each lending itself best to certain kinds of entries, transitions, gathering places, and focal points. Consider the Italian Renaissance garden, largely the story of dramatic views, terraces, and rooms, with shapely trees and falling water playing important parts. What but the landscape of Tuscany, and of the Alban and Sabine hills near Rome, would have influenced this style? And the great French parterre gardens must certainly have been suggested by the very flat topography of northern France. The English landscape garden, too, corresponds to the rolling pastoral nature of the countryside. One can hardly imagine the Persians, for example, of having conceived of "all nature as a garden."

Most modern gardeners will not be working on such a large scale, but the small garden also has its precedents, influenced by the social divisions already executed on the land form. The Surrey school in British gardening—so influential for the modern flower garden—looked back to the medieval garden, emphasizing the use of indigenous plants and materials in informal schemes. And the urban garden has much to learn from the Japanese tea garden. Gathered in tight quarters from an early date, the Japanese developed a small garden form capable of producing the repose of country places. The concentration of symbolic elements (water, country lighting, selected plantings) plus the laying of irregular paths relaxes both the visitor who walks through the garden and the one who simply observes it.

In a sense, anyone who contemplates a garden—even the gardener—is a visitor to it. The landscape itself must look at home. The demands on the garden designer, then, are double: first, to compose a picture that is appealing and appropriate from all entrances to the garden, and next, to assure that the vantage points from transitions and gatherings present a variety of engaging scenes. Whether vistas focus inside the garden or outside it, whether the garden itself will be seen from a picture window and/or from deep in the woods, the task of matching taste to land form remains the same.

Sight-lines and enclosures are the major tools. By playing one against the other—by squaring the circle or vice versa, as it were—the designer influences the garden's apparent size, its mystery, its harmony, and the uses to which it can be put. The difficult path, for example, made of irregular stones at different heights, can change the visitor's view with every step, making even the smallest and most closed of gardens seem capacious. And on a country or estate garden, the longest of vistas can be brought into the garden frame by arranging the middle-ground to make a picture out of the view.

Flat sites and formal layouts are typically French, and Vaux-le-Vicomte is considered one of the greatest achievements in the French landscape style. The gardens were designed in the seventeenth century by André le Nôtre for Louis XIV's finance minister—and the king was so impressed that he immediately arrested the owner and commissioned le Nôtre to work at Versailles. Vaux's central axis extends across an entry court and through the chateau, crosses parterres and canals, and then becomes a rough grassy allée before disappearing over a distant hill. The garden consists of grass and gravel—warm pink for the paths, deep red for the parterre beds—clipped evergreens, water, and statuary, set within dense bosquets of clipped green- and purple-leaved trees.

LANDMARKS

A large abstract sculpture and a rough drive running between a line of trees mark an entrance to an art center set in rolling hills. Here are landmarks at the largest scale.

Masses of spectacularly colored 'Hinodegiri' azaleas banked along a front walk are spectacular in spring and partially evergreen through the winter.

Ornately pruned evergreens flank the front of a city dwelling, providing an eye-catching year-round display but using only a minimum amount of space.

Creating a sense of place in the garden depends, first of all, upon marking the spot where the residence begins. The first glimpse should encompass the garden's symbol, the landmark. It is both a sign of the character of the garden and a beacon to show the way.

People are used to finding their way in city or country with the help of landmarks: the yellow house, the street light opposite the driveway, a cluster of pine trees. Yet these are haphazard elements in the surrounding landscape that tell you nothing of the garden you are approaching. These objects are, if anything, misleading, for they make visual impressions that might detract from the experience of the garden rather than support it as a prelude.

Unless you enjoy the effect of startling contrasts, you will find it important and valuable to create a welcoming street identity that not only marks the spot as a special one, but prepares the visitor for a memorable sequence of garden events.

With landmarks, the local topography takes on a special importance, as does the surrounding density of buildings or woodland. These things determine the distance of views to the property. From how far away can you sight the house and garden? Can the house be seen at all? Is it lower than the surrounding things or higher? Or is it the only habitation within view?

If the approach to the house and garden is open, the challenge is to develop a landmark that will be visible from a distance. This situation occurs in a country house setting on open parkland or agricultural fields, and in flat or gently rolling landscapes. Because the views in such settings are long, landmarks must be large enough to be seen from the first opportunity. An outstanding bosque of trees or a monumental sculpture will draw attention to the spot. Extensive solutions to mark the entry drive—an allée of trees or hedges, a long border of flowers or turf, or even a

watercourse accompanying the roadway—are both landmarks and garden experiences in themselves. A tall allée of native trees, a linear orchard, or an aqueduct emphasizes the garden's continuity with the surrounding land use. A pleached or hedge allée prepares for greater formality and, if dense, turns the entry into a tunnel, momentarily divorcing the residence from the landscape. A subtle compromise—and a less costly one—is a hedge clipped to below eye level. The look is formal, but you can still see the landscape beyond.

Often the house in a rural situation will not be visible from the road, due to woodland or hills. It is then important to give the landmark some architectural presence as well, to foreshadow the identity of the house. Here the formal gateway is most appropriate. It needn't contain an operating set of gates, though. Two pillars of substantial proportions will convey the same message, but in a friendlier tone.

When house and garden are set in a denser location—in a suburb or row of city houses—detail is the key to creating an effective landmark. Since the property will be visible from a comparatively short distance and since house numbers are likely to be the main piece of information when locating the place, a landmark that is small-scale and highly detailed will draw attention to it as an individual, private place. This quality is especially valuable in a setting where all the houses look alike, because it will suggest the garden's distinctive character. Landmark solutions at this scale rely, therefore, on the more gardenesque or decorative devices. If the site is undulating or craggy, an earth mound or jutting layer of native rocks might be revealed, or sculpted from the site, to mark the spot at streetside. Vibrant color comes into play at this scale. It can be used to make the chosen landmark come forward: Bright colors will help the eye to pick out the landmark easily. For this reason, a

massed flower planting—whether in the ground or in containers—is a fine, if seasonal, marker for such entries. Flowering plants that also offer attractive foliage are the best choices, since they will stand out even when the flowers are gone. Plants with a strong form—such as shaped hedges, bonsai, or other specimen plants—are also good choices.

A piece of sculpture is an extremely effective signal to the visitor that he is arriving at a personal place. Indeed, the smaller the scale, the more personal and immediately welcoming is the arrival that is signaled by the landmark. At the smallest, densest scale of urban living and garden-making, a pot of flowering plants by the front door, a windowbox, or a wall tile with the house number will be most inviting.

For a stepped entry, banks of pink and white azaleas lead up to a large rhododendron; a solid green hedge alongside defines the path. Color is used in masses: Pale pink builds up to a slightly deeper pink, with white separating the two shades. Imagine how very different (and perhaps less effective) the bank would be if the plants had been set randomly rather than grouped by shades. The soft edges enfold arriving visitors.

LANDINGS

The entrance to the residence is best treated as a part of the garden, and it offers the first opportunity to relate architecture to the garden's form. Detail is all-important here, but the trick is to prevent the combined elements from seeming too cute or precious.

For this reason, statuary is seldom a good idea at the front door, unless you have matched pieces that respect the ornamentation of the house. Older residences occasionally preserve dismounted remnants of architectural detailing that may be just right to frame the door.

Framing is the key concept and simplicity the best guiding principle. The symmetry of a pair of urns planted with single, formal evergreens—say, dwarf spruce—will set off almost any doorway as the principal entrance to house and garden. Balanced plantings stretching away to either side add to the sense of focus. In urban situations, windowboxes and a pair of suspended container plantings serve the same purpose.

If the residence has a bonafide porch—even when only two steps lead up to it—the landing will bear more detailing, but you may first wish to expand or extend it. The porch must be generously sized in proportion to the house. In a renovation, this often means extending the width and depth of the landing so that a party of several persons can be comfortably accommodated. Generosity, in garden design, begins at the front door. The landing becomes a terrace between house

A wall of variegated ivy and a pot with an evergreen topiary grace an English doorway. The light leaves of the ivy seem to capture the sunshine, a treasured commodity in Great Britain, and the topiary adds a touch of formality. For summer color a pot and a hanging basket feature wax and tuberous begonias. The ordered sequence of plantings draws the visitor on.

Brightly colored annuals in pots line the steps of a broad porch, and hanging baskets draw the eye up to the door. The pots are filled with salmon and pink tuberous begonias; urns alongside contain deep red geraniums. Fuschia and lobelia cascade over the edges of the baskets, and pansies and gerbera daisies carry color into the beds below.

Evergreens in tubs and the glossy leaves of a camellia frame a doorway in all four seasons; impatiens add summer color. The total effect is symmetrical but relaxed.

Spires of hollyhock, sedums, chives, and alchemilla line a path to the front door of Sheila MacQueen's cottage garden.

and garden, mediating building architecture and garden architecture, serving as a common ground for the two.

Once the landing area is grounded, it is important to give it a sense of enclosure that is welcoming and enfolding. Often, a railing will be enough. Its material might harmonize with the style of either the house or the garden. A complete arbor will look fine, provided the residence has enough elevation to keep it from looking cramped. Wood usually looks best in this case, even on a brick residence. If the porch is wide enough, benches may even be built into the arbor. Railings, but especially arbors, can be softened, and their effect enhanced, by the use of climbing plants. In choosing these, pay particular attention to climbers whose foliage is dense and attractive enough to remain interesting once the flowers are gone.

In urban or suburban situations, when a forecourt is built-in, provide plenty of detail to focus attention inside it, directing it toward an internal patterning or feature, such as a fountain or specimen plant. Forecourts in spacious settings provide a foretaste of intimacy in contrast to the open nature of the arrival sequence. In these, architecture, planting or earth forms may be made to frame the view, or can be layered against it, repeating the distant forms and lines.

Of course, framing does not always mean symmetry. A single or mixed climber can serve as a charming, irregular doorframe or marker. Cottage and country styles suggest informal, spreading climbers, while urban entries may call for distinctive topiary or a single climbing rose. The urban row house provides the opportunity for a true community approach, if owners agree to match a single style or species of planting at each front door.

ENTRIES

Coming into the garden proper is the completion of the arrival sequence, but it is crucial that the whole garden plan not be given away at first glance. Entry to the garden is gained from the interior of the house, or from an outside area beyond the garden itself, such as a streetside wall or an alley. The first type might be called an inside-outside entry, while the second could be referred to as a landscape entry.

In the majority of urban and rural properties, houses are sited in the first third of the property, closest to the street, with most of the exterior space located behind the house for privacy's sake. In such cases, the house itself is one garden wall. The most typical sequence of experience consists of sighting a landmark, coming into the arrival garden on foot or by car, alighting at the landing, and entering the house itself. Passing through the house, you get a first glimpse of the garden through windows. Windows onto the garden proper are a year-round opportunity to "enter" the garden without getting wet, cold, or overheated. Windows also preview the garden, hinting at the pleasures to come, but revealing only a segment. Most gardeners will frame their view using existing windows, but in older houses with few openings to the garden it is worth considering replacing a solid door with a windowed one, or even replacing part of a wall with a sliding glass door. It is rewarding to compose garden scenes for the benefit of window frames. Layered textures and colors will draw the eye out into the garden, and a focal point, such as a mossy, upright rock, birdfeeder, or a specimen tree, will anchor the scene.

Partially revealed scenes are good ideas for landscape entries as well. The view into the garden must entice by virtue of concealment and the promise of surprise. Even a flat, small, rectangular space can be made seductive with planting screens or with turf sweeping around a bend of shrubbery. This device also helps

A pair of rounded yews, stands of yellow achillea, pink and white impatiens, and roses line a grass path in a Connecticut garden. The yews pinch the path, providing privacy and enclosure for the porch beyond. Classical columns supporting a dense canopy of wisteria define the space within and make the entry all the more inviting.

suggest spaciousness. If the site slopes up or down, the contours themselves can screen the entire garden from view. On a tiny site, it is best to use the structure of the house to make a garden entry that conceals most of the garden space. Latticework, canvas shades, and more elaborate treatments with pergolas at the point of entry from house to garden can be adapted to frame one view while screening others. Moreover, since the change of overall scale from outside to inside is dramatic—the ceiling lifts up to the sky, the floor broadens, the walls drop back—a sense of enclosure or screening at the transition will soften the change in scale.

There are at least six types of landscape entries, in terms of form. The most architectural, formal, and non-revealing is the solid wall that mimics a house facade, with a solid door set in; but unless you are aiming for a secret garden it is best to provide a limited view through the gate, to entice the

visitor. Take the door out altogether to create an opening in the wall, which itself might be made of shrubbery. Remove the top from the portal, and suddenly the entry is simply an open space between two "walls." Or drop the height of the walls and set in a gate, and the garden becomes much less formal, more open to the outer world. The most abstract and elegant is an entry that is free-standing: say, two stone pillars flanking a path; two Irish yews standing sentry; or rustic posts and a header.

The bolder and simpler the entry solutions become, the more they require the context of a large-scale landscape. Highly detailed entries with minimal exposure of what's beyond are most appropriate to small gardens, whether flat or contoured. If the garden is expansive, however, it cannot possibly be comprehended in one glance, so the entry can afford to be more revealing.

Moongates are excellent frames for an entry view, and they make dramatic transitions. Here, an unusual moongate marks the entrance into a woodland garden. Note the mixture of Far Eastern and Western influences: The gate and the foreground specimen stones contrast with the open terrace and flower borders. Floor, edge, and gate are all made of concrete.

For the entrance to a rose garden, a brick arch wreathed with ivy. Along the path, the form is repeated and counterpointed in a line of slender, rose-covered arches.

A rustic arbor marks a break in a walled garden. With a wire grid stretched across the wooden frame, vines can climb up and over the path, carrying the garden across the gate.

City landscape entries must secure the garden from unwanted guests, but even a locked entry can give the passerby a glimpse. Wrought iron is the best choice. It is sturdy but open in construction, and it can be worked to reflect the garden's inner character.

In an open rural setting, on the other hand, the merest suggestion of an entry will suffice. An opening in a boundary line—a perennial border, for instance—will give entry to the garden proper, while subtly reinforcing the line of demarcation between public and private. Then, the boundary line itself becomes more important than the point of transit through it. The difference on either side of such an entry could be as simple as a change in mowing heights. Other soft edges could consist of plants—ivy trained to cloak a wire fence, a low, mixed hedge, or a planted wall, suggesting a horticultural framework for the garden's design.

CORRIDORS

An allée of mature trees (maples, in this case) can be an evocative element in the landscape, suggesting the axis of a former garden or the line of a long-abandoned roadway, making an informal corridor.

A narrow dirt trail winds off the main path into a rock garden. Both path and planting are geared for slow going, scaled to suit a collection of dwarf evergreens, low shrubs, and mats of ground-hugging alpines.

The most important organizing tool in all garden design—and the most often overlooked—is the corridor. It organizes sight-lines, so it profoundly influences the character of the enclosure. And by linking landmark, landing, entry, and gathering place, corridors control the dynamics of the garden, the pacing of experience. On any site, they offer the opportunity to diversify the view by turning the visitor's eye, redirecting attention.

The obvious role of the corridor is to convey a person or vehicle from point to point. Its design purpose is to enrich the garden experience, especially on flat sites. There, irregularly shaped stepping-stones or cobbles will force the visitor to pause and change direction frequently, refocusing the attention on fresh aspects of the garden site. Such a corridor treatment is appropriate to informal styles and small distances, since it focuses the eye close up. Most important, it awakens the body to a fresh sense of distance, balance, and time.

The simplest kind of corridor, and the most delightful for large-scale wild gardens, is a path mown through taller grasses and wildflowers. It gives the sensation of undulating terrain and greater distance on the flattest sites. At the other extreme, a carpentered framework makes a very complex corridor for flat sites, with sides and overhead coverage, like a hall in a house, or a tunnel. Enclosure intensifies the sensation of passage through a corridor, creating a dark contrast with open space at the beginning and end.

More or less enclosure means more or less surprise at the far end. A low hedge constrains the walker, but does not limit the view. It lends itself best to parterre treatments, where most of the garden experience is the sight of living geometries. Pergolas or pleached allées reach a compromise, asserting a more total enclosure, but leaving gaps for the wandering eye.

Tight, covered allées and high hedges conceal the whole view, framing the tunnel's end, in anticipation of things to come. These work best on large sites, as transitions in a garden of multiple rooms.

Allées number among the most elegant uses of corridor space. The repetition of trunks draws the eye inward and down the length of the walk or drive. Trees of irregular growing habit can enliven the land, but should only be used in that fashion on flat ground. The greater the change in grade along an allée, the more necessary it becomes to use substantial trees or evergreens for an unchanging, strong pair of lines converging at some distant point. Generally, the length of an allée is best balanced by increasing the scale, especially the corridor width and the size of trees or shrubs.

Time and cost are factors when developing such a dominant landscape form as an allée. Gravel, even turf, used instead of pavement will significantly reduce the installation cost—though maintenance time will increase, since gravel has to be raked and rolled, and turf must be mown, trimmed, and fertilized.

Maturity can take years to achieve if slow-growing trees are used, yet fruit trees, poplars, and small ornamentals such as redbuds (*Cercis* spp.), plums, and crabapples can circumvent the waiting period. Of course, this quicker growth also means a shorter lifespan for the allée. Still another option is to plant a mixed allée of fast- and slow-growing trees, the second to take over for posterity as the first begins to die out.

This sort of connective architecture makes a very powerful line in the flat garden. It can be used equally well in urban or rural settings, although in the city it must usually be linked with building architecture, especially in the densest situations.

No matter what the topography, at least one corridor in any garden should

Billowing box hedges line a grass path, creating a loose but narrow channel. Flowering dogwood adds a lacy touch to the otherwise green landscape.

Pleached hemlocks, Tsuga canadensis, *create a tunnel of shade and a closed transition. Appropriately, this allée is called the Ghost Walk.*

Lavender-studded spires of Echium fastuosum *are echoed by smaller pink flowers farther along an informal and wild-looking path.*

*Crested iris (*I. cristata*), pale blue phlox, pink and white trilliums, and hostas carpet the ground beneath dogwoods and birches along a narrow path.*

A Japanese-inspired footbridge deliberately slows passage along a wooded path lined with pachysandra, ilex, azaleas, and bamboo.

A path through the gardens at Tresco Abbey brings blossoms to eye level, running beneath a wisteria arch and along a dry stone wall dripping with flowers.

suggest an axial spine—to give the garden its backbone. In wild and Oriental garden styles, the corridor can be purely visual—the eye will follow every line that is suggested to it, so that axes need not be literally straight lines upon the ground plane. Here is where sweeps of turf, landmarks, borders, and borrowed scenery come into play, leading the eye along the spine of the garden.

All corridors, at whatever scale, can be reinforced with edging materials, patterns, or side paths to direct the visitor's view. A corridor might contain within itself a transition, such as a change in paving detail or materials. A shift from coarse to fine plant texture can mark a transition. Branching paths, done in contrasting paving, add to the mystery of a country or woodland garden, offering a choice of explorations off the main axis. The corridor should, indeed, play a hinting game with materials and partially revealed views, subtly directing the visitor's attention.

VERTICAL CHANGES

Railroad-tie steps with gravel treads wind through a rock garden with andromeda, azaleas, cotoneasters, junipers, tulips, and a purple-leaved Japanese maple, leading to dogwoods in a grassy meadow above.

Transitions bind a complex garden together while holding possibly overwhelming spaces at bay. Paving unifies this three-room garden, at the same time clearly marking the passage from one space to another. The foreground planting at the head of the steps focuses the visitor's attention.

In a green woodland garden, weathered logs articulate grass treads along a series of steps that cut between banks of junipers, azaleas, and a weeping Sargent hemlock, Tsuga canadensis *'Pendula.'*

A subtle modulation or a precise change of key between garden spaces happens when the garden has a slope. Design solutions for vertical changes call for creative transitions and, more often than not, encompass the relationship between house and garden.

Built into the house-and-garden transition is a dramatic shift in scale. Inside, space is contained by floors, walls, and ceilings, relieved only by windows. Outside, space is more fluid. The expanse of sky overhead makes everything seem to lift, especially if there is a drop in grade.

There is no better opportunity to create transitional space and movement than between house and garden. In fact, this transition can be quite complex and interesting, blending architectural and garden forms as does a vine-covered pergola. Instead of two or three miserly steps set down at a back door, make a porch or deck, add railings and pots of flowers to ease the change from inside to outside. In constructing a deck or patio on a rising site, though, be careful to level the ground beyond the structure so as to produce the most gentle slope possible. Otherwise, the garden may seem overly tight and cramped.

Using the vertical element in the landscape is especially valuable for the garden of rooms. No matter how slight, any variation in grade is an opportunity to enlarge the space by organizing the vertical dimension. Vertical changes need not be along a corridor. A moderate down-slope might be carved out in subtle terraces, so that each level becomes a single, very broad step. Down-sloping paths can exit from different points along each terrace, making the visitor pause and change direction.

With a larger space, a garden of discrete terraces is an attractive, more formal solution. It is important to remember, though, that the cut-and-fill required to make flat terraces is considerably more expensive than simply using, or reinforcing, a gentle slope. Here you will need the advice of a landscape architect. Generally, the cut should be slightly larger than the fill, to assure an even and sightly progression of "rooms," but exact propor-

In springtime masses of azaleas provide color alongside a narrow stone stairway, with ivy and ferns below them. A small bluish-green spruce punctuates the top of the steps; a Japanese maple with dark leaves draws attention to the terrace above.

tions will vary with the surrounding site.

In any garden, steps lead through a rich transitional dimension—psychological and physical—and so are garden essentials. Even one small step can work magic in the flat garden. Vertical changes on slight grades don't need to be heavily engineered, so you can exercise the option of blending natural and structural materials. Brick-edged and turf-surfaced steps are a classic compromise, and work well as transition between formal and informal areas.

Wood has a softening effect: It can be used to box in gravel steps, or it can be cut in rounds from a log and staggered down a small slope. Railroad ties, like stone slabs, can be set into a grass slope for an informal woodland or rustic detail. Perhaps the most subtle possibility is the grass ramp. An element in classic Italian and French gardens, it is becoming popular again today.

If steps are to become a major focal point in the garden, then they must be treated as objects in themselves. Decoration and ornament are needed touches. The traditional and very grand example is a flight of stairs that connects two architectural terraces in formal fashion. Often such a flight will incorporate a landing, urns, statuary, even water stairs in the middle. Such grand pieces of garden architecture are mostly treasures of the past, but they embody lessons of scale and proportion that are important to study for steep sites and major flights of steps.

EXPLORATION

*Between a pair of large ilex, black-eyed Susans (*Rudbeckia hirta*), Queen Anne's lace (*Daucus carota*), and two low, flower-covered posts mark an unpretentious entrance into a pine forest; the wildflowers emphasize the contrast between sunny garden and shady woods.*

A very special element in the garden is discovery. For children, it is everything. For adults, it suggests the excitement of childhood. Gardens harbor many opportunities to integrate this element at every scale.

Looking to the nature of the site itself will guide the kinds of discoveries that can be built into the design. Flat ground is like a clean slate in regard to designing discoveries. In order not to give away the whole scene, and to imply expansiveness, screens can be erected or developed to conceal parts of the garden or dramatic views. This uses the flat ground plane to create the sensation of coming around a corner. Such screens as a mass of shrubbery, a rocky outcrop, and wooden latticework intrude upon the sight-line and work to this purpose. Pruning "up" a tree—removing its lower branches—can frame a view through tree trunks. The Japanese have much to teach about the art of revealing and claiming distant views. By the removal of tree limbs and shrubbery that obscure the view, and the erection of vegetative screens to conceal unwanted elements in the foreground, the gardener creates layers in the garden that culminate in the distant scenery.

The most informal type of exploration travels along a corridor into an uncontrolled, naturalistic area of the garden, where the unexpected is allowed to happen—where plume poppy (*Macleaya cordata*) might seed itself in a miniature forest. Call it a "ramble" as did nineteenth-century landscape architect Frederick Law Olmsted, and think of it as a means of preserving the habitat for wildlife and native plants. With patience, a ramble can be created from scratch, and it is equally at home on flat, undulating, or craggy ground.

Enclosure is all-important in developing a secret and secluded destination within the garden. Here, the densest hedging and the most solid walls and gates are most appropriate. Overwhelming the visitor with a marked vertical dimension is not out of place. Small details within this retreat—white benches, statuary, a simple fountain—make the secret garden into a lovely space for private meditation.

Taken to the limit, the ultimate enclosure/discovery is a maze. Best used as a folly, mazes are a very formal test of optimism, which is an essential ingredient in exploration. A low boxwood maze is both more practical for the home gardener and less intimidating to the visitor. The whole game may be seen at a glance, and the pattern—no matter how complex—will complement a surrounding parterre design.

The great reward of exploration is the discovery of a new landscape. Even if the garden is flat and closed, consider such possibilities as a treehouse or belvedere, if you have a view to capture. The treehouse can also focus the view down onto the garden itself. A viewing mound can be made from earth excavated in digging a pool or leveling a site; engineering and earth-moving equipment will be required to ensure structural integrity. Such an elevation can be quite candidly artificial—even approaching the artistry of earth sculpture—yet it will reward the explorer with a survey of claimed landscape in the outer world.

For any exploration feature, there should be some hint to draw the visitor onward. The sound of water splashing in a fountain beyond a hemlock hedge will draw the curious to find the secret passage into that spot. A spot of bright color, or the heady scent of flowers in bloom, will accomplish the same thing. Sculpture can also be used to draw a person toward the edge of discovery.

A path of weathered stepping-stones bends around a bank of red and white azaleas, suggesting that something is to come around the corner. That message is reinforced across the lawn, with a line of multi-colored tulips and a solitary dogwood.

A simple frame set on top of the roof deck of a contemporary house incites curiosity and invites exploration, offering a viewing platform from which to survey the bay and surrounding scenery, and promising a novel spatial experience as well.

GATHERINGS

A large tree, a niche cut out of the surrounding planting bed, and pots of annuals define a separate seating area on a terrace in California.

In a small garden a detail like a recessed arch can suggest a spot to set a table and chairs. Ferns, a camellia, and a pot of geraniums add interest.

In gathering places, detailing, scale, and amenities all contribute to the sense of having found the right spot.

The design of gathering areas depends largely upon the size and topography of the site. If the garden is terraced, then the levels will dictate the number and arrangement of the spaces. Creating a second level in a flat garden—by adding an elevated deck, for example—will likewise create two independent gathering spaces. Multiple gatherings are particularly desirable when you need both passive and active uses, for children as well as adults, for example.

Much depends, too, upon your attitude toward living space. Look to your interior style and arrangement to guide you in deciding between an open ground plan or a garden of many rooms. Almost always, it is possible to choose between open or closed plans.

The terraced garden will have as many gatherings as it has levels, yet the entirety can still be oriented outward, toward the surrounding landscape. Another option for blending these ideas on a large plot of land is a sequence of gatherings that counterpoint open and closed spaces, or concentrate closed rooms nearer the house, increasing the volume and openness of the gatherings with distance.

Gatherings need to be furnished as thoughtfully as living rooms in the home. The style should harmonize with the general design character of the garden, and the type should be suited to the activities planned for the gathering. Just as in interior design, it is important to group furniture for ease of conversation, and to pull the pieces away from the walls or edges. Fixed seating should be chosen with views in mind. In a multi-purpose garden room, however, a good solution is to use light, movable furniture. Aluminum-tube frames latticed with natural or synthetic webbing are ideal for this purpose. Even some relatively heavy wooden furniture can be mounted with a wheel at one corner to facilitate moving it.

The arrangement of furnishings will suggest a first, psychological level of enclosure. Walls, railings, and shrubbery give the second level, ensuring a sense of security and privacy. These devices will also help channel the visitor's view. A third effect of enclosure can be achieved with light. Floodlighting should be arranged to demarcate the gathering place, while selected garden areas can be spotlit, or given a mysterious glow by uplighting.

Designing gatherings involves a great amount of planning, second only to planning the garden's overall structure. Once the site's essential qualities have been assessed—light and shadow, topography, natural amenities—one must assess one's own needs. Each space in the garden will have a function, just as each corridor does.

Carefully consider whether multipurpose or single-purpose rooms are more practical and pleasing. Many city and suburban "spaces" are gardened under the assumption that only multi-purpose rooms are possible. Certainly, the togetherness afforded by one big garden room, where adults and children relax, play, and work within sight of one another, is appealing. And contemporary house design tends to bias us toward concentrating many functions in a consolidated space.

But richness of experience often comes from diversity, and it is indeed possible to differentiate gatherings within even the smallest of gardens. Here, careful use of materials comes into play. The floor may be perfectly level, but the flooring material need not be homogeneous. With a single step down, another space and another use can be suggested.

Floor and wall materials that contrast with one another can help to diversify even the smallest space. Floors can be made out of gravel, paving, wood, grass, ground cover—and mixtures thereof. With

Cloth-covered cushions make seating comfortable on a flagstone terrace with Chinese details. Chrysanthemums pick up the reds of dogwood leaves and berries.

A seating area defined by bands of contrasting paving and blocks of planting—a row of oak-leaved hydrangeas, H. quercifolia, and a bed of hostas.

A vine-covered pergola, pots full of red geraniums and glossy pittosporum, a line of white impatiens, and a perimeter of large-leaved tropical plants give this San Antonio terrace style. Morris and White, designers.

walls, anything goes: hedging, tree trunks, fencing, steel, masonry, canvas, vines. Ceilings start with the sky and end at trellises and branches. Materials should express the style and character of the place. Generally speaking, the more formal materials—flagstone, bricks, and the like—should be placed nearer to the house, with the less formal materials deeper in the space. In larger areas, layers of formal and informal treatments can alternate through the garden.

Overlooked opportunities to carve out a new space for the garden include turning a corner of the residence and using the side area that lies beyond. Sunlight and shadow can be managed to create different gatherings and to enhance the sensation of transition between them. A shady trellis with hanging bunches of grapes implies shelter, rest, and refreshment, while a sunny oval of turf, circled with a path just wide enough for tricycling or strolling, clears a play space. The motion of shadow across the site during the course of a day will dictate to some extent where space is made for vegetable production or afternoon tea, but the effect of shadows can be used for its own sake as well.

The fulfilling element in every garden gathering is its animation. Corridors are visible evidence of movement; landings, too, are passageways. But gatherings require designed animation to complete the environment and the picture it makes. When people are looking at a gathering space, it is doubly important that it contain motion. Light and shadow make a gathering place dynamic. So, too, does water playing in fountains and streams, carp darting in pools, and birds flitting from feeder to bath. The sound of a breeze, rippling through ornamental grasses or revealing the silvery underside of a leaf, will not be overlooked, nor will the scents that fragrant plantings supply.

DINING

Spaces for dining are, first and foremost, garden spaces. Designing them is mostly a matter of detailing the garden gathering for specific use, and appropriately furnishing, lighting, and equipping it.

Avoid the common solution of replicating the typically static indoor dining room on an outside patio or deck. Outdoor pleasures are the music of birds, wind chimes, crickets, and water, and the sensual refreshment to the skin of moving air. If sights and sounds, scents and touch are gently stimulated by the garden, the palate will be encouraged to follow suit.

The adventuresome flavor of dining outside peaks in the picnic; all that is required is a blanket on the ground or a portable table—or even trestles and a broad plank of wood. With picnics, you enjoy the luxury of following blooms around the garden throughout the season. Opportunities for picnics can also be built into the garden by putting a platform deck or little terrace at some distance from the house and furnishing it for dining. It can be screened in to exclude insects, and architecturally detailed as a teahouse or gazebo. An even simpler alternative is to encircle a small tree with a round table and benches to make a canopied and fruitful setting.

More permanent dining areas need to be protected from the vagaries of weather; come rain or shine, the party can go on. Wind and direct sun should be excluded; consider planted screens as opposed to walls. The living screen will disperse wind, without creating eddies in its lee. In a cool climate the afternoon sun may actually be a boon, but where the climate is hot, consider adjustable shades or awnings to shield diners from glare and discomfort. Sound flooring is important so tables and chairs don't rock. Avoid deckboards or unmortared bricks where you expect to entertain formally, since the cracks are not only unstable for furniture but create traps for narrow-heeled shoes.

For safety's sake at night, and for ambi-

Far left: A square of bricks is a handsome and practical floor for a wooden table set in the shade of massive beech trees. Surrounding the table, grass, pachysandra, ferns, and rhododendrons create a secluded, green glade, completing the outdoor dining room with horticultural walls. David Benner, designer.

Near left: Building a deck beneath a tree provides shade, enclosure, a delicately detailed canopy, and ideally, brings seasonal changes—spring flowers, fall color, and a tracery of winter branches.

Below left: Baskets of petunias and impatiens in reds, pinks, and whites hang from the eaves of a decorative wooden arbor, giving colorful definition to the edge of a brick terrace.

ence, lighting contributes a great deal to detailing a spot for dining. Candles are lovely, but many a meal that begins in daylight ends in near-total darkness when only candles are used. Don't expect candles to ward off insects either. Rather than lighting the table itself, light up nearby trees with spots, and pick out steps and walks with low-level lighting. The pools of light will illuminate dining areas indirectly, while visually enlarging the space.

Other built-in fixtures may be especially useful in permanent dining spots. Siting them in close proximity to the house or a pool means that lines for natural gas, water, and electricity will be economically at hand for cooking and clean-up facilities and appliances. Consider, too, adding a buffet ledge outside a kitchen window as a pass-through. Constructed barbecues are best built from local stone or other masonry to match the house or landscape. Fixtures such as gas grills can be skillfully blended into a carpentered countertop; firepits can repeat other rocky forms in the garden. Even brick barbecues can be part of a larger, multi-purpose wall or floor in the garden. Site all barbecues so that the prevailing breeze takes the smoke out of the garden.

PLAY SPACE

Play in the garden is not an invention of California designers. Features like elaborate playhouses and sporting fields, water tricks, and croquet lawns have been employed for centuries. The range of activities to which garden spaces may be put depends in large measure upon the number and ages of its occupants and their particular pleasures. Although "pleasure ground" is a traditional term for the entire garden, this discussion is concerned entirely with active play.

A child's garden should be well set off from the overall garden but easily visible from the adults' gathering places and from vantage points in the house. There is no reason to segregate it as though it were a dog run or utility area. Its special needs can be well integrated in the garden plan.

A playhouse or treehouse gives the area a scenic identity and a scale that is the child's own. But a playhouse can be located according to the garden's geometries; its small scale, especially in smaller gardens, will give the illusion of more distance and depth.

Spaces for fixed play equipment can be designed to have a second life after the children have grown. A sand pit can become a planting bed or a lily pond in its second generation; a circle of shredded bark or cork where a swing once dangled from a tree limb can become a shady, quiet gathering spot. Swings, slides, and climbing apparatus are available in endless configurations in timber, as well as in metal and finished wood. Choose them according to the style of the garden. The surface for play equipment areas should be flat and well graded, with shredded bark, wood chips, or grass for soft landings. If nothing else can be guaranteed about children's behavior, it is certain that they will fall. Even the design of a sand pit calls for special care. Wooden coping is better than brick, stone, or concrete, and the bench it forms should be at a comfortable height for the child to sit.

Two kinds of play spaces may be necessary for mobile equipment and toys. A tough lawn containing ryegrass and fescue is perfect for badminton and volleyball courts or the like. When not in use, the space reverts to a simple garden gathering. Tricycles, bicycles, skates, skateboards, and wagons require large, smooth-paved surfaces, or tracks around the garden. Such circulation systems double as pathways and even running tracks for adults. Asphalt, concrete, and mortared pavements will all serve, and can be tinted and detailed to harmonize with a wide variety of styles.

A contemporary play structure built with cedar posts is a place to climb, swing, slide; the height of the lowest ladder rung prevents small children from climbing above their limit. Mulch provides a soft, carefree surface below. Timber play structures can be built with children's help, and they are a much more sculptural addition to a garden than ordinary swing sets.

*Circuit paths are ideal for wagons and tricycles and are adaptable to a range of styles. **Above:** A geometric scheme with a sandbox set at the far end of the loop, away from the front gate. Brick edging helps keep sand and grass separate. **Right:** For a hillside garden, a path that weaves with the undulating ground plane. Closely cropped circles are for putting practice. Mark Sutter, designer.*

WATER AND PLAY

In Pennsylvania a long narrow pool for swimming laps and pavilions inspired by a similar pair at Hidcote Manor. Clipped evergreen hedges surround the pool, leaving just enough room for a flagstone path, a strip of grass, and beds for summer flowers.

Some of the first garden patterns were based on irrigation systems, and topography still has much to do with the placement of water in the garden. Of course, it flows downhill, and water stairs, small pools, and waterfalls are well suited to a steep site. Large pools that masquerade as natural seem odd, however, if located anywhere other than the low point of the garden. If higher, they should be incorporated into a gravity-fed series of water features at various levels, for swimming, sound, reflection, fish, or water plants.

Flat sites can be equally at home with moving water, as long as it is formally channeled, as in a Moorish-influenced, brimming canal, or the kind of runnel Sir Edwin Lutyens favored. Pools on flat sites should be compatible with the garden's other geometries, whether irregular and curvilinear or formal and rectangular.

One way to suggest natural contours in the pool is through paint on its interior walls and floor. Gray-blue to black shades will, in effect, make any pool a reflecting pool. The changing reflections of clouds and trees immediately tie the pool into the garden as a whole.

A swimming pool is a kind of aqueous gathering place and should be furnished as such. The bogeys of pool design are details like the diving board, the slide, and the metal steps. If the choice is made in favor of conventional equipment, then it is advisable, regardless of litter, to mass plantings at those points around the pool in order to screen them. Ingenious alternatives to the diving-board problem include layered stones or decking stacked up at poolside. The fullest and most attractive effect for the actual water level requires a coping edge that is slightly raised, so that the water is level with the surrounding paving. This also introduces connotations of an ornamental pool.

In fact, the most inventive water play in the garden combines fountain, spa, and pool as one element, concealing each use with color, ornament, or decorative configuration. The pool for lap swimming needn't be absolutely straight, wide, or even very deep; the spa, for relaxing, can have a sculpture or a fountain at its center,

A potted bursera on a podium in front of a free-standing wall provides a striking backdrop for a lap pool in Santa Monica. Emmet Wemple, designer.

Ilex, vinca, and box-edged beds filled with tulips and iris surround a formal pool; fountains spout from the coping.

A wooden deck carries the material of the house into the garden, surrounding a pool.

and it can be tinted dark to conceal the fixtures.

Fountains provide continual water play and animation in the garden. They can also be designed for wading or cooling your feet while sitting on the edge. As a rule, the simpler the fountain, the more pleasing to the ear and eye, regardless of the general grandeur or overall scale of the garden. Choose more elaborate fountains with great care. It takes a fairly formal, architectural setting to accept, say, a nymph pouring water from an urn. One excrescence in an otherwise beautiful, informal flower garden—supposed to be Cupid riding on a spouting dolphin's back—was known to visitors as the "angel riding a pig."

CONTEMPLATION

Contemplation is a focused act of concentration, requiring both mental discipline and freedom. The garden space that is designed for contemplation needs to be both strict and relaxed. Careful and rigorous selection of elements will limit distractions. Enclosure is all-important, as is the elimination of interior clutter. The sense of privacy is a paramount goal.

The sculpture garden is especially sensitive to interference from color. Deep green backgrounds and simple floorings are called for. In a raked sand garden with subtly placed stones, everything ought to reiterate the monochromatic richness of that palette. Moss gardens do well with a canopy of small trees, but they should spread well above the ground level, providing a changing pattern of shadow for the moss.

Any garden viewed from a fixed vantage point can become a garden for contemplation. Oriental gardeners—because they have usually regarded the garden as a symbolic miniaturization of rural scenes—offer important guidelines for the contemplative's garden, whether it be viewed through a window, from a porch or patio, or from the edge of a courtyard.

Care and restraint in placing the elements of the scene are most important. Stones, specimen plantings, and ruralia (like water basins and pathways) should be placed asymmetrically to keep the scene in motion, but each should present its best side. Keep the whole scene uncluttered so that each element can be appreciated for itself as well as for its part in the constructed landscape. The archetypal contemplative garden—the Japanese *tsuboniwa*, or courtyard garden—may be as small as 4 feet (1.2 meters) square. It may contain as little as one stone, one dwarf maple tree, a water basin, and two or three stones to suggest a path. These few elements, when arranged with sensitivity, provide a scene more graceful and quiet than many a full acre of woods.

Above left: Peacock urns, their backs brimming with feathery artemisias and campanula, are the sole occupants of this imposing secret garden. **Above right:** Hummocks of moss in a raked sand sea beneath a spreading pine are a complete landscape in miniature in the hojo garden at Tofuku-ji. **Far right:** In the shelter of a ruined stone wall, a bench becomes a private retreat.

WORKPLACES

Garden work is often a gardener's greatest pleasure. Though workspace must first be functional, thoughtful design can capitalize upon these needs to make a more satisfying garden plan.

Bins for composting organic material, cold frames for nurturing tender plants, and storage for trash cans, hoses, and so forth ought to be treated in a straightforward manner. They should be sturdily built and conveniently located—never disguised as wishing wells or overly detailed. If tucked against a hillside, a building wall, or a garden wall, they will appear more knit into the surrounding fabric of the place. Natural screens—such as simple palisade fencing or even a thick shrub border—can conceal these necessaries while adding a new and pleasing contour to the garden.

Structures such as potting sheds, greenhouses, and conservatories are, by virtue of their bulk, dominant garden elements. Potting sheds and greenhouses (cool or heated) must be located for the necessary exposure to sun and protection from wind. Aesthetically, the mass of such structures makes it important to site them carefully. If they are free-standing, their form should be balanced with plant masses or other architectural elements, such as pergolas or fences. Otherwise, the structural mass can serve as part of the enclosure for a terrace or other garden gathering.

The conservatory itself may well be placed as a sort of closed porch between house and garden. In winter the lush contrast with exterior spaces is arresting, poignant, and comforting. In other seasons the conservatory makes a softer transition to the garden proper.

Broad beds of pale peach and purple irises flank the entrance to an open and smoothly contoured English conservatory; alongside, paths are neatly edged with a line of rounded bricks.

Top left: *In front of a small greenhouse, a mixed border with osteospermum, fuschia, and columns of contrasting evergreens balance a stone trough filled with alpines. The garden side of the building is softened by a stand of lupines and a mass of pink-flowering woodbine, Lonicera periclymenum.* **Top right:** *Gravel is a tidy-looking, practical floor in a greenhouse with a wall of epiphytes grown on pieces of bark.* **Left:** *A solar greenhouse and cold frame, surrounded by a vegetable bed. The marigolds not only add color and fullness to the early garden, but if matched with certain companion plants, they can be effective in discouraging insects as well.*

CHAPTER FOUR

ELEMENTS OF THE GARDEN

by Susan Littlefield and Michael Van Valkenburgh

PAVING • TURF AND GROUND COVERS • STEPS
WALLS AND FENCES • GATES AND WINDOWS
STRUCTURES • SEATS AND BENCHES • WATER
ORNAMENTS • LIGHT • THE PLANT PALETTE

PAVING

Gravel is a relatively care-free surface, made comfortable for walking with the addition of a firm path. Here, sections from a tree trunk sweep around a rounded flower bed.

On terraces and along paths, paving is for feet—to keep them dry, mud-free, and off of vulnerable plants. It is part of the garden's architecture, outlining the places for people and articulating movement, suggesting where they gather and which way they walk through the garden. Pavement gives a garden its basic underlying structure, both visually and spatially, for it leads the eye just as effectively as it leads the foot. More generally, the ground plane establishes the base from which the rest of the garden grows. In plan, scale, and materials, therefore, the treatment of the ground, whether it is hard or soft, is fundamental to the structure of the garden as a whole.

As paving is essentially a functional element, functional criteria help determine its form. A terrace should be large enough to handle the activities of family and friends; paths should be generously proportioned for comfortable passage—at least 4 feet (1.2 meters) wide for more than one person to walk abreast. Generally, the scale of all paved surfaces should be proportioned to suit the size and scale of the garden. Materials are also determined by functional constraints. How much use the surface will have is influential, as are prevailing weather conditions. A climate with plentiful rain demands a hard, readily drainable surface: either concrete, slightly pitched to facilitate runoff, or paving stones set with porous joints. A snowy climate suggests a smooth surface that will be easy to shovel but not slick when wet or icy—concrete, either brushed or dressed with pebbles, for instance.

For a well-integrated scheme, the paving materials and their handling should reflect the character of both the adjacent buildings and the surrounding landscape. "To be fair, it must be fit," as landscape architect Charles Eliot said. In the landscape, indigenous materials generally tend to be the most "fit": Redwood is at home in California, granite and brick in the

Stone for garden use is available in many sizes, shapes, and colors, from finely textured pea stone to smooth water-worn cobbles. In selecting colors, consider surrounding architectural and natural materials; size is determined by both visual and practical constraints.

COMPARATIVE COST AND MAINTENANCE OF PAVINGS

SURFACE	COMPARATIVE COST (1-to-10 scale)	MAINTENANCE REQUIRED (1-to-10 scale)
Bark or chippings	1.0	5
Bricks	2.0	2
Cobbles (loose)	2.5	5
Cobbles (in concrete)	4.8	3
Concrete (plain)	1.5	2
Concrete (w/aggregate)	1.9	2
Flagstone (new)	6.4	2
Flagstone (used)	4.2	2
Gravel	0.5	7
Setts (new)	4.5	2
Setts (used)	4.0	2
Slate	10.0	2

*Top left: An elegant pavement with a most unusual ingredient—horses' molars. **Top right:** Stepping-stones provide a meandering path in a Japanese garden. **Bottom left:** Concrete paving softened with plants. **Bottom right:** Muted gray pebbles at Findhorn, Scotland.*

eastern United States, and the local honey-colored stone is a lovely feature in England's garden landscapes. Paved surfaces, and terraces in particular, help weave the house and garden together, and that unity is accomplished most successfully when the materials and proportions of the building are expressed in the surrounding pavements. Paths can carry that continuity further into the garden.

There, ground plane plays an active role as well. A lawn that bends and disappears around a corner draws attention to the garden beyond; broadly sweeping walks suggest leisurely passage, while a narrow path channels movement directly from one destination to the next. In Japanese gardens, paving patterns articulate rhythm and movement with artful combinations of textures, patterns, and materials. Where passage is most important, the path is straight and even. When the paving becomes rugged and irregular, it forces a slower pace, typically in response to some change in the larger landscape, such as the opening of a view or the appearance of a special tree.

Among paving materials, concrete is one of the most durable and the easiest to maintain, but it suffers from unimaginative use. Concrete need not look cold, bland, or institutional—it can be brushed to create different textures or topped with pebbled aggregate, providing a wide range of colors and patterns. Joints can be marked with wood slats, brick, or granite blocks, creating crisp patterns and effectively reducing the scale of the paved surface. In a garden that will be used by children, a loop of smooth paving provides an ideal route for bicycles and roller skates; with forethought it can be an attractive and integral feature of the garden plan as well.

Bricks are warm in color, fine in scale, and endlessly variable in pattern. They can be arranged in concentric circles around an old tree or set in linear patterns like herringbone, basketweave, or bond. The herringbone pattern and basketweave, in particular, are extremely attractive, but it is comparatively difficult (and

A brick path at Dumbarton Oaks, lined with a narrow row of brick and cobblestones.

A concentric circle in the brick paving gives a tree center stage, focusing the space.

Circles of brick scoop into a concave step in an English garden. John Vellam, designer.

therefore expensive) to lay out. Bricks are unusual-looking when set with their long narrow sides exposed, as nineteenth-century architect Sir Edwin Lutyens used them in the gardens that he created in collaboration with Gertrude Jekyll. Flagstone provides an interesting counterpoint to brick, as do cobbles or granite blocks, whether woven into the design or laid alongside to define the edge. If traffic will not be too heavy, bricks can be set in a sand and concrete mix. Laying them in mortar provides a more durable surface but adds considerably to the cost, as it involves laying not only the brick but a concrete base as well.

Stone can be costly, but where locally available it is a practical and elegant surface. Flagstone is one of the most familiar paving stones, and like brick it can be set in sand with grass or turf joints or mortared in place over a concrete base. Cut granite is available in a range of colors, sizes, and finishes, from large slabs to setts—3-inch (76.2 mm) blocks that are sometimes arranged in circles or fan-shaped scallops.

Squared or rounded cobbles create a rougher surface; marble is smooth and refined but best suited to hot climates. Combinations of different stones, or of stone with brick or concrete, can be handsome but should be composed with restraint, as busy patterns with too many materials are apt to detract from a harmonious plan. One unexpected matching that looks lovely is an island of granite setts surrounded by timber decking.

Wood decks and boardwalks are useful when an elevated platform is desirable or where uneven ground puts level space at a premium. Where the climate is wet, however, wood can prove too slippery. In flat areas, gravel and finer materials like pea stone, sand, or brick dust are practical for paths and places that will be driven on. As the small grains are relatively mobile, a containing edge is necessary—made of wood, stone, or even metal, if plants alongside the edge will spill over. The finer the aggregate, the easier it will be to keep clean. On a surface that will need to be raked, for instance, the gravel should be a

half-inch (12.7 mm) in diameter or smaller. Wood bark can be used on an informal path: It decomposes over time but can readily be added to. Crushed shells and the hulls of nuts or cocoa beans are attractive where locally available, but they will also need periodic replenishing. Such soft, organic material paving has one additional advantage: It absorbs sound, making the garden seem quieter. Perhaps the simplest of all outdoor surfaces is packed earth: It can be dusty, but in the right spot it is a handsome garden floor, not suitable for rainy climates.

The roof garden has special paving needs. Light timber decking is a common solution, though as with all roof surfacing it must be underlain with a long-lasting, waterproof surface. The best idea is to lay it on battens over bituminous sheeting. But timber is by no means the only solution. Where weight is not a limiting factor, cement tiles—lain or textured—offer opportunities for more complex patterning. And cobbles set in vermiculite create a varied texture and pattern.

TURF AND GROUND COVERS

A carpet of tiny-leaved baby's-tears, Soleirolia soleirolii, *will thrive in warm climates with shade, rich soil, and plenty of moisture.*

Where foot traffic is not likely to be too heavy and shoes need not be kept dry, the ground can be carpeted with less durable materials—plants, generally, and grass, specifically. Grass has been an integral part of almost everyone's image of a garden since the French created formal gardens with long turf panels and the English introduced the landscape style, with acres of rolling lawn dotted with stands of mature trees. With its soothing green color and even texture, grass hugs the ground, capturing light and shadow and emphasizing the natural contours; it creates an attractive foil for surrounding plants and provides a soft, safe surface for play and relaxation. Lawns also provide a handsome foreground to landscape scenes, and, because grass has a low profile, it can seem to melt into the distance, weaving the near and far together into one picture. Turf is most successful given plenty of rainfall and cool, moist air; but even in the most favorable climates, it requires regular mowing, weeding, and feeding. In less than ideal conditions, a lawn can be an endless struggle to maintain. Many varieties and mixtures of turf are available today, specially formulated to meet a wide range of growing conditions: Fescues and the bluegrasses are best in cool places; Bermuda, St. Augustine, and zoysias are subtropical grasses, more tolerant of heat. Selecting an appropriate mix will limit maintenance headaches considerably. The addition of a mowing strip—a hard surface 6 to 10 inches (152.4–254 mm) wide, set between the lawn and the surrounding beds—also helps keep edges neat and mowing easy.

But perhaps the most effective way to reduce lawn care is to think critically about how much grass is necessary in your garden before planting it. Turf serves two basic and essentially different purposes: The first is functional—it provides a close-cropped surface for strolling, playing, and picnicking; the second is visual—grass creates an even green carpet that underlines the garden's open space. For functional requirements, few soft surfaces can compete with grass; but visually, other finely textured ground covers can replace or work in harmony with turf.

Some, in fact, are easier to maintain and better adapted to local growing conditions than even the most carefully selected grass mixtures. Chamomile, the small-leaved mints, and the many varieties of low-growing *Thymus serpyllum* will tolerate light foot traffic. Baby's tears and indigenous mosses create soft green mats, but they do not respond well to treading feet. In such cases, the addition of a few stepping-stones will serve light pedestrian traffic and contrast nicely with the finely textured plants. Larger-leaved, more upright ground covers like vinca, duchesnea, ivy, or pachysandra create a less manicured ground plane, effective from a distance or where a coarser texture is desired. In larger gardens, a meadow mown once or twice annually will bring an ever-changing variety of wildflowers and grasses, providing a loose alternative to an ordinary lawn. If local wildflowers are particularly limited or slow to settle, special seed mixes can be tailored to suit specific soils and climates.

In a more architectural setting, when a continuous hard surface is not entirely necessary, combinations of soft and solid materials can create a rich ground plane. Grids with alternate squares of stone and grass are familiar features in Japanese gardens—they are crisp, geometric variations on a more casual American practice of encouraging mosses, thymes, or plump houseleeks to fill in the joints between paving units. In England's benign climate, summertime brings seas of pale blue flax, alyssum, campanula, and brightly colored aubrietas to stone terraces. To the south, blocks of sun-loving herbs such as lavender and santolina alternate with large paving stones in French gardens.

LAWNS FOR TEMPERATE SITUATIONS		
BOTANICAL NAME	COMMON NAME	TEXTURE AND USE
Agrostis canina —*canina-fascicularis* —*montana-arida*	Velvet Bent Brown Bent	Fine Fine
Agrostis stolonifera alba	Creeping Bent	Fine For damp soils
Agrostis stolonifera 'Palustris'	Fiorin	Rough For damp soils
Agrostis tenuis	Browntop, Common Bent, Colonial Bluegrass	Fine
Festuca ovina	Sheep's Fescue	Fine For lawns and playing fields
Festuca rubra	St. Ives' Fescue, Red Fescue	Fine Tolerates shade and poor soil
Lolium perenne	Perennial Ryegrass	Rough For playing fields and in mixes with Fescues and Bluegrasses
Poa pratensis	Kentucky Bluegrass, Smooth-stalked Meadowgrass	Fine For lawns and playing fields
Poa trivialis	Rough Bluegrass, Rough-stalked Meadowgrass	Tolerates shade For playing fields

Grass—the quintessential ground cover—mowed in bands echoing the adjacent beds.

Creeping juniper, Juniperus horizontalis *'Blue Rug,' grows well in dry, sunny places.*

Mosses create a soft mottled floor if conditions are right. David Benner, designer.

STEPS

The Horseshoe Steps at Dumbarton Oaks near Washington, D.C., surround a fountain; the foliage on the stone balustrade is repeated around the basin. Beatrix Farrand, designer.

Steps mark changes in level, and in gardens they are often associated with views as well. No matter how slight the grade change, a set of steps provides an opportunity to stop, look over the level below, and catch one's breath before proceeding. The landing at the top of the steps is particularly important for that reason, and in its treatment it should reflect the overall garden plan. A broad landing with a bench encourages contemplation; a balustrade suggests hesitation with its choice between continuing left or right. A narrow landing, hardly differentiated from the adjacent path, downplays the approaching change in grade.

As a set of steps is often an extension of a garden path, it should be either well related to or consciously contrasted with the path in dimensions and materials. As with paths, the rhythm of steps is variable and can be effectively linked to events in the surrounding landscape. Wide treads and low risers are most comfortably proportioned for a leisurely pace, but they require a fairly gradual change in grade. Where a sharp grade necessitates steep stairs, the introduction of a landing every three to eleven risers will make the climb much less arduous. In general, regular landings and uniform ratios between risers and treads are far safer than irregular arrangements, and odd numbers of steps are more comfortable to climb than even sets. One or two steps alone are difficult to see and therefore somewhat hazardous.

Outdoor steps can double as places to sit or to picnic. If circulation is less important than other functions, the widths of the treads can be varied—several stairs can be stacked to create a ledge for sitting, or a level can be extended to make room for a planting bed or small fountain. Such details are quite architectural and are best incorporated in a structured section of the garden.

Because steps are linear, their edges are visually important. The sides can be

Round pavers of pre-cast concrete overlap to make a smoothly flowing set of steps along a gravel path. Steps curve as they meet an outcrop of boulders; pachysandra softens the edge on the inside of the curve, creating an effective foil to the rock and concrete.

Railroad-tie risers carry a brick path up a gradual slope in this relatively informal transition. The steps also mark the point at which the path emerges from between box hedges before sweeping around the edge of an open lawn.

Broad grass steps edged with a narrow band of brick mark a change in grade. Seen from above, the grass seems to continue without interruption, enhancing the view from the house to the garden. The result is a neat compromise between formal and informal.

terminated by a wall, or softened by plants spilling from adjacent beds. Stairs are a choice location for growing special plants, incidentally, for passers-by intently watching their feet are likely to notice fine details. Succulents and alpine plants can be encouraged to hug the faces of the risers, or to fill in the joints along the outside edges of the treads. To emphasize the linear quality of an outdoor stairway, the top of the tread is often extended slightly over the supporting riser, creating a sharp shadow line. Incorporating a band of contrasting material, larger paving units, or a rounded or bevelled edge, further highlights the line along the edge of the step.

Stone steps, whether of granite, marble, flagstone, or another locally available material, are a handsome addition to any garden. Stone can be elegant or rustic, suitable to the most elaborate or the very simplest of plans. Because garden designers and architects have been creating steps for as long as they have been creating gardens, variations are virtually endless—from straight runs of steps to sweeping, curved staircases with balustraded platforms from which to survey the grounds below. Thomas Church designed elegant steps suitable for smaller gardens by setting a convex flight above, a concave flight below, and a graceful circular landing in between.

Brick steps usually need a solid stone edge to hold them in place, but they can provide a smooth transition along a brick path, particularly where the grade is not too steep. Concrete steps can require foot-ings and reinforcing, or they can consist of separate slabs set like paving stones. In steps, as in pavement, concrete can be combined with other materials. Railroad ties are appropriate and sturdy steps in informal settings. Where the grade change is gradual (not over 5 degrees), they can be extended with long earth treads between the ties. Wood headers also serve this purpose, and gravel or wood chips can be added to define the treads.

Where traffic is light and growing conditions are favorable, grass treads are also feasible. Even steps completely sheathed in turf are a possibility—or they were once, when gardeners had the time and the means to invest the necessary hours in trimming each tread and riser by hand.

WALLS AND FENCES

The edges that surround a garden can be soft or solid but they create a frame and thereby establish the setting for the garden. A solid stone wall provides quite a different boundary than one defined by a mass of trees; and even a planted boundary can be varied with the introduction of evergreen and deciduous species grouped to frame occasional views of the surrounding countryside.

Conditions in the larger landscape will help determine the quality of a garden's edge, and that quality in turn will effect the development of the garden within. Where views are appealing, the perimeter can be open and the garden itself simple, complementing rather than competing with the distant landscape. Unpleasant surroundings, on the other hand, favor the development of an internally oriented garden with a few eye-catching details judiciously arranged. In addition, the treatment of a garden's edge will depend on surrounding noise levels, wind conditions, the character of indigenous materials, and the adjacent architectural details—for edges are essentially architectural elements, defining and sheltering the garden within.

Walls are the most permanent garden enclosures and perhaps the most treasured, for in terms of materials, workmanship, and protection a lovely old wall is an invaluable and practically irreplaceable feature. At any height, a garden wall is a handsome foil for flowers and foliage, providing warmth and shelter for precious plants. If constructed by the dry-wall method or planned with intermittent pockets of soil, a stone wall can support a wealth of special things, from volunteer stonecrops, valerian, or ferns to carefully nurtured phlox, saxifrages, rock cresses, mignonettes, and wallflowers.

Brick walls demand masonry construction and are therefore better suited as support for vines and climbers planted in the ground below. They are attractive when set in Flemish bond—with headers and stretchers alternating in every course—or in English garden-wall bond—where full courses of headers and stretchers alternate in sets of two to five. Ordinary English bond tends to look boring. Remember, too, that a brick wall has one drawback as compared to a stone wall: It cannot follow the undulations of a landscape unless it is stepped. Nonetheless, brick walls can curve, and the undulating line of a serpentine wall provides regular pockets of sheltered sunshine. Stucco walls are a familiar element in warmer climates with their uniformly dappled surfaces in soft pastel shades. They are an effective backdrop for the bold leaves, brilliantly colored blossoms, bright sun, and dark shadows typical of tropical landscapes. Concrete block is somewhat less romantic, but it can be an effective and relatively inexpensive wall, improved with a smooth surface and a veil of greenery. Masonry walls can be punctuated by a stone cap, wood coping, or iron railings. Heavy cast-iron chains, suspended from piers or pillars above a wall, provide graceful scalloped support for vines and climbers. Garlands of bougainvillea line the perimeter wall at Vizcaya in Florida; for a similar effect in temperate climates, follow Gertrude Jekyll's suggestion of using clematis and allowing the flowers to tumble down and mix with peonies and roses in the beds below.

Concrete walls, however, are worth more than passing mention. They are relatively inexpensive, and they can be brushed and molded in a variety of ways. They can even mime brick or stone.

Fences tend to be more open than masonry walls, and they can be built in a

In Kyoto just one of the almost infinite number of variations on the bamboo fence: double rails with short-angled lengths crossed in between and tied in place with pieces of twine.

Large blocks of cut stone make a rugged wall, well suited to expansive rural landscapes. In a garden setting, plants can be coaxed to colonize crevices that have been filled with soil.

A low stone wall topped with a trough for planting gets a coping of brightly colored portulaca in summertime. The wall marks the transition between a flagstone terrace and an open lawn.

A crisscrossing iron fence designed to support espaliered fruit trees. Extending the branches in one plane assures that an equal amount of sunshine will reach all the ripening fruit.

Like bamboo, pickets can be arranged in many different ways. Here, angled slats cross over regular uprights, creating a fence that is light looking, yet sturdy enough to support heavy vines.

Stained latticework, each joint embellished by a small metal tack, is combined with glass to provide a weatherproof architectural screen between interior and exterior.

A brick wall, solid below and capped with a frieze of rounded bricks above, allows for exchange of breezes, views, and bits of ivy between terrace levels at Dumbarton Oaks. Beatrix Farrand, designer.

An irregular wooden fence constructed of pieces of driftwood or salvaged lumber has instant patina and can be effective visually, as long as the surrounding planting is equally informal.

Retaining walls are one of the most efficient means of changing grade in a garden; but they need proper footings, drainage, and reinforcement to protect them from frost damage and buckling.

variety of materials. In wood they range from elaborately crafted structures with white pickets and finials in virtually any style from Chippendale through Victorian to rustic constructions of palisade or split rails with the patina of rough unpainted wood. The split rail fence has a strong horizontal thrust, so it should always follow the lay of the land.

Fences can be more or less solid, depending on privacy constraints or noise and wind conditions. In texture, degree of detail, color, and scale the design of a fence should reflect its importance in the overall plan. Boldly graphic patterns capture the eye, and they are best used in moderation for that reason. White stands out in gardens—be it on fences or in flower beds—so before whitewashing, take a good hard look at the fence to be sure it won't become too dominant.

Fences vary in their effectiveness at tempering traffic noise and gusty winds. To muffle noise, the enclosure should be as solid, as high, and as deep as possible; in baffling winds, some permeability is desirable because it breaks the wind and discourages turbulent eddying around the fence. Introduction of a 45-degree baffle along the top of a fence line also helps mitigate strong winds. Permeable fences have the additional advantage of allowing light and breezes into the garden and affording occasional glimpses of the landscape beyond.

Wrought-iron fences seem to suggest a boundary rather than proclaim it: They are urbanely diplomatic borders, and particularly handsome with lush green leaves poking out between the black pickets. Round, sculptural plants like hosta are spectacular against wrought iron, as are gray and silver leaves, or twisted tendrils of morning glories (*Ipomoea* spp.) trained to climb up and along the rails. In Japan, less enduring materials like bamboo, cane, reeds, and grasses are interwoven to create sturdy fences with exquisitely elegant details. Although these are materials that some people think of as tropical, they are perfectly at home in the cold, snowy winters of the Far East.

GATES AND WINDOWS

Breaks in the solid masses that define garden spaces serve two somewhat different purposes. First, openings mark a transition from one section of the garden to another, the way doors do; and second, openings frame views within or beyond the garden, as windows do. These two roles can overlap—for in garden design, movement and views often develop hand-in-hand. In that any opening is inherently part of an enclosure, its treatment should be considered in relation to the enclosure itself. Where boundaries are clearly delineated, openings can be structural elements such as gates or windows. In addition, for looser edges a void can be just as effective—a break in a mass of trees, for instance.

A gate ordinarily is an integral part of a fence, with some extra detail added to emphasize its role as an entry point—a curved top, a touch of color, special hinges and handles, or an unusual pattern. They can be solid or transparent, depending on the need for privacy and desire to suggest what lies beyond. But gates need not always be variations of the fences that they articulate. A clipped hedge may be highlighted by the tracery of a wrought-iron gate; along a garden's periphery, a hedgerow may be interrupted by a rustic wooden gate opening out to a distant view.

Openings can also be suggestive—transitional elements that order garden space rather than punctuated points in a well-defined line. Where that is the case, free-standing arches or a rose-covered arbor serve as gateways. Every opening in a garden is a gate of sorts, but some are

Top left: A high gate at the entrance to a city garden. *Above:* *Lattice on top of a solid wooden gate suggests openness without sacrificing privacy.* *Right:* *Handsome brickwork around a bull's-eye window.*

A rustic arch covered with roses creates an open and alluring invitation to enter a small rose garden. The low picket fence is just enough to suggest enclosure without blocking views of the brightly colored flower beds.

Below: *A narrowing path and an ivy-covered arch focus attention on the entrance to a walled garden, and the open woodwork in the gate allows views of what lies ahead.*
Bottom right: *The circle of a rough stone arch is carried across the top of a simple wooden gate, creating a combination of window and gate at the door to an enclosed, informal garden.*

more literal than others. In less structured sections of the garden—where the planting parts to make room for a path or a visual axis, for instance—the gate post might be a specimen tree, a striking arrangement of shrubs, or a piece of sculpture. And finally, the experience of passing through a gate can be more than purely visual. A gate creates a pause, and this in turn provides an opportunity for noticing a particularly fragrant plant, a tree with patterned bark, or leaves that whisper in the breeze. Low gateways mark the entrances to the garden, outside Japanese tea-houses, forcing visitors to bend over and physically acknowledge the fact that they are entering a special place.

In gardens as in buildings, every wall has the potential for a window. Chinese garden walls are often punctuated with small unglazed openings, and each one varies slightly, in response to the particular view being framed. In formal gardens, neatly trimmed windows often pierce topiary hedges, providing glimpses into the neighboring garden rooms. Like a view or a gateway, a window offers an enticing suggestion of pleasures ahead.

Lattice walls enclose an English city garden, providing a frame for climbers and creating windows and niches for choice potted plants. John Vellam, designer.

At Lyndhurst Castle an archway so heavily decked in roses that it has become a flowery bower. Surrounding evergreens make the roses sparkle and enhance the sense of enclosure.

STRUCTURES

A garden is a pleasure ground, and in order for it to be pleasant it must be comfortable, with shady nooks, places sheltered from wind and rain, and private spots for quiet contemplation. The essence of these spaces is that they provide protection and still maintain a gardenesque character: For although they are architectural elements, they should be experienced as part of the outdoor landscape. Garden structures can be associated with a house or free-standing. Structures close to the house probably receive the most use, and they should therefore cater to functional requirements, such as passage between house and garden or eating and entertaining outdoors. Free-standing garden structures are more fanciful and can be treated as sculptural elements in terms of form and placement. They belong in pleasant settings—a promontory with a commanding view, the edge of a brook or pond, or a sunny clearing in the midst of a dark stand of trees. Ideally, the addition of an architectural feature further defines and enhances the picturesque setting.

Pergolas often abut the house, adding a ceiling and walls to the floor of a terrace or deck. A pergola articulates the transition between house and garden, merging interior comforts with outdoor pleasures: It is an ideal place for alfresco dining, sitting with a book, or simply enjoying the open air. Overhead, a pergola can be filled in to make a solid, waterproof roof, or left as a series of beams, suggesting (rather than creating) a protective canopy. Vertical supports range from plain to ornate, but whatever their form, they should be arranged to provide easy passage and a becoming frame for the garden beyond.

Climbing plants and vines bring the garden onto and into the pergola, and soften the structure's lines. Flowering vines can be coaxed to drape garlands of brightly colored blossoms over the breakfast table; fruits and vegetables that climb can be trained on pergola supports, bringing the kitchen garden right to the back door. If a rampant grower is chosen, it might eventually fill in the openings in the canopy overhead. Evergreen climbers assure a year-round mantle of leaves—and the introduction of a few flowering vines adds extra summer interest.

With trelliswork and climbing plants, arbors are much like pergolas, but generally they are free-standing. They are often long and tunnel-shaped, with climbers trained to climb up both sides and tumble over the roof—an ideal arrangement for developing flowers and fruit because it provides maximum exposure to the sun. Grapes and roses are the classic clothing for arbors, but the possibilities are limitless. Vining plants range from the sublime to the commonplace: Wisteria, passion flowers (*Passiflora* spp.), morning glories (*Ipomoea* spp.), and scarlet runner beans (*Phaseolus coccineus*) flourish on arbors, and even tomatoes and squashes can be trained to climb overhead. Arbors, being linear, are logical canopies for garden paths, where they provide a cool, fragrant shade embellished by clusters of ripening grapes or views through backlit sprays of pastel-colored roses. Pleached trees can also create arbors—laburnum has panicles of yellow flowers in spring; hornbeam provides dense shade even on the hottest summer day. An arbor can also be an enclosing element, marking one side of a formal garden or terminating a garden axis. Not every arbor need be linear, however. A shell-shaped structure provides a sculptural support for climbers and can be scaled to suit a small garden.

Gazebos and summerhouses are more substantial structures architecturally, and they demand choice situations. Generally, they are objects to look at as well as places for having tea, reading, or resting in a cool summer breeze. Gazebos are lacy, open structures in wood or ironwork, typically painted white. In plan they are usually circular, hexagonal, or octagonal, with a raised floor edged by a decorative balustrade. The very simplest version is a rustic shelter pared down to the bare essentials, with a solid roof sup-

An extended rose arbor suggests a long, low tunnel, providing a sweetly scented, shady canopy from which to admire shrubs and perennials in the adjacent beds.

An arbor protects a secluded seat, marking the end of a garden path.

A tunnel of lattice arches leads into an Oxfordshire garden. Anne Dexter, designer.

Far left: *A white gazebo with a conical roof seems to float above a Pennsylvania pond, enhancing the summer scenery and providing an inviting spot for a late afternoon retreat. The striking design, light color, and suprising placement make the structure stand out, commanding the surrounding landscape. Renny Reynolds, designer.* **Left:** *Simple lines, a low, broad roof, and soft green paint keep this pavilion from detracting from a colorful perennial border nearby, where achillea, delphinium, foxgloves, oenothera, and salvia are massed along a grass path.* **Below left:** *A rustic gazebo, complete with all of the essential details—wooden piers resting on a raised stone base, a shingled roof, and a handsome ornamental top—handled simply enough to fit in the corner of a wooded garden.*

ported on rough wooden posts. The most ornate gazebos are rather like wedding cakes, embellished with intricately detailed railings, brackets, and cornices, and with a special finial or ornament marking the peak of the roof.

Summerhouses are somewhat more serious buildings, structurally speaking, but they can be every bit as fanciful as gazebos. The walls are likely to be solid, perhaps even built of masonry, and they may include windows and doors. A second story might feature a light, breezy room, with excellent views over the gardens below. Summerhouses are often planned with striking silhouettes or unusual polychrome color schemes, for their role as garden sculpture is as important as their value as shelters. Classical temples and ruins have inspired many summerhouses. During the Romantic period, picturesque cottages were added to English gardens and occasionally occupied by hired hermits, who were considered equally picturesque. Nash's towering Chinese pavilion at Kew inspired a flurry of Oriental garden houses, including a brightly colored teahouse built on the cliffs in front of a Newport mansion. Summerhouses are among the most whimsical garden elements: They are the gardeners' follies, designed purely for pleasure.

SEATS AND BENCHES

Primitive but elegantly designed, a chair with an arched back and sapling seat.

An archetypal iron bench with delicate detailing at Mill House in Oxfordshire.

A peaceful place to sit is one of gardening's great pleasures, and both the spot and the seat ought to be inviting and comfortable. The most appealing benches, whether permanently installed or movable, are set in quiet niches just out of the mainstream of garden traffic. Some back against a wall or a bank of trees and shrubs, others are more exposed; but to the front, every seat should offer a lovely prospect of the garden or the surrounding landscape. Benches are a bit like pointers in this sense, for they mark the location of particularly choice features—a nice view or the shade of a favorite tree.

The most permanent garden seating is built as an integral and relatively immobile part of the plan, in the form of seat-height walls, approximately 18 inches (457.5 mm) high, that line the edge of a terrace or retain a raised planting bed. Seat walls are a great convenience in climates where keeping furniture outdoors year-round is impractical, for they are perennially in place and ready to use. As built-in elements, seat walls complement a garden rather than clutter it, as some garden furniture is apt to do. In planning walls for seating, keep in mind that long straight stretches are not the most conducive to conversation: Angles and corners create nooks that are far better suited for socializing. In terms of materials, seat walls often grow out of the paved surfaces that they border. A contrasting cap highlights the sitting surface: Its width can vary to assure comfort and convenience.

Stone benches can be considered permanent seating, depending on their construction and weight; but generally, even the heaviest masonry seats are freestanding and potentially movable. They can be simple cut slabs, or complete carved benches with arms and upright backs. Occasionally a stone bench is adapted for planting: Chamomile is a time-honored plant to use in benches because it stands up to even the most portly seat and is delightfully fragrant. Stone is an attractive foil for plants of all kinds—and a bench, like a piece of sculpture, looks handsome set in a green bower.

Wood is the most familiar material for garden benches and the most versatile. The classic wooden bench is an English one—a sturdy, straightforward design built in teak, which is one of the most durable and weather-resistant of all woods. Still, other woods will make a garden seat of nearly equal elegance and durability. Oak, African mahogany or walnut, afzelia, agba, keruing, afrormosia, iroko, or utile are other suitable materials. There are formal Chinese Chippendale benches and elongated Empire styles with gracefully curving lines, painted white or weathered to muted gray. Playful variations include deep-seated wooden porch swings and joggling boards—a sagging seat that bounces and has become a garden institution in parts of the American South. To the north, Adirondack and Appalachian craftsmen make primitive garden seats of heavy twigs complete with branches and bark. Wicker is essentially a variation, although it is less weatherproof (and so treasured now that it seems to have graduated from gardens altogether). Still, white wicker is an unmatched choice for summer gardens, provided one has space to store it in the winter.

South Carolina is known for its garden benches with wood slats set between ornamental wrought-iron ends. Both wrought and cast iron have been worked into many fanciful bench designs, some geometric and some inspired by natural forms like ferns and tree stumps. Woven wire benches were featured in Victorian gardens, but they must have been more amusing to look at than to sit on. Finally, hammocks are seasonal garden seats, of a kind: suspended between two trees, or on a wide porch, a hammock is a blissful hideaway for a weary gardener's afternoon nap.

A slightly sculpted back and seat create comfort and smooth lines.

A seat built on a bridge is a tranquil spot for enjoying the scenery.

For a sunny spot in a pine woods, a rustic log seat is just right.

An informal bench, with carvings of partridges, set against a hedge.

Roses and liriope frame an ornate wrought-iron garden bench.

A simple wooden bench set in a corner of the garden at Great Dixter.

WATER

A rocky stream with a small waterfall creates a niche for moisture-loving plants— ranunculus, primulas, and hostas. Douglas Wright, designer.

Pansies and English daisies rim a low, formal pool at Butchart Gardens in British Columbia. A bed set in the water contains irises; lily pads float alongside.

A lovely small-garden idea: an old pump gushes water into a trough. The rustic quality of the fixtures suggests a relaxed, nostalgic tone. Vic Shanley, designer.

Water is captivating: It grabs our attention and lures us to its cool edges. It is usually far more compelling than any other garden feature, and its treatment is therefore one of the most important details of a garden's design. Being a natural element, water has its own intrinsic properties, and where it is incorporated in a garden—particularly when introduced to a previously dry landscape—those properties should be respected and upheld. Water's inherent characteristic is that it runs downhill, collecting in low spots. Even the most carefully designed and impeccably planted pool will look awkward if perched high in the garden. The character of the water is every bit as important as its situation: Be it formal or informal, highly ornamental or starkly simple, it must fit the site. Scale and proportion also demand careful consideration, for too large a body of water will loom in the landscape and one too small will seem diminutive and trite.

Self-contained bodies of water can be left in their natural state, enlarged, reduced, or reshaped; if the landscape is dry, water can be introduced. In very general terms, still water can be characterized as formal or informal. For an informal pond or wetland, nature is by far the best model. Local ponds tell a tremendous amount about the contours of the land at the water's edge. A careful observer can see the progression from aquatic plants to riparian trees to shrubs and wet-loving plants that bloom in spring, change color in fall, or produce beautiful crops of winter berries that attract birds.

Formal pools, on the other hand, can be built in various shapes and materials, from rectangular to elliptical, concrete to marble—and they tend to be free-standing elements in the garden, set in the midst of level open space, helping to define it. Their edges are crisp, typically, and their details architectonic. Pools can be raised slightly above the ground plane or set flush; they can be deep or shallow, dark or light. For glassy reflections, dark-surfaced containers are the most effective aesthetically. A pool can be edged with materials such as flagstone, fieldstones, brick, or tiles. The shallow reflecting pool at Dumbarton Oaks is lined with multi-colored pebbles, set in abstract patterns in the center and as a sheaf of wheat (the garden's symbol) at one end. The surface of this pool is strikingly graphic and equally effective with or without water.

This brings up one of the most important considerations in designing a pool or a pond, for that matter—its appearance out-of-season, without water. Because a pool tends to be the focus of the garden, it has to be a successful year-round feature with a clear shape, strong lines, and refined proportions. Statues are often associated with pools, and they do add interest, but a sculptural tree or a collection of spectacular water plants can be every bit as striking. Lotus, papyrus, rushes, grasses, and water lilies are bold plants, dramatic in form and texture, and some even have interesting winter features like large seed pods, golden leaves, or spiky textures.

Depth is another important consideration in designing ornamental pools. A depth of around 21 inches (525 mm) is good for the safety of children, since it is not so deep as to be dangerous if they should stray in. A pool for water lilies can be comparably shallow, and a simple reflecting pool can be still shallower.

Finally, there are swimming pools. If free-standing, a pool for bathing should be treated like any ornamental pool. It does not have to be brilliant blue and outfitted with the standard chrome equipment, for starters: Stone decking, a dark lining, and a few large rocks to dive from will do the job far more attractively. Where safety is a pressing consideration, the swimming pool can be set in a separate garden room, closed with a gate. A lawn and a flower border nearby are worthwhile additions—grass for sunning and flowers for the pure pleasure of seeing and smelling. Wading pools are still easier to fit into a coherent garden plan, as they lend themselves to sloping-sided treatments, with indigenous or harmonious natural materials like pebbles or river stones lining their edges and bottoms.

Streams and brooks are great garden assets, for they bring movement, sound, and wonderful opportunities to use ferns, rocks, and a whole retinue of moisture-loving plants. Moving water is a prominent feature in any landscape, but it tends to be less dominant than a free-standing body of water—perhaps because it is usually an extended line rather than a solitary object. In any case, a stream acts as an axis of sorts, and the surrounding garden should be developed with and around it. A stream can be informal, with a circuitous course, a rough or rocky profile, and irregular banks; or it can be a canal-like channel. A line of water marks the main axis at the Villa Lante, and on one parterre it runs down the middle of an outdoor dining table, bringing fresh water to chill the evening's wine. At the Alhambra, a runnel lines the handrail of a staircase, tempting hot fingers to trail in the cool water. The rate of flow in a stream or channel affects the form of the garden along its banks: The edge of a swiftly moving stretch of water is best treated simply, for instance, allowing attention to focus on the movement and sound of the water itself. A more serene spot, alongside an eddy or a backwater where the water collects, is a more appropriate place to develop with special plants and a secluded seat.

Fountains are emphatic and commanding focal points in the bodies of water from which they arise. They can have one or two elements: Always, there is the water itself, which can be forced into powerful jets or allowed to gurgle gently; often, there is some form of sculpture, which may serve as the water's source, or be purely decorative. The most ornate fountains are spectacular affairs with multiple tiers of water and monumental sculpture, like the Basin of Apollo at Versailles. Some of the most humble and understated fountains are found in Japanese gardens, where a rock with a depression on top may catch water dripping from a bamboo pipe. In between the two extremes there are fountains in every conceivable size and shape. The best ones work in the context of the body of water with which they are associated and the character of the surrounding garden. Elaborate waterworks are most effective in very simple spaces, generally; where the plan or planting is complex, on the other hand, the water feature should be relatively simple. Any fountain with a towering jet should be placed so that the jet falls between the sun and the spectator, at some time of day, creating a scintillating, luminous scene.

In planning a fountain, think of sight—how high the water should rise, how wide the basin should be, how many different levels and layers there should be, and at what angles the jets should be set. Also consider sound. Water can be "played" with lovely results, but it produces a very persistent noise, and in most circumstances shouldn't be encouraged to drown out all the surrounding sounds.

The most adaptable fountain, perhaps because it is the simplest, is a solitary jet rising directly from the surface of the water. It is elegant enough for the most formal scheme and understated enough to fit even a relatively natural-looking pond. Think first before centering the fountain that is selected—that is a universal impulse, and it is not always the most interesting alternative.

A birdbath in an herb garden, surrounded by garlic, chives, marigolds, and opal basil.

ORNAMENTS

Ornaments are the accessories that give a garden punch and personality. They appeal to both sight and sound, and they can be used to emphasize important places in the garden or simply to enrich the existing scenery. A statue might mark the end of an axis; a stone trough may provide a focus in the center of an herb garden; a simple fountain can introduce the trickling of water to a shady bower. Statuary is one of the most familiar forms of garden ornament, whether classical or modern, representational or abstract. It can be free-standing, set against a hedge or wall, or recessed in a special niche, depending on how the piece works three-dimensionally. Obelisks and orbs, sundials and fountains are often used to articulate central points and cross-axes; sculptured figures tend to be more directional and are therefore more effective facing into an open space or out over an important view. Statuary can be equally at home in informal or formal settings, depending on its form, material, and subject matter; and in almost any setting it seems to have a particular affinity for water. Even abstract sculpture looks fine in modern gardens.

Many objects that are not statues *per se* are sculptural, and although they may be less formal than expertly chiseled marbles, they can be every bit as effective. Wellheads, millstones, hitching posts, decorative chimney pots, and all sorts of architectural fragments can be incorporated into gardens, especially when they are drawn from the surrounding architecture. Rock can be strikingly sculptural: The Japanese use it constantly, and occasionally even create entire gardens using only sand and stone. Special trees can be outstanding features. Beeches are massive and muscular, birches delicate; the lacebark pine has exquisite detail and a poinciana covered with red flowers is a breathtaking sight from far away. Colors, textures, forms, and branching patterns vary tremendously, and they change throughout the year, making trees the most enticing sort of outdoor sculpture. Using natural materials as ornamental accents is somewhat different than using statuary, however. Trees and rocks are irregularly shaped, so their balance is dynamic, and for that reason they can be used quite freely. A group of rocks, for instance, might be set off center, or a tree be partially

At Hever Castle, a backdrop of climbing roses creates a striking frame for a classical bust set on a column.

An ornamental chimney piece given a special setting between a crown of roses and a carpet of lamium and hosta.

Ivy and low-growing campanula nestled at the foot of an old stoneware jar weave it into the garden scenery.

hidden behind a wall; whereas a bronze in a similar situation demands a more straightforward treatment.

Decorative containers combine sculpture and plant material, and they should be sturdy, slightly over-scaled pieces, suited to the outdoor environment. There are classic terra cotta pots in all shapes, sizes, and styles; simple stone troughs and elaborate sarcophagi; cast-iron urns and wooden Versailles boxes, designed to be easily moved in and out of orangeries and glass houses. Containers can function as fillers, softening places where plants would not otherwise grow, or as focal points, adding an emphatic architectural touch. Pots can punctuate corners, steps, terraces, and walls, housing plants that simply won't do elsewhere in the garden because they are too fussy or too exotic, too brilliantly colored or too delicately detailed to stand on their own in the midst of other plants. Boldly sculptural things like yuccas, cannas, and some of the low-growing sedums are ideal pot plants, for they demand to be admired on their own pedestals, free of competition from encroaching neighbors.

The introduction of sound adds tremendously to a garden. Sound tends to go hand-in-hand with movement, and is equally worth planning for. Certain plants respond to wind, for example: Aspens and poplars flutter, willows whisper, pine trees sough, and long-stemmed grasses swish and rustle. Chimes and bells bring music, again in response to breezes; and although some chimes are lovely to look at, they need not always be in a visually prominent place. Hearing the sound without seeing the source might be a more beguiling arrangement. Mobiles and moving sculptures are usually silent, but like chimes and trees they bring wind and motion into the garden. And water, with its own rhythm, can always be coaxed to sing and dance.

Excepting peacocks and a few other species, most birds do not qualify as ornaments in the landscape—but their darting presence, plumage, and song enriches a garden tremendously. Some landscapes are planned for attracting birds, with abundant food, water, and shelter. Hawthorns and hollies, junipers, apples, crabapples, cherries, and any number of viburnums provide fruits and berries for birds, and add interest to the garden as well, particularly in fall and winter. Hedgerows and understory shrubs provide protective cover and nesting materials. Pools for bathing and drinking are small water features—even the simplest will catch the eye. A handsome container surrounded by specially choice plants will please both birds and bystanders. Feeders are most fun where they are readily visible, but they can generate a lot of litter, which is better left invisible. Banks of trees and shrubs nearby will encourage even the shyest birds to venture forth and try the feeder.

Birdhouses are as varied as the birds that occupy them; but if there is a specific bird that one longs for, no run-of-the-mill house will do. Birds are choosy tenants: Dimension, location, and design must be custom-tailored if they are to commit themselves to moving in. Swallows like shelves; woodpeckers prefer pieces of hollow tree trunk; wood ducks nest in boxes hung low over water; and purple martins insist on being way up high in multi-storied apartments. These last are perhaps the most eccentric avian residences, like miniature turn-of-the-century summerhouses perched proudly in the middle of their gardens on 20-foot (6-meter) poles. For those who are not quite so choosy about the birds they attract, houses can be more whimsical and locations less scientific: Some birdhouses are more sculptural than ecological, after all, and should be treated accordingly.

Gardens can also be planted for butterflies—they flock to flowers and shrubs like buddleia, the milkweeds, asters, and *Sedum spectabile*. Butterflies are easy to please, for they seem to like plants that are sweetly scented and brightly colored. Bees can be lured to gardens also, with generous clumps of flowering thymes, mints, cranesbill geraniums, salvias, and poppies.

For an oriental garden, a thatched bird feeder inspired by Japanese shrines.

A dovecote to suit the choosiest doves, with shingles echoing the rounded doorways.

A Chinese pavilion mounted on a wooden platform adds both color and ornament in a protected corner.

LIGHT

Night lighting creates drama and extends the use of a small garden in San Francisco. John Wheatman, designer.

In lighting gardens for nighttime use, two basic considerations apply: One is safety and the other is aesthetic appeal. Steps are the most critical garden features to light in terms of safety; and well-traveled walkways must also be lighted, particularly where the paving is rough or irregular. Gathering places like terraces and decks can be lit for ambience, on the other hand, and aesthetic considerations are paramount in using light to define or enhance nighttime scenery. In either case

the aim is not to recreate the brilliance of daytime but to play light against dark, creating a comfortable setting. If you succeed in capturing a bit of the magic for which nighttime is famous, so much the better.

The key point in lighting for safe movement through the garden is to illuminate the ground plane, and one of the most straightforward approaches is to concentrate the light almost exclusively on paved surfaces. Low lights can be set on 12- to

18-inch (305–457.5 mm) posts with caps that deflect light down; or incorporated in bollards, again with a baffle that directs the light away from sensitive eyes and onto the ground plane. This type of lighting hits the paved surface and the very edge of the surrounding planting, thereby creating a strong contrast between dark and light areas. On steps, light sources can be attached to the stairs themselves, to the underside of railings or to a wall alongside—in all arrangements, a deflector is still necessary to focus light onto the paved surface.

For major paths, brighter light may be appropriate, in which case lamps on poles are effective. These fixtures are important objects visually, and should blend with the house, the paving materials, and the general plan in both design and detail. Lampposts are available in stone, metal, or wood, and they can be coordinated with surrounding objects like benches, railings, and fences for a clean, unified effect. Contemporary styles are available with plain shafts and simple geometric globes; other lamps have ornamental posts and paneled shades. For the very traditional, even gaslights are still a possibility.

Lighting for mood can be general or specific, involving either an area or an object. Generally, ambient light is far more subtle and appealing than focused light: A terrace lit by the glow from inside the house or by light reflected from an adjacent tree is far more comfortable than a floodlit one, for instance. If light fixtures seem necessary, they can be attached to the walls of the house or set around the garden on decorative poles. Specific objects—trees, most often, in gardens—can be lit from above or below. Uplighting is particularly effective when canopies are in leaf, for it creates a ceiling that holds and reflects light. Water also seems to invite light, and as with trees, subtle effects are by far the most desirable. In terms of planting for nighttime pleasure, white flowers are spectacular: They sparkle in the dark, reflecting even the faintest light, and tend to be fragrant during the evening hours. Petunias, nicotiana, jasmine, silver-leaved and variegated plants are lovely at night; moonflowers *(Calonyction acu-* *leatum)* open their great white blossoms just as the evening star begins to shine.

Not all lighting need be permanent, however. Torches can be exotic bamboo poles sputtering flames or elegant wrought-iron fixtures creating soft halos throughout the garden. Candles are always romantic, and glass lanterns make them practical to use outdoors—set on top of tables, lined up along steps, or on top of a low wall. Votive candles carefully nestled in sand in small, open paper bags give a warm glow; and Japanese lanterns are always festive. Strings of tiny white lights threaded in trees are occasionally used year-round, but they are far more effective if saved for special occasions. Light, after all, is an ephemeral element: It should be not static but adaptable, ready to take best advantage of the changes that are so constant in gardens.

Soft light pinpoints architectural features in a Japanese-influenced garden. Artistic Lighting Inc., designers.

Here the focus is on plants—climbers and mounds of sedum—and a raised pool beneath a pergola. Brophy, designer.

THE PLANT PALETTE

The gardener's taste is important in developing the plant palette, but existing flora and environment can also play decisive roles. Every garden, urban or rural, is part of a larger landscape context. Consider the existing plant patterns and species on or surrounding the garden site as possible elements of the palette. They may be replicated or counterpointed by new plantings. Near the sea, for example, a gardener might choose to reinforce the indigenous plants, creating drifts of them where there were only whisps before. In gardens reclaimed from other land uses, the surviving hedgerows, orchards, or specimen trees may be edited or reshaped to form the new garden's bones.

Where the gardener intends to counterpoint the existing vegetation, it is especially important to consider the site conditions and its micro-climates. Water, wind, air quality, amount and timing of sunlight, summer and winter temperatures, and soil conditions will all affect the plants' ability to thrive. Some of the limitations can be overcome by good, high-maintenance gardening: by irrigation, windscreens, soil improvement, and fertilizers. Others are genuinely limiting. Few conifers, for example, will survive in shade, nor will plants with gray or gold foliage. High winds make it difficult to plant evergreens that are already large, as the trees may well topple over. Frost, too, can present difficulties. If you are planting marginally hardy plants in an area subject to frost, it can be killing to place them where the morning sun will strike them in winter. Frozen water left on the foliage from the night before will do worse damage if the foliage is exposed to direct sun.

Whatever the garden conditions, the palette will consist of three layers or "stories": an upper story of trees, a middle story of shrubs, and a lower story of herbaceous plants. Of course, not every garden will contain all three layers, and some members of each—dwarf trees and shrubs or climbing herbaceous plants—may occur in other than their accustomed layer. Still, these stories contain the plantsman's entire repertoire.

This page, top: The rich greens of broad-leaved evergreens complement delicate ferns and impatiens. Center: 'Roulette,' a hybrid narcissus, is a welcome sight in a spring garden. Bottom: Arum italicum, with its tracery of white, grows in mild climates and rich, moist soil. Opposite page, top left: Spires of foxglove are a strong vertical element in flower borders, lifting the eye above masses of lower-growing annuals and perennials. Top center: Euphorbia characias is treasured by the English, for it is a striking addition to a mixed border, and the yellow-green flowers are useful in complementing and modulating a great many color combinations. The variety here is 'Lambrook Gold.' Top right: Delicate azalea blossoms. Middle left: A mat of Epimedium alpinum var. rubrum is a choice ground cover for partial shade. Middle center: The crepe-paper blooms of an oriental poppy. Middle right: Sculptural leaves and seed pods of the water lotus. Bottom left: The rich purple of a bearded iris is highlighted by a background of finely textured gray leaves. Bottom center: Pale-lavender flowers above clumps of blue-green hosta. Bottom right: A vigorous, recurrent-blooming, climbing rose named 'Dortmund' provides a vertical focus in an informal, meadow garden.

Trees

Trees extend above garden walls, forming a composition with the surrounding landscape. Trees also form the garden ceiling, the least finite space-shaping element in the garden. A ceiling is seen but no touched, and it may be spare or dense, depending on the species of tree selected. Albizzia and honey locust, for example, have thin foliage, while linden and hornbeam are more dense. The quality of a ceiling will be different with each.

The first use of trees in the garden is to provide visual enclosure, blocking unwanted views. If it is important to produce the screen as quickly as possible, choose fast-growing trees like the poplars and/or site the trees as close to the garden gatherings or viewpoints as possible. Ordinarily, the trees available from a nursery will be 10 feet (3 meters) tall or less, though it is sometimes possible to buy them much larger. The same trees make excellent shelter from the wind, typically reducing the wind speed in their lee by half.

Trees may frame a view, as well as block it, emphasizing a part of the surrounding landscape while masking the rest. There are two ways to proceed. One may leave a gap in a dense group of trees, making a high, narrow frame. Or one may prune out the lower limbs of a grove, producing a horizontal and interrupted frame. Many

Trees can be used formally or informally; allowed to assume their natural branching patterns or trained to more linear or sculptural configurations. **Left:** *An allée cut through a wooded thicket, lined with saplings that have been pruned to encourage long, lean stems.* **Top right:** *A pear tree espaliered against a wooden fence. Once considered a highly productive method of growing fruit, espalier is now used as an ornamental element, to give attractive graphic definition to flat garden surfaces.* **Bottom right:** *Pink dogwoods and azaleas line a woodland path, surrounding it with a cloud of bloom.*

AVERAGE RATE OF TREE GROWTH					
A = 20ft/6m, B = 30ft/9m, C = 40ft/12m, D = 50ft/15m, E = 60ft/18m, F = 80ft/24m or more					
TREE	AT 20 YEARS	AT 50 YEARS	TREE	AT 20 YEARS	AT 50 YEARS
Acacia	C	E	Magnolia, Southern	B	F
Ailanthus	B	E	Magnolia, other	A	B,C
Alder	B	D	Maple, Field	A	C
Almond	A	C	Maple, Japanese	A –	A
Apple	A –	A	Maple, Silver	B	D
Arbutus	A	C	Maple, Sugar	A–B	E,F
Ash	B	D	Oak, Pin	B	F
Aspen	A +	E	Oak, Scarlet	A–A+	D,E
Beech	B	D	Oak, White	B	F
Birch	B	E	Oak, other	B	D
Catalpa	A	D	Pine, Aleppo	A	E
Cherry, Japanese	A	C	Pine, Corsican	B	E
Chestnut spp.	B	D	Pine, Scotch	B	D
Cedar spp.	A	D,E,F	Pine, Swiss Mountain	A	B
Crab apple	A	C	Pines, other	B	F
Cypress, Arizona	A –	C	Plane	A	D
Cypress, Italian	B	F	Poplar, Black	E	F
Cypress, Lawson's	B	E	Poplar (Cottonwood)	B	F
Cypress, Monterey	B	F	Poplar, Grey	D	F
Cypress, Mourning	A +	E	Poplar, Lombardy	E	F
Cypress, Swamp	B	D	Poplar (Quaking Aspen)	C	F
Elm, American	B	F			
Elm, Cornish	B	D	Redwood	B C	F +
Elm, English	B	D,E,F	Rowan	A	C,D
Elm, Wych	B	E,F	Sophora (Japanese Pagoda Tree)	A	D
Fir, Douglas	D	F			
Fir, Giant	D	F	Spruce, Serbian	B	E
Fir, Noble	C	E	Spruce, Sitka	E	F
Gingko	B	E	Sycamore	B	E
Gleditschia (English)	A	C	Thuja (American arborvitae)	A	D
Gleditsia (Honey-locust)	B	F			
Hawthorn	A	C	Thuja (red cedar) (giant arborvitae)	C	E,F
Hemlock, Canada	D	F			
Hemlock, Mountain	D	F	Tulip Tree	C	F
Holly, English	B	C	Walnut	B	D
Holly, Japanese	A –	A	Whitebeam	A	C
Hornbeam, American	A –	B	Wellingtonia	C	F
Hornbeam, European	A	D	Willow, White	C	E,F
Laburnum	A	B,C	Willow, others	B	C,D
Larch, American	A +	E	Yew	A	B
Larch, European	B	E,F	Yew, Japanese	A	D
Lime	B	D	Zelkova, Japanese	A–B	E,F

Japanese gardeners are masters of this latter art, working with pines, Japanese cypress, cryptomeria, bamboo, zelkova, or evergreen oak.

While trees are often planted in rows as screens, they can create many moods in the larger garden when they are placed in free-standing groups.

A bosque is one way of planting trees. The plants in a bosque are geometrically arranged and equidistant, perhaps as close as 10 to 15 feet (3–4.5 meters) on center. Bosques were commonly used in Renaissance gardens, and have found wide use in the twentieth century. The landscape architect Dan Kiley masterfully uses bosques to counterpoint expanses of lawn in his gardens. A bosque may be as small as four trees, or indefinitely larger. The form of each tree is surrendered to the character of the bosque, since the tree canopy and branches become intertwined and inseparable. Inside a bosque the trees, planted on a grid, form long corridors of space. The closely spaced trees lose interior branches, due to the deep shade inside the bosques; this creates a high, vaulted space. The measured repitition of elements and the contrast of light and shade create a dramatic walk. The geometry of the bosque makes a clear statement that it is manmade.

A grove is another common planted form, but is quite different from a bosque. It is composed of one or two types of trees closely and irregularly spaced, as an abstraction of forest patterns. Unlike a forest, however it has no understory plants. As in a bosque the identity of individual trees is sublimated to the identity of the stand. Again, the ceiling is high, but unlike a bosque, the grove has no interior corridors, since the trees are placed randomly. Since the trunks do not align, they tend to

Certain trees are predisposed to grow in colonies or groves—bamboo, birches, hazels, poplars, eucalyptus, and locusts, to name just a few. Where space allows, a uniform expanse of trees creates a strikingly serene landscape effect.

In a formal garden the woodland grove can be taken one step further, becoming an orchard or bosque, where similar trees are planted at regular intervals. Such blocks of trees become geometric elements in the landscape, appearing at once relaxed and refined. Dan Kiley, designer.

aggregate visually, and from a short distance a grove can appear dense and impenetrable. A grove is often used as part of an informal woodland composition.

A glade is the volume of space formed by an opening in a bosque or grove. The glade's placement is an important design consideration, as pockets of sunlight are made by the glade, which is itself open to the sky. The sunlight makes patterns on the ground, set against the shadows of the adjacent canopy. Trees that border a glade often have branches closer to the ground than the adjacent forest, making a closed and secret place. In woodlands, glades are appropriate sites for wildflowers and other flowering plants, since sunlight is available.

An allée, on the other hand, is a double or multiple row of closely spaced trees that parallel a centered path. It may be open or enclosed at the top. Allées function as corridors to connect destinations and also highlight views of objects at their terminus. Columnar trees, like Lombardy or Bolleana poplars, are commonly used to form an allée. Another kind of dramatic corridor can be made by cutting a tunnel through the branches of a mass of closely planted evergreens such as hemlocks or arborvitae.

Single specimen trees or closely spaced masses are sometimes placed in a landscape as outstanding elements. Plants that function this way require strong year-round visual qualities. The designer must understand the relationship between such plants and the spaces in which they are located. Common examples include copper beech, and plants with dramatic forms like amelanchier or white birch. Sometimes, more exotic plants like smoke trees or cut-leaf Japanese maples are appropriate.

Azaleas crowd a narrow flagstone walk in a Connecticut garden, structuring movement along the path as they change from deep pinks in the foreground to paler pinks and whites in the distance. A.E. Bye, designer.

Shrubs

Shrubs are among the most important garden plants. The placement of shrubs is compositionally important, since their size and volume are almost always articulated at eye level or below. Shrubs are commonly used to form garden walls that define space and block views. Clipped hedges and dense shrub borders are two examples. Garden walls should not become transparent in winter, and for this reason are often made with thick evergreens or densely branched deciduous shrubs. The wall must be sufficiently opaque and dense, but not overbearing. Its height must satisfy its purpose and be calibrated with a consideration of its effects on the garden's character. Gardens may also incorporate walls that function as transparent screens, marking edges but also allowing glimpses into other spaces. A garden wall made with plants requires considerable effort to craft the most appropriate solution.

A hedge is commonly composed of a single shrub species and is planned with precise dimensions to be controlled by pruning. (When hedges are low enough to be seen over, they are referred to as edges; they must be pruned several times each year. Not all plants tolerate pruning, and it is best to make hedges with plants commonly used for the purpose. Best of all, for its rich foliage is the evergreen, English yew (Taxus baccata). It is dense, fine-textured, and lends itself well to pruning. Hollies such as Ilex aquifolium are other excellent choices, dense but more luminous than yew. All tend to grow slowly, but if you plant a quicker-growing species at the same time, you can get relatively instant results until the more lovely, stately choice grows in. Good, fast-growing species include privet (Ligustrum ovalifolium), the honeysuckle Lonicera nitida, and several of the barberries (Berberis spp.). Of course, the drawback to quicker-growing shrubs is that they must be pruned more often.

Low hedges are ideal for framing beds and providing a firm outline for formal garden spaces. Sometimes, they may constitute the whole formal plan, as in a maze created with low hedges or a hedge checkerboard.

One alternative not to be overlooked is the tapestry hedge. The Japanese are fond of mixed shrubbery hedges that present varied color and flower through the season. The famous hedge at Entsu-ji garden in Kyoto contains no less than six species: a camellia, a sasanqua (Camellia sasanqua), a tea bush, a gardenia, an oak, and a Chinese hawthorn. The technique has also long been practiced in England and Europe, where yew, holly, and beech make an attractive and much-used trio.

The shrub border is another type of garden wall, but it is less formal than a hedge. Shrub borders may be composed of one or several species, and they are usually not pruned. To achieve a continuum of density, a gradation is created by starting at ground level with lower shade-tolerant species. Taller-growing species can be planted in ascending order behind those at ground level. Species diversity and low maintenance are attributes of the shrub border.

Alone or in combination with herbaceous plants, the shrub border offers an unparalleled opportunity to weave a garden area into a complex of complementary textures. The variables in foliage are size, number, and luminosity. Generally, you will achieve the loveliest tapestries by grouping plants with common characteristics. Coarse, matte foliages mix well, as do fine, luminous ones. If you intend the shrubs to set off a statue, featured plant, or array of bright flowers, the best foil is a pattern of dense, dark foliage.

Perhaps the finest among all mixed shrub borders is the ericaceous border. Members of the family Ericaceae are varied in appearance and accomodate themselves well in many garden situations. A mixed border might beautifully combine blueberry, mountain laurel, azaleas, and rhododendrons: all Ericaceae.

A checkerboard of sand and neatly clipped shrubs pattern a Japanese courtyard.

Rhododendron, boxwood, and dogwood surround a lawn at the Tyrconnell garden.

Herbaceous Plants

The ground plane is the third layer of garden space. Aside from turf and ground covers (see page 136), herbaceous and perennial plants are its main constituents. Unlike the garden ceiling, the ground plane is opaque, so it leads the visitor's eye quite persuasively. Planting patterns should mesh with the slope of the land to give a pleasant sense of depth and breadth. Where the ground slopes up

from the vantage point, one solution is to plant in depth, providing irregularly spaced points of interest for the viewer's eyes. In this situation, a bed that draws a line across the visitor's view often makes the garden too static. Where the ground slopes down, the gardener has a fine opportunity to play with perspective. One good idea is to frame a descending path with flowering plants. One can make the path grow narrower as it descends, and the framed space will seem to telescope, giving the viewer an increased sense of depth.

Flat ground gives the widest variety of options, the three most popular of which are detailed below. For all schemes with herbaceous plants, though, it is best to plan in associative groups that provide interest throughout the year. If a plant dies to the ground in winter, for example, it should be placed near shrubs or other plants that have winter foliage interest. And bulbs, whose foliage dies quickly, are best planted so as to conceal the dead leaves: among other plants, in masses, or in grass.

The first option for planting herbaceous

Clumps of pansies and tulips bring brilliance to a spring border. Colors and textures are arranged in contrasting blocks of single hues in order to maximize the visual effect, and a line of glossy-leaved evergreens in the background offsets the vivid flowers. Such basic, bright colors are typical of bulbs and annuals; perennials tend to lend themselves to softer, subtler compositions.

CHARACTER OF FLOWERING PLANTS

PLANT	HEIGHT (in inches)	COLORS AVAILABLE	SUN TOLERANCE	PLANT	HEIGHT (in inches)	COLORS AVAILABLE	SUN TOLERANCE
Achillea	19–45	red, white, yellow	full sun	Dicentra	12–28	pink, red, white	full/partial sun
Aconitum	36–48	blue, yellow	partial sun	Dictamnus	19–36	pink, white	full sun
Aethionema	4–8	pink	full sun	Digitalis	30–72	pink, red, white, yellow	full/partial sun
Ajuga	2–6	blue, red, yellow	partial sun				
Alchemilla	12–18	yellow	partial sun	Doronicum	6–36	yellow	full/partial sun
Allium	9–48	red	full sun	Draba	1–3	yellow	full sun
Alyssum	3–18	blue, yellow	full sun	Echinops	36–48	blue	full/partial sun
Amsonia	18–36	blue	partial sun	Erigeron	3–24	blue, pink, white, yellow	full sun
Anaphalis	10–36	white	full/partial sun				
Anchusa	18–60	blue	full sun	Eryngium	18–36	blue	full sun
Anemone	4–18	blue, red, white	partial sun	Eupatorium	24–72	pink	partial sun
Anthemis	6–30	orange, white, yellow	full sun	Euphorbia	14–48	red, yellow	full sun
				Festuca	9	blue	full sun
Aquilegia	18–36	blue, pink, red, white, yellow	partial sun	Filipendula	18–60	pink, white	full sun
Arabis	2–9	white	full sun	Gaillardia	12–36	orange, red, yellow	full sun
Armeria	3–12	pink, red, white	full sun	Gentiana	4–24	blue, white	full sun
Artemisia	18–60	red, white, yellow	full/partial sun	Geranium	6–24	blue, pink, red, white	full sun
Asperula	3–10	white	partial sun				
Aster	8–40	blue, pink, red, white	full sun	Geum	18–24	orange, red, yellow	full/partial sun
				Gypsophila	3–36	pink, white	full sun
Astilbe	12–40	pink, red, white	full/partial sun	Helenium	36–60	orange, red, yellow	full sun
Aubrieta	3–6	blue, pink, red	full sun	Helianthemum	6–12	orange, pink, red, white, yellow	full sun
Baptisia	48–60	blue	full sun				
Bergenia	6–12	purple	full/partial sun	Helianthus	36–72	yellow	full sun
Caltha	9–18	yellow	full sun	Heliopsis	36–48	yellow	full sun
Campanula	4–36	blue, white	full/partial sun	Helleborus	12–24	pink, white	shade
Catananche	18–36	blue, white	full sun	Hemerocallis	24–40	orange, red, white, yellow	full/partial sun
Centaurea	12–48	blue, pink, red, white, yellow	full sun				
				Heuchera	18–24	pink, red, white	full/partial sun
Chrysanthemum	6–36	purple, red, white, yellow	full sun	Hosta	18–28	blue, white	partial/full shade
Chrysogonum	6–9	yellow	partial sun	Hyacinthus	8	blue, pink, red, yellow, white	full sun
Cimicifuga	60–84	white	full/partial sun				
Clematis	climbers (to 30')	blue, pink, white, yellow	shady base, tops in full sun	Hylomecon	8–12	yellow	full sun
				Iberis	4–15	pink, red, white	full sun
Convallaria	5–12	white	partial/full shade	Incarvillea	12–24	pink, red	full sun
Coreopsis	12–36	yellow	full sun	Inula	12–24	yellow	full sun
Corydalis	4	blue, red	partial sun	Iris, bearded	12–48	blue, pink, red, yellow, white	full sun
Crocosmia	18–36	red, yellow	full/partial sun				
Delphinium	18–72	blue, pink, white	full sun	Iris, dwarf	6–10	blue, pink, red, yellow, white	full sun
Dianthus	4–8	pink, red, white	full sun				

CHARACTER OF FLOWERING PLANTS

PLANT	HEIGHT (in inches)	COLORS AVAILABLE	SUN TOLERANCE	PLANT	HEIGHT (in inches)	COLORS AVAILABLE	SUN TOLERANCE
Iris, English	18–24	blue, white	full sun	Polygonum	4–48	pink, red, white	full/partial sun
Iris, Siberian	30–48	blue, pink, white	full sun	Potentilla, fruticosa	48	orange, white, yellow	full sun
Iris, spuria	24–48	blue, white, yellow	full sun	Potentilla, others	3–24	orange, pink, red, white, yellow	full sun
Lamium	6–14	pink, red, white	partial sun				
Lathyrus	16–70	blue, pink, red, white	full sun	Primula	4–24	blue, orange, pink, red, white, yellow	partial sun
Lavandula	12–48	blue	full sun	Prunella	9–12	blue, pink, red, white	partial/full shade
Leontopodium	4–9	white	partial sun				
Lewisia	3–9	white	full sun	Pulmonaria	6–12	blue	partial sun
Liatris	18–36	red, white	full sun	Pyrethrum	18–36	pink, red, white	full sun
Ligularia	24–50	orange, yellow	full/partial sun	Ranunculus	4–24	pink, red, white, yellow	full sun
Limonium	6–18	blue, pink, white	full sun				
Linum	8–18	blue, red, white, yellow	full sun	Rudbeckia	12–40	yellow	full sun
Lobelia	6–36	blue, red	full/partial sun	Salvia	18–48	blue, pink, red	full sun
Lupinus	12–48	blue, pink, red, white, yellow	full sun	Santolina	30	white	full sun
				Saponaria	3–6	pink	full sun
Lychnis	6–36	blue, orange, pink, red, white	full sun	Saxifraga	2–18	pink, red, white, yellow	full sun
Lysimachia	18–36	white, yellow	full/partial sun	Scabiosa	9–28	blue, white	full sun
Lythrum	18–40	pink, red	full sun	Sedum	3–24	pink, red, white, yellow	full sun
Malva	36–48	pink	full sun				
Mertensia	24	blue	partial sun	Sempervivum	2–15	pink	full sun
Monarda	24–36	blue, pink, red, white	full/partial sun	Silene	6–12	pink, white	full sun
				Solidago	24–72	yellow	full sun
Myosotis	6–12	blue, pink, white	partial sun	Stachys	12–24	pink	full/partial sun
Nepeta	12–18	blue	partial sun	Stokesia	9–18	blue, white	full/partial sun
Oenothera	12–24	yellow	full/partial sun	Symphytum	24–48	blue, pink, red, yellow	full sun
Pachysandra	9–12	greenish-white foliage	partial/full shade				
Paeonia	6–36	pink, red, white	partial sun	Thalictrum	24–60	blue, pink, white	full/partial sun
Papaver	6–36	orange, red, white, yellow	full sun	Thymus	2–8	red, white	full sun
				Tradescantia	12–28	blue, pink, red, white	partial sun
Penstemon	12–30	blue, pink, red	full sun				
Phlox, maculata, paniculata	24–48	pink, red, white	full sun	Trillium	12–18	red, white	partial sun
				Trollius	12–24	orange, yellow	full/partial sun
Phlox, others	6–15	blue, pink, red, white	full/partial sun	Veronica, herbaceous	6–24	blue, pink, red, white	full sun
Physalis	18	red	full/partial sun	Vinca	6–18	blue	partial sun
Physostegia	18–42	pink, white	full/partial sun	Viola	4–8	blue, orange, red, white, yellow	full/partial sun
Platycodon	8–12	blue	full sun				
Polemonium	18–28	blue, white	partial sun	Yucca	36–48	white	full sun

Note: Heights are given in inches, for plants under average conditions. Use the figures for comparison in planning a bed or border.

Annuals create a colorful border at the foot of a clump of birches in a quarry garden at the Royal Botanic Garden in Hamilton, Ontario. Surrounded by steep walls and rocky outcrops, this tiered planting begins low with blue **Salvia** *farinacea and pelargoniums, then builds up to a drift of* **Nicotiana** *'Nike Mix' in a range of pinks, reds, and whites with a few lime greens.*

plants is the parterre, a geometric pattern of distinctive and often colorful annual and perennial flowers arranged in a planting bed. The edges of a parterre are frequently framed with low evergreen hedge, which may also be repeated as part of the internal parterre composition. Parterres are usually placed to be viewed from above, since their patterns are most easily understood from such a vantage point. A common arrangement is a raised terrace with slightly lower parterres nearby.

The perennial border allows the investigation of ground covers and herbaceous plants selected for leaf textures and flower colors. A perennial border can be either geometric or irregular in its outline and internal composition, and is a diversely expressive planted form (see page 72).

Since most perennials bloom for a short period, numerous species are needed to establish interesting patterns throughout a growing season. At the end of the nineteenth century, the English designer Gertrude Jekyll perfected the design and use of the perennial border. Her writings on this topic remain excellent sources. Beatrix Farrand's perennial borders, designed in the first half of this century, are among the finest American examples. At any scale, the border is among the garden's glories.

French intensive beds are obtained by planting tightly in a rich soil bed, elevated slightly with a stone or wood edge. These edges establish areas of visual interest on the garden floor in seasons when dormant herbaceous plants are not visible. French intensive beds are usually rectangular and

less than 6 feet (1.8 meters) wide—twice the length of an arm's reach. They offer design possibilities for combining elements from parterres and perennial borders.

A meadow is composed of one or several taller grasses, often with wildflowers. The height of meadow plants often exceeds 2 to 3 feet (600–900 mm) and it moves with the wind, gently animating the landscape. A meadow is a low-maintenance landscape, requiring less fertilizer and moisture than a lawn. A meadow can turn a pleasant brown in dry summers. The cutting of a meadow usually occurs only once a year, after biennial wildflowers have set seed. Unlike a lawn, which can be beautiful in a small area, a meadow usually requires a large expanse to be effective.

CHAPTER FIVE

DESIGNER'S CHOICE

by Susan Littlefield

LUIS BARRAGÁN • JOHN BROOKES
ROBERTO BURLE MARX • • PAMELA BURTON
A.E. BYE • ENGEL/GGP
FALCON & BUENO • BARBARA FEALY
INNOCENTI & WEBEL • DAN KILEY
LOIS LISTER • DIANE McGUIRE
OEHME, VAN SWEDEN & ASSOCIATES
RUSSELL PAGE • MICHAEL VAN VALKENBURGH

LUIS BARRAGÁN

A rimless watering trough set beneath an avenue of towering eucalyptus trees in a plaza designed for horses and riders. Any ripples in the trough spill over into a narrow gutter, assuring mirror-smooth reflections. The white wall captures shadows on a vertical plane.

As Luis Barragán sees it, "A beautiful garden is the most efficient refuge from the adversities of contemporary life." His gardens are integral to the houses that he designs, and they tend to be abstract spaces, expressed simply and directly with indigenous Mexican materials: tile, stone, and stucco in bright sun beneath brilliant blue skies. They serve not only as refuges, but as the souls of his houses, courtyards in which nature is a permanent but controlled presence. Barragán has been most inspired by the architecture, patios, streets, and squares of his own country and by Moorish gardens in Spain. He admires the gardens of the Alhambra, and the Patio of the Myrtles in particular, for it contains what every garden should, in Barragán's opinion—"nothing less than the universe itself."

Serenity and silence are two of Barragán's greatest goals, and he believes that they both begin with enclosure. "Any work of architecture which does not express serenity is a mistake. That is why it has been an error to replace the protection of walls with today's intemperate use of enormous glass windows. . . . Walls create silence." And from that silence, he suggests, "You can play with water as music . . . in my fountains, silence sings."

Water takes many forms in his gardens, from mirror-smooth reflecting pools framed in polished stone to narrow canals, gur-gling sluiceways, and aqueducts that thread along the top of high walls. Often, glassy surfaces are ruptured by water spilling from simple square channels; always, the vessels are sculptural, designed to be as striking with water in them as without. The surrounding ground plane is simple: packed earth, tile, smooth river-run cobblestone, or rough brick.

"Landscape architecture is architecture without a ceiling," Barragán believes, and his outdoor spaces are stages for a constantly changing play of light and shade. Flat expanses of water capture moving clouds; stuccoed walls reflect the tropical sun and strike dramatic shadows. Within his gardens, Barragán incorporates only a few freestanding elements, and treats them all as sculptural objects. Walls punctured with doors or monumental gateways subdivide space and channel movement. Massive fountains contain great volumes of water. Plant forms are every bit as sculptural as the built elements, although as natural objects they provide a striking contrast to Barragán's architecture. He uses native trees and plants for the most part, silhouetting them in front of walls or setting them just beyond. "There is mystery," he suggests, "when you see part of a tree, behind a wall." Rocks and exposed outcrops can also assume a sculptural role, contrasted against stark architectural forms, as can a more formal arrangement such as the collection of terra cotta pots that fills a corner of a patio in Barragán's office. In the courtyard of the stables at Los Clubes, even the horses and riders have a frieze-like quality as they pass in front of great pink and purple walls.

Perhaps Barragán's most ambitious creation—the subdivision of *El Pedregal* (The Rockery) near Mexico City—survives only in memory. In the late 1940s, he acquired 865 acres of land covered with lava flows. Here, gardens were to be the spiritual center of the dwellings, the houses limited to 10 percent of each plot and serving mainly for sleeping and cooking. With stairs built into the rock and pools and walls integrated into the weird spaces, he made model gardens using the local cacti, wild flowers, and trees. Brightly colored gates marked the boundaries. Today, massive development has eradicated most traces of Barragán's impressive and unusually attractive plans.

Bright colors are perhaps the most graphic and therefore most memorable features of Barragán's houses and gardens—and al-though they seem fundamental to his compositions, he does not always begin his projects with color in mind. Choices about color are made at various points during his design process: In one project he may find that the very first forms define their own colors, but for another he might wait until the space is built. Then he visits it at different times of day, in changing light, and gradually begins to visualize the final color scheme. "Color is useful to enlarge or shrink a space," he suggests. "And it is also useful to add that touch of magic a space needs." However, he warns that careless use of color can disrupt the sense of serenity: "One has to be on guard against using an indiscriminate palette of colors in order not to frighten it away."

"Gardens, to me, should be poetic, mysterious, bewitching, serene and joyous," Barragán explains. "I believe in emotional architecture. It is very important for humankind that architecture should move by its beauty—because life without beauty is not worth being called human."

The stable yard at San Cristobal, where horses are exercised. Views between the house and stables are screened by a rust-colored wall with a sluiceway running through its center that spurts water into the pool below. A pink wall, cut to reveal its depth, shields haystacks.

JOHN BROOKES

John Brookes is a master of smaller gardens, although he lives in a relatively large English one in West Sussex where he is director of the Clock House School of Garden Design. His thoughts and practices are not, however, limited to confined spaces. ''A garden should always serve as an extension of the house, both practically and visually,'' he wrote in *The Small Garden*. From there, the possibilities are virtually endless, limited only by the site and the designer's imagination. ''You can use bold ideas over a small area which might become monotonous on a large site,'' Brookes points out. At the same time, however, he warns that restricted spaces should not buzz with eye-catching details. For a garden of any size, he thinks in terms of broad, simple lines, and of the shapes they describe—because it is within those shapes that people concentrate their activity.

Most Brookes gardens begin with a terrace sheltered by a pergola. ''These are something of a cliché for me,'' he explains, because they make ''one feel *in* the terrace rather than *on* it.'' Pergolas also provide shade, dappled sunlight, and support for a wealth of climbers such as clematis and roses, golden-leaved hops, or English ivies. For year-round interest, Brookes likes to dress his pergolas with a combination of deciduous and evergreen plants. He prefers simple designs with which ''the fully grown plants will be shown to their best advantage,'' and he warns against making the pergola's vertical supports too heavy for the horizontals.

Walkways lead from the terrace, binding the different parts of the garden together. Brookes prefers an understated paving pattern here, with small units of a material that is used on the exterior of the house, if possible. This repetition, he feels, defines the garden as an architectural extension of the building.

Changes in level are useful, because they draw the eye into the garden. ''Diagonal slopes, steep terraces, flights of steps and raised planting beds in the garden all provide focal points,'' Brookes suggests, which are ''particularly advisable in a small site or an awkwardly shaped one, where boundary walls can look very conspicuous.'' Existing contours can be modeled to shape natural changes of grade, but where space is limited, he finds that low retaining walls are a more efficient means of articulating levels.

''Plants more than anything else transform a two-dimensional garden plan into a three-dimensional reality,'' Brookes claims. He works with trees to underline the garden's structure, fills in the spaces he has defined with shrubs, and finally adds decorative details with herbaceous and flowering plants. He favors fullness—bold masses of plants with things spilling over paths and edges—and he prefers to use species that are either native to or regionally identified with the area in which he is working. This preference is articulated in his books *A Place in the Country* and *The Garden Book*.

''Because of our supposedly miserable, dull climate (which incidentally allows us to grow a far greater range of plants than

On John Brookes' terrace at Clock House, variegated ivy climbs from wall to pergola. Evergreen shrubs and climbers provide year-round interest; pots of seasonal flowers add summer color.

Marigolds in a stoneware pot and golden hop, **Humulus** lupulus 'Aureus,' growing against a wall. From July to September the hop will be covered with clusters of small cones—the brewer's hops.

*Above: Herbs in a walled garden include artemisia, thymes, green and purple basil, salvia, lavender, rosemary, alchemilla, and spires of velvety-leaved verbascum. In the background a eucalyptus, a chartreuse-leaved honey locust (*Gleditsia triacanthos *'Sunburst') and variegated ivy echo the silver and golden leaves and flowers.* **Right:** *Purples, dark greens, and variegated leaves make welcoming surroundings for a Clock House entry court.*

almost anywhere else in the world) we are obsessed with colors,'' Brookes admits, adding that without a strong sense of order, colors can quickly become ''unrestful and disturbing.'' He sets warm colors in front of cooler ones to enhance a sense of depth; if exotic tones are incorporated, Brookes recommends bringing them close to the viewer, lest they play too dominant a role in the overall composition. Selecting plants and colors is challenging, but it is a great pleasure for John Brookes, who terms it ''the carrot,'' that lures him through the less leafy parts of garden design.

ROBERTO BURLE MARX

*B*razil is rich with tropical plants, samba rhythms, and romance, and all three come together in the gardens of Roberto Burle Marx. As a musician, painter, and accomplished plant collector, he is an unconventional combination of artist and ecologist. He paints with plants, alternating swaths of brilliantly colored tropical foliage with stretches of cropped grasses and patterned pavements that sparkle in the Brazilian sunshine.

Gardens are an art form to Burle Marx, and he believes that the best art takes its inspiration from nature. Garden designers must be keen observers therefore, constantly studying how plants grow in nature, where they grow, and why. In an effort to make nature more comprehensible, the garden artist introduces order. His compositions consist of themes and variations, orchestrated by the same principles that guide a musician or a painter. Clear thinking is essential, says Burle Marx, and it is the result of endless simplification.

Simplifying is not always easy for gardeners who love plants, and Burle Marx is certainly a plantsman. He has collected tropical species of philodendron, bromeliads, anthuriums, palms, and orchids; many of his discoveries bear his name. This love of plants and his awareness of their tremendous diversity dominated his early design work. "They were marvelous salads," he remembers, "but not gardens. Minus is more in gardens."

His gardens are his expressions of Brazil—of the wealth of tropical flora and of the glory in the natural world—and he is quick to point out that although simplicity is very important, "it is easiest to express yourself with a rich vocabulary." Editing that vocabulary is the key to making a successful garden. Every plant must have a reason for being what and where it is in order to contribute effectively to an overall composition.

Volumes are expansive in Burle Marx's gardens. Open spaces and planted areas are scaled not only to architecture but to the larger landscape as well, in an effort to weave the gardens into their sites without detracting from Brazil's spectacular scenery. His largest gardens unfold like extravagant carpets, in valleys rimmed by snow-capped mountains. Planting is kept low in swirling beds that exaggerate the height of the rugged peaks. The bold patterns, with their broad sweeps of vividly colored plants, suit the imposing scale of the surrounding landscape.

The lines in these gardens are simple, strong, and organic, like winding rivers or topographic contours. Typically, they are drawn with masses of plants, because Burle Marx feels that tropical plants are most dramatically displayed in blocks with uniform colors, textures, and forms. Rhythms develop as the garden weaves across the site, and it is marked in contrasting plant forms. Beds of ground cover ripple, stretches of lawn flow, and stands of giant cactus strike a staccato note. Burle Marx is adamant in his insistence that each plant assume its natural form: No clipped hedges or pruned shrubs, for luxuriant growth is an integral part of tropical landscapes. He introduces color after the structure of the garden has been defined and uses it to bind the various shapes and textures together. Some plantings are seasonal, with colors and patterns that change throughout the year, because, as Burle Marx muses, "expectation is a marvellous thing in a garden."

Burle Marx's own garden is set in the midst of the Brazilian jungle. **Opposite page, top left:** *The spiky leaves of bromeliads with their stiff flowers add bold texture and bright color to a mound of finely cut leaves alongside a pool.* **Opposite page, bottom right:** *Stone steps surrounded by the lush vegetation typical of the tropics.* **Above left:** *Where green is the predominant color, texture and leaf forms provide interest. Great lichen-covered boulders, water loving plants, orchids, and rosettes of reddish-pink bromeliads accent a corner of the garden.* **Above right:** *In a more formal pool, circular lily pads contrast with sharply angled coping; the light concrete rim and adjacent beds of cobbles offset the dark water. Set off-center, a stone column with a bromeliad cap provides a strong vertical accent.* **Right:** *A wall built by Burle Marx with cut stones and architectural fragments collected from sites that he has worked on. Bromeliads crown the top; niches are filled with orchids and other epiphytic plants.*

PAMELA BURTON

A detail in a corner of a garden outside an artist's studio that was designed as a metaphor for two contrasting California environments—the oasis and the desert. Lush greens and fragrant flowers allude to the oasis, with finely textured zoysia grass, a neat mound of liriope, and the glossy leaves and white flowers of jasmine.

"*L*andscape architects are not merely space planners who advise clients, specify irrigation schemes, design planting plans, and recommend megadozing," says Los Angeles landscape architect Pamela Burton. "They also create cultural meaning in their work." Almost every designed landscape has implicit meaning, she points out, because it reflects the designer's attitudes. Some also have explicit meaning, expressing specific ideas in their plans and planting. Medieval gardens, for example, were designed as miniature versions of paradise, and in Japan, gardeners combined rock and sand to create abstract landscape scenes.

Pamela Burton designs gardens with explicit meanings, using symbolism, historical references, and mythical allusions to introduce intellectual themes. She begins each garden conceptually, with an abstract idea from which all secondary details emanate. The idea can be general or specific: creating a metaphor or a place for the rituals of daily life, expressing a historic garden type, or translating a work of art into garden form. Her most recent garden is an interpretation of two Milton poems, lamenting the loss of rural values with a cast of mythological characters that Burton "translated" into plants. Aurora is personified in bougainvillea 'Texas Dawn,' Zephyr is a tree that whispers in the wind, and the three graces are introduced as citrus trees. One section of the garden, entitled "Hydrotopia," is developed around a swimming pool with a path that passes through a range of watery environments, from a desert to polar ice caps, symbolized as mountains.

Burton designed another garden in the image of a Persian paradise—a walled enclosure shaped by paths intersecting in a circle that represents enlightenment. The Los Angeles paradise is actually an entry court marking the transition from street to house, with a flower-lined path that leads through an arch to a courtyard with trees, fragrant flowers, and a round central well in glazed blue tile.

Metaphor is another favorite Burton medium. For a sculptor she created a garden with two 15-foot (4.5-meter) squares representing desert and oasis. The desert is entirely sand and doubles as a work space; the oasis contains a California pepper tree, grasses, and gardenias—capturing sound, shadow, and scent, among the most universal garden elements.

Almost all of Burton's designs incorporate daily routines, such as walking, entering, or resting, that she interprets as acts of ceremonial importance. "I like to investigate the idea of ritual in my work," Burton explains, "the idea that something takes on new meaning in its daily repetition." Thus, the paradise garden involves "the rituals of entry and passage from public to private space"; another garden, fitted out with grassed terraces rising to a rose-covered gazebo, "provides a sanctuary, set beyond the vicissitudes of daily life, to be used as a place of communal celebration and solitary meditation."

The oasis section of the garden seen through a gate framed by a stand of bamboo and a ficus-covered wall. A California pepper tree, Schinus molle, *whispers in the breeze, introducing sound and movement. Shrubs and flowers below were chosen for fragrance.*

Studies for the oasis/desert garden: Oasis on the left, with soft greens, and desert on the right, re-created with somis sand. Each section is a 15-foot (4.56-meter) square, cut from a concrete parking slab. The desert square serves as a stage for sculpture.

Throughout, Burton uses symbolism, metaphor, ritual, history, and mythology to create meaning in her work. Beyond these abstract concerns, however, she insists that her gardens have little in common. "My approach changes every time," she claims. Each project elicits a different point of view, but some general characteristics and attitudes do appear in many of her designs. As a landscape architect and an architect, Burton sees no boundary between landscape and architecture. Her interior and exterior spaces are connected with pergolas and structured garden rooms. The outdoor spaces tend to be enclosed and internally oriented, providing retreat or escape from what she sees as a harsh external environment. "The intentions in landscape are the same as the intentions in architecture," she believes, suggesting specifically that landscape architects take inspiration from postmodern architects, drawing on events and elements from the past in an effort to enrich their work.

A. E. BYE

"When you look at these gardens you may wonder what, if anything, we did," A. E. Bye acknowledges. "If that is so, that is exactly the impression we wanted to make." His gardens are not gardens in the traditional sense of flowers and patterned beds, but transitions where earth, rock, native trees, and woodland plants weave buildings and architectural spaces into the surrounding landscape. Bye's goal is to protect the diversity that exists in nature by preserving the existing character of the places where he designs.

His work has been influenced by several American designers. Frank Lloyd Wright has been a source of inspiration in his use of local materials and native plants brought to the edges of his buildings; and Jens Jensen's work with the Wisconsin prairie was instrumental in Bye's studying the intrinsic qualities of native landscapes. But most of all, Bye's gardens are a tribute to the natural

environments in the part of the world that he knows best, the eastern United States. For over 30 years he has studied and photographed landscapes from the tangled Okefenokee Swamp to the rolling hills and deciduous woodlands of southern New England where he lives and practices. His photographs are provocative depictions of nature, and he refers to them constantly in his work. A picture of the Maine coast, for example, inspired a garden in front of a contemporary house on the Connecticut shore, where Bye created a rugged composition with rocks, pines, and low-growing junipers.

Photography has sharpened Bye's ability to identify the mood of a particular piece of land, and mood is often the essence of his gardens. Serenity or stability, mystery, delicacy, and even humor occur in nature, Bye suggests, and any one mood might express the character of a residential property. "Above all," he explains,

A serpentine wall at Gainesway Farms contrasts with the linear wooden fences typical of the Kentucky countryside. The wall is a ha-ha, which allows for uninterrupted views of the landscape from above and keeps livestock from wandering into the garden.

Along the edge of a gravel drive, Bye planted a line of native shrubs—rhododendrons, mountain laurel, and leucothoe—that stands out against the dark clearing in the woods beyond. Rocks define the edge and frame the composition.

A watering trough set in an allée of oaks is a focal point in the stable area at Gainesway Farms. The jets of the fountain are kept low to avoid exciting the thoroughbred horses. Crushed brick covers the ground, its warm terra-cotta color a handsome complement to the lush green of the surrounding pastures.

Another fountain at Gainesway Farms began as a wall, 8 feet (2.43 meters) high by 30 feet (9.12 meters) long, screening the house from the parking area. On the garden side, the wall is punctuated by a row of stone channels, spouting streams of water into the basin below. The lighting is important, as the fountain is featured at night.

"the existing conditions found on the site suggest the final composition." Once he is familiar with those conditions, he finds that his vision of the completed project is likely to be intuitive and almost instantaneous.

Details take longer to design, but they too are inspired by the local landscape. Bye's contours are extensions of the exisiting ground plane, steps are carved out of existing slopes, and rocks and plants are brought from adjacent woods to the edges of buildings. Generally, his vegetation is layered: thymes, succulents, and grasses or ferns and wildflowers carpet the floor beneath an understory level of broad-leaved evergreen shrubs with small flowering trees and a canopy of mature deciduous trees.

He preserves indigenous plant material whenever possible because it provides continuity with the surrounding environment and requires minimum upkeep. For one project he transplanted pieces of the forest floor as if it were sod, successfully reintroducing the native forest complete with mosses, partridgeberry, ferns, small birches, and seedling hemlocks. As Bye points out, "Native landscapes can continue for a long time with little change if they are suitably maintained." When he finds that introduction of non-native material is necessary, he chooses plants that resemble local species in form, texture, and color.

Bye's admiration for and understanding of natural materials is nowhere more evident than in his use of rock, from outcrops and sculptural groups of boulders to the graceful sweep of a stone wall or the straight line of a gravel moat marking the edge of a house. "Rocks are elements of permanence against the variables of plant growth," he explains in his book *Art into Landscape, Landscape into Art*—and permanence is one of the most important aspects of all of Bye's work. "I like gardens to have an ageless quality," he reflects, "like a Shakespeare play or a Beethoven sonata. They should be designed in such a way that there is a message for everyone."

ENGEL/GGP

For a courtyard set in the center of a house, Engel/GGP created this water garden. The top pool, visible from the rooms on the second story, empties through a stone wall into a rectangular trough on a veranda below. Stands of **Cyperus alternifolius** *fill the lower pool.*

As David Engel sees it, photographers record nature on film, painters interpret it on canvas, and garden designers fit somewhere in between. "We do not attempt to copy nature," he asserts. "The evidence of man is always in our work—but we strive to make the elements that we use feel natural." His is a romantic view of nature, inspired by classic English landscapes, by the work of Frederick Law Olmsted, and by the gardens and philosophy of the Far East. The Oriental influence comes from Engel's years of study in Japan, and it infuses Engel/GGP's work with intensely expressive energy.

Movement is integral to their gardens: They are not static compo-

sitions, but landscapes to be explored. "You shouldn't see a garden all at once," partner Dennis Piermont explains. "Pathways should lead through constantly changing spaces." Paths articulate movement through Engel/GGP's gardens in typically Japanese fashion: where a relatively quick gait is appropriate, the path is a smooth, narrow channel; if a slower pace is necessary, an irregular pattern of rough-hewn stone appears. When an important view opens up, the paving does also, underlining the change in the surrounding landscape.

Engel believes that natural elements are inherently expressive; they influence our subconscious, evoking emotions such as excitement, pleasure, or fear. He likes to use them abstractly, and says: "We are willing to let materials symbolize things," describing sculpted mounds of azaleas that resemble rolling hills, rocks like mountain peaks, and pavements swirled with bands of different colored stone that recall rippling waters.

Rock is a favorite Engel/GGP material, and it is used in every size, shape, and situation from crushed gravel paths to bluestone terraces, rough stone walls, and seemingly natural outcrops that are as artful as any piece of outdoor sculpture. Engel is a master with rock; he spends days in the field looking for just the right boulders, and then supervises their placement to be certain that their arrangement expresses a sense of natural balance.

"We use elements and materials to create tension," he explains, because in the right dosage, tension makes a composition dynamic. Engel/GGP's gardens are exercises in the Oriental art of occult balance, with straight lines played against curves, and verticals offset by horizontals. Engel particularly likes to create interplay between natural and man-made elements, with a rough fieldstone supporting the elegant column of a wooden trellis or a

sculptural pine balanced by a slab of cut granite. Unusual juxtapositions and artful transitions are also characteristic of Engel/GGP's use of materials. Paving patterns intermingle; ground cover or a gravel gutter soften the line at the base of a wall.

Engel/GGP chooses plants for year-round character rather than for beauty during a brief period of bloom. "In wintertime, bare branches are as important as evergreens," Dennis Piermont emphasizes. "We may use trees like beeches that are muscular, or amelanchiers for delicacy. Japanese black pines have a wonderfully contorted look; and for contrast, we might use hollies and azaleas sheared into soft billowy shapes."

Whether rough or refined, Engel/GGP's use of details is imaginative. The design for a bench support came from a patterned window in a Japanese garden; a bamboo water pipe rests on a wooden block inspired by the bridge of an Oriental stringed instrument. "Don't be held down by convention," David Engel remembers one of his favorite Japanese teachers saying. "Do something new." And Engel is quick to add, "Not just to be new but to create an effective and beautiful solution."

Outside the house a flight of granite steps leads into a strolling garden, through clumps of multi-stemmed amelanchiers and mounds of sheared azaleas set amidst boulders. Engel's interest in and knowledge of Oriental gardens is clearly in evidence here.

Around the corner a swimming pool is set in cut white granite and grass, the two materials intermingling. The surrounding wall is concrete block—stuccoed and capped with ceramic Japanese tiles— kept low enough to allow views of the valley below.

FALCON & BUENO

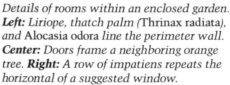

Details of rooms within an enclosed garden.
Left: *Liriope, thatch palm (*Thrinax radiata*),*
and Alocasia odora *line the perimeter wall.*
Center: *Doors frame a neighboring orange*
tree. ***Right:*** *A row of impatiens repeats the*
horizontal of a suggested window.

Teresita Falcón is an architect and Juan Antonio Bueno is a landscape architect; together they practice in Miami, where a warm subtropical climate allows for an easy flow between interior and exterior space. "Gardens mark transitions," Bueno explains. "They are part of a progression that begins inside of the house, moves through the porch and the garden and then extends into the broader landscape." As an interdisciplinary team, and as husband and wife, Falcón and Bueno advocate an integrated approach to designing houses and gardens. They begin their work separately, "but by the end of a project our exchange of ideas has been so constant that the interior and exterior designs are completely integrated. Conceptually, we consider the house and the garden as one."

Their gardens are outdoor rooms, precisely structured around the house and becoming softer and more natural as they extend farther from the architectural core. Because most of their work has been on relatively small sites, the garden spaces that they have designed tend to be on the architectural end of the spectrum. Generally their gardens begin in intimately scaled courtyards with tile floors enclosed by stuccoed walls. Farther into the landscape, the ground may be decked or planted; walls are defined by sheared hedges or colonnades of architectonic palm trees. Planting is generally restrained, in deference to the sharp lines and clear colors of architectural surfaces. Large-leaved philodendron, alocasia, and live oaks with their twisted trunks become sculptural elements; flowers set in precisely patterned beds and pots are more decorative.

"In designing and combining elements, we like to select ideas and fragments from a number of different styles," Bueno explains. He suggests that this inclination might be rooted in bicultural experience: "We grew up in Cuba, so we know two cultures and two traditions. We have learned to take the best from each."

South Florida is a richly eclectic environment as well: people come from north and south; architecture ranges from Spanish

Left: Plan for a Miami garden with lattice-covered pergolas extending the house into the garden. Architectonic lines are carried through blocks of clipped hedges and a royal-palm obelisk that marks the main axis of the house and the apex of the wedge-shaped property. Right: A leafier detail in another Florida garden.

Colonial and Bahamian to Tropical Art Deco and postmodern. The plant palette includes everything from stately palms, tropical ferns, and exotic orchids to rampant vines with pale pastel blossoms and window-box varieties of geraniums and petunias. In the midst of this diversity, Falcón & Bueno's work is consistently tropical in character. "We like our designs to be responsive to the indigenous Florida landscape," Bueno says, "not just in terms of native materials like palms and cut keystone, but in our understanding and use of vernacular forms and cultural traditions."

Ultimately, Falcón and Bueno believe that a garden should be a private place, a shelter offering both freedom and protection. Their designs seek harmony between satisfaction with what has been and anticipation of what is to come. "In Spanish, there are two words that express this very well," Bueno says. "*Recuerdos* and *ensueños:* which translate roughly as memories and daydreams. A dreamlike quality, reflecting the past and the future—that is what we want to capture in our gardens."

BARBARA FEALY

Barbara Fealy is a landscape architect practicing in Oregon, where houses are tucked into forests of towering firs and great maples. Spring brings a burst of understory bloom to her gardens, with rhododendrons, azaleas, mountain laurels, woodland flowers, and bulbs. After this blush of color, Fealy finds that most Oregonians are quite content with their shady retreats. "Our summer gardens are more green than they are brilliant," she explains, "and that means that they must have good anatomy. If the lines and masses are well related and there is a smooth flow as you move around, then it really doesn't matter what names the plants have—they will carry the design." Pots of annuals can always be moved into spots of sunshine, she suggests, to provide accent and summer color.

Most of Barbara Fealy's planting is more permanent, however, with shade-tolerant species drawn from a rich assortment of native plants. Oregon grape and huckleberry, wax myrtle, abelias, gaultheria, and a lovely ground cover called kinnikinnik (Arctostaphylos uva-ursi) grow in the woods around Portland, and they suit Fealy's design ideas perfectly. "I like relaxed spaces with a natural feeling...spaces that have a relationship to the settings that surround them."

"Fitness" is one of Fealy's main objectives in designing gardens,

A generously proportioned Portland terrace set in a frame of evergreen shrubs. The planting makes the most of spring, with a pair of flowering trees, banks of azaleas, and large terra cotta pots filled with yellow tulips. Smaller pots of marigolds will carry the bright color into summer. The smooth surface is concrete, topped with a pebbled aggregate and highlighted with bands of darker stone.

and terraces carved into rolling hillsides are essential elements in Fealy's designs. Typically, they are smooth, simple, and crisp surfaces, offset by the verticals of boulders and dense mounds of coarsely textured evergreens. Fealy is particularly fond of a pale-gray flagstone that is quarried locally, which she uses whenever possible. For larger areas an aggregate of crushed rock is set in concrete and articulated with flagstone or wooden joints to achieve a more refined scale.

Once she has completed her plan for a garden, Fealy supervises construction and planting. "If I have gone that far, I want to see that the garden says what I want it to say. Things can always be improved or polished, and that's possible when I'm right there on the site." During construction she makes minor alterations, embellishments that, in Barbara Fealy's opinion, add immeasurably to the richness of the garden's design.

Beneath a canopy of towering trees, great mounds of rhododendron capture sunlight in springtime, creating a more human scale around a small circular pool edged with stones.

In another woodland garden, gravel paths wind between crowned beds. Within the beds, planting has been kept low, to suit the lines of the contemporary house: Patches of moss surround rocks alongside stands of stiff-fronded ferns and drifts of multi-colored azaleas. The garden is colorful in spring, cool in summer.

whether they are large or small, exposed on the cliffs of the Pacific coast, nestled in firs on a hillside near Mount Hood, or set at the edge of the broad Willamette River. She vividly remembers Stanley White, one of her favorite teachers, saying that if the plan didn't fit the site as well as his open palm fit his clenched fist, the design could not be successful. To that fitness Fealy adds the importance of a graceful composition. "Gardens have to be well designed in order to look beautiful," she explains, particularly now that people seem to have so little time for gardening. "The shape of the lawn and planting beds, the arrangement of the walks...all of the elements should be well arranged and there should be a certain gracefulness in the way the parts are joined."

Although the gardens that she works on are not always large, their spaces and the masses of plants that define them are generously proportioned to suit the scale of the Oregon landscape. With sweeps of lawn, massive rocks, and banks of native plants, her gardens fit neatly into their forest clearings. "I love big boulders," Barbara Fealy admits. "They make a garden feel like it reaches into the forest and that creates a nice, natural transition."

Oregon's rain nurtures emerald-green grass, and it also necessitates a system of dry surfaces for walking. Paved paths, patios,

INNOCENTI & WEBEL

For nearly 50 years Innocenti & Webel has been designing American gardens. Although not necessarily formal in style, their gardens are architectural in spirit, with classic details expressed in traditional materials: gravel drives neatly trimmed with granite sets, flagstone terraces, stone steps, brick paths, and lead sculpture set in leafy bowers.

After studying in Europe, Umberto Innocenti and Richard Webel opened an office on Long Island in the 1930s. It was the era of the suburban estate, with large houses set in clearings carved out of the native forest. Innocenti & Webel's gardens provided handsome settings for a variety of building styles, relying on architectural elements to establish graceful lines and human proportions around the house, then reverting to natural materials and forms toward the surrounding woodland. The firm is active today from Maine to Florida, New York City to Fort Worth; although gardens tend to be on smaller sites with fewer people to look after them, Innocenti and Webel's ideas still have a classic feel to them. "Architectural elements are more efficient, particularly where space is limited," Webel points out. "Why use 20 feet [6 meters] of planting when you can do the same thing with an 8-inch [200 mm] wall?"

An Innocenti & Webel design begins with the building, establishing a proper setting and a favorable orientation. Terraces, walls, and arbors give structure to the spaces immediately outside the house. Evergreen shrubs are neatly trimmed; vines are trained on trellises; fruit trees are espaliered against building walls. Seasonal flowers decorate terraces and pools in terra cotta pots or large wooden boxes with French or Chinese Chippendale detailing. To assure a smooth transition from built to unbuilt space, familiar plants are repeated. Dogwood might mark the edge of a terrace, for example, and then be carried through the garden and into the woods beyond; a stretch of lawn might narrow to become a grass path winding toward a wilder section of the garden.

"Create a change in level to make a garden more interesting," Innocenti & Webel suggests. As architectural features, walls and steps tie the house and terrace to the garden beyond, and in their detailing they establish the appropriate scale and style. A brick terrace fits a colonial house; flagstone surrounded by a seat-height wall may be better suited to a house in the French style. "In any case, the garden should reflect the character of the house and the scale of the surrounding landscape," Webel emphasizes. "It should look as if it could only have been made that way."

Pools are incorporated as design elements. "We like swimming pools that look like ornamental pools," Webel adds, "with strong architectural character which can be attractive throughout the year." The pool's shape and proportions should relate to the house or surrounding garden spaces; details should be crisp. "We often set a piece of sculpture at the edge of a pool, with a recirculating fountain, and then surround it all with paving or set the pool directly into the lawn."

Designing gardens comes down to one basic principle, according to Webel. "Simplify, simplify, simplify. Restraint is everything. And taste, which is essentially the ability to use restraint. Look to the great French gardens for inspiration," he suggests. "They are still modern today."

Left: Neat geometry in a Long Island garden, with six triangles of wax begonias punctuated by standard roses, set around a central square of roses. Right: A similar theme, handled differently in Texas, with gravel paths and box-edged beds with periwinkle and clumps of the pink crape myrtle, Lagerstroemia indica. *The strong outline of the parterre carries the garden through the winter months.*

DAN KILEY

Trees planted in bosques are a typical feature in Kiley's gardens: These are redbuds, Cercis canadensis, *set 20 feet (6.08 meters) on center in crushed rock. The bosque is a violet mist when flowers bloom in spring; in summer it becomes a shady foil for the Henry Moore sculpture and the sunlit lawn beyond.*

When Dan Kiley talks about his work, he starts by saying that he lives in Vermont, with the land as well as on it. Living in the country, he believes, is the best way to learn about the nuances of nature—to know how to "travel lightly," in his words, and "not to stumble over the rocks or step on the hepaticas." But Kiley's gardens are quite different from the rolling landscapes that he loves in northern New England. His own farm, for instance, has rows of Lombardy poplars, sugar maples, and quaking aspen, as well as a long driveway that winds between banks of purple and white lilacs.

Kiley thinks in classical terms; his gardens are crisp, geometric

extensions of the houses they surround. They are suited to their sites, as any garden has to be if it is to grow, but they are shaped by both architectural and ecological principles. "When you organize space in a geometric, simple way, you get much more out of it than you would if you put a loose row, a woodland sort of thing. Efficiency of space makes it imperative that you organize. I'm not against a loose landscape," Kiley emphasizes, "but first you have to have architecture of the space outside."

One of his goals in designed landscapes is to recreate the excitement of a walk outdoors, through woods and clearings, across fields, hills, and valleys. He wants to capture that kind of movement and variety in his gardens, but the progression must be ordered and scaled to relate to the architecture nearby. Where those efforts are successful, Kiley believes that landscape design is "poetry of space," an abstract expression of nature interpreted, edited, and organized by an artist.

Ordered architectural space is fundamental to Kiley's compositions. To unify different parts of the garden, he uses classic elements such as lines, axes, and nodes; to ensure a sense of continuity, he creates arcades and open spaces that can be passed through or looked across. He is distrustful of principles because they suggest that there is always a set answer. He does, however, abide by one or two of his own: "Don't break a straight line unless there is a good reason to," he advises, observing that in nature, straight lines and simple modules can provide endless diversity as they undulate over uneven terrain and change in the play of light and shade.

He uses trees in lines to shape outdoor corridors and rooms with leafy canopies and roughly colonnaded walls. Allées of horse chestnuts, lindens, and honey locusts connect terraces and trellises, shaded bosques and open meadows. The ground plane is either a green carpet of ivy, pachysandra, or grass; or a floor of gravel, flagstone, or granite. Details tend to be hard-edged and extremely simple: water rests in stone pools; fountains spout vertical jets. "Never mind copying scenes of nature," Kiley insists. "I find direct and simple expressions of function and site to be the most potent."

He praises architects, Le Nôtre, and the clean partnership between beauty and utility that shaped the formal vegetable garden at Villandry. He admires philosophers and the precise ordering of space in Japanese houses. Of his own work, he is perhaps most proud of the garden that he designed for the Millers in Columbus, Indiana. The garden there is an extension of Saarinen's interior, with outdoor rooms that wrap around a central core, unfolding and eventually merging as they move out into the landscape. Allées and bosques echo the centrifugal floor plan, underlying one of Kiley's most fundamental convictions—that in nature, geometry need never be static.

A wooden pergola built around an existing oak tree. The pachysandra bed is slightly mounded, to give it extra emphasis. At the corners, each post rests on a stone square—Japanese-fashion—and is wreathed with a twisted vine.

Another bosque, this one with small-leaved lindens, Tilia cordata, set in trim squares of pachysandra. Along one side of the trees, a narrow trough sits in full sunshine, its fountains providing a sparkling contrast to the lindens' dense shade.

An allée of moraine locusts, Gleditsia triacanthos 'Inermis,' runs between a gazebo and a glass-enclosed dining pavilion. Grass thrives in the trees' light shade; stepping-stones handle foot traffic. Notice the fountains capturing light beyond the linden bosque.

A long, low porch surrounds architect Eero Saarinen's Miller house, encouraging an easy flow between interior and exterior spaces. Flat beds of ivy extend the ground plane into the garden; a weeping beech brings the garden to the edge of the house.

LOIS LISTER

"So often I find a house in a marvelous setting with a superb view—but when you go outside, you're absolutely nowhere. There's no place to be, no place to put anything. To make it a garden, you need to turn it into *somewhere*."

Creating that sense of place is the essence of garden design, according to landscape architect Lois Lister. English-born and a long-time gardener, Lister practices in Toronto, making gardens that are practical, livable spaces stretched out-of-doors. Rather than define separate rooms, which Lister feels "people don't have the time or strength to use even indoors," develops a series of spaces that flow easily into one another.

Paths, views, and places to sit are among the basic elements

with which Lister works. Stone or brick paving skirts the house and circles around the garden, providing firm, dry paths that incidentally make ideal routes for tricycles. Grading—one of the least costly and most effective tools at the garden designer's disposal, in Lister's opinion—is used to give the house a proper stance, to shape an attractive entry, to suggest spaciousness, and to frame views. "So many people seem to think of their gardens as foursquare—a lawn, centered and surrounded. But that is the hardest sort of garden to keep up," Lister warns, "because everything is constantly in view. Even one unhappy plant will stand out." Where appropriate, she prefers compositions that incorporate a variety of levels.

Clear plans and clean details are the hallmarks of a Lister garden, softened by foliage and flowers that spill over the crisp edges. Beds are set in paving or outlined with stone; grass is treated like a "carpet on a hardwood floor," surrounded by paths or granite mowing strips. "If the plan doesn't work without a plant in it, it won't do," Lister insists. "With beds outlined, paths and mowing strips laid, and perhaps a few trees put in place, the structure is set and the garden should look completely composed. If not, I don't think there's anything that anyone will be able to do to correct it."

As a gardener, Lister thinks constantly about plants. She doesn't make final planting decisions until construction is finished, however, when clients can see the final picture and play a more active role in plant selections. She works with some large trees and many small ones, shrubs, and a rich palette of herbaceous plants and ground covers, focusing on species that have value in more than one season. Light, airy plantings are her ideal, brimming with whites and delicate flowers that seem to float above their foliage. "Daylilies score high," she says, particularly the lovely light yellow variety, 'Hyperion.'

*Left: Masses of alyssum, marigolds, and portulaca spill over the edges of cobble and flagstone walks in a Toronto garden. Low-growing pines and yews add year-round structure to the flower beds. **Right:** Lister uses wide steps with low risers and broad treads whenever possible, because they're pleasant to climb and they ensure a smooth flow between levels. Cotoneaster and roses carpet the banks alongside. **Below:** An unusual stone bench set in the lawn like a free-standing sculpture. Across the path a stand of the silver dogwood,* Cornus elegantissima, *highlights the shrub border with light leaves in summer and red stems in winter.*

A well-furnished garden is every bit as basic as a well-furnished house, in Lister's mind. Freestanding benches double as outdoor tables; "slow" steps generously proportioned hold pots and serve for sitting; walls are seat-height. "In our climate, we have lots of days that aren't quite warm enough to merit going inside and bringing out a chair—but if a seat or a table is already there, it's perfectly easy to slip outdoors and enjoy a moment of sunshine." During Toronto's long, cold winters, a swimming pool can easily give a garden a somewhat desolate look. "I try to avoid that by designing the garden so that you would like to have the pool there, as part of the composition, regardless of whether anyone ever puts a toe into it."

For nighttime gardens, Lister likes the glow that comes through windows from inside the house: She adds just enough outdoor light to make movement safe, on steps, for instance, with perhaps an occasional uplight for drama. "The lighting should preserve some mystery," she believes, "but avoid creating dark uncomfortable shadows. For it is a feeling of comfort and shelter, above all, that gives a garden its sense of place."

DIANE MCGUIRE

A broad flight of railroad-tie steps turns at a gravel landing, cutting through a bed of low-growing evergreens with mugho pines, ground-hugging junipers, bayberry (Myrica pensylvanica), and a rose.

The transition from garden to seaside is marked by the lines of clipped turf, rough grass, and a low stone wall. In the meadow beyond, a few trees frame the view and provide scale.

Diane Kostial McGuire is an academic practitioner: a landscape architect, scholar, and historian. Garden history, social history, and, more specifically, the previous history of the places where she designs are all grist for her mill, and they are the forces that shape her gardens. "All properties have histories, in one way or another—and I feel that the other uses, the previous ones, should be incorporated in their gardens."

The garden behind New College in Oxford is a lovely example of respecting history, according to McGuire, with its roses and clematis clambering over a section of the ancient city wall. "Incorporating the past into the present is something that the English do more effectively than we do," she reflects. "It gives a depth of meaning that the garden wouldn't otherwise have."

Her practice has taken her to many different places and projects, from postage-stamp yards on Beacon Hill that "were never intended to be gardens," to the grounds of an Italianate villa built by a nineteenth-century gentleman who longed to recreate the Villa Lante in the wilds of Arkansas. She has contributed to a number of restoration projects, which always begin with research—"detective work" that McGuire loves. Once her documentation is complete, she shifts to the role of advocate and designer in her effort to reestablish or protect places created by past gardeners. She has put herself in the shoes of such venerable individuals as Henry Wadsworth Longfellow, in restoring his gardens in Cambridge, Massachusetts, and Beatrix Farrand, as consultant for the

Above: *At the foot of the railroad-tie steps, the angled edge of a flagstone terrace is distinctly architectural, in contrast to the broadly sweeping curve of the evergreen planting and the smooth contours of the sloping lawn.* **Right:** *Multi-stemmed Japanese maples at a fork in the driveway, their fall foliage complemented by the purplish leaves and red berries of a deciduous barberry, the rich green grass, banks of low junipers, and several large boulders.*

17 acres of formal gardens that she designed at Dumbarton Oaks.

"It's an ideal professional world, actually, combining teaching and landscape architecture, as it allows me to take on the kinds of projects that I am most interested in." She can develop a fairly specific point of view, and she finds that with that direction, she can apply herself to virtually any design situation. "You have to do your homework," she emphasizes. "But once you understand the history of a place, its people and its plants, you can project yourself into almost any era, anywhere, and work within its particular parameters."

Recently McGuire has become particularly interested in the ancient stonework of the Mayan ruins, the Egyptian pyramids, and the gardens of China and Japan. Although she is quick to acknowledge that this interest is not likely to lead directly to any design projects, she explains that studying materials and understanding how they were used in different vernaculars is fundamental to understanding the people who used them—and more importantly, to understanding their ideas about designing gardens.

The ideas that inspired past gardeners are what most intrigue Diane McGuire. She looks at gardens not as outdoor decoration, but as art: cultural artifacts that reflect the attitudes and values of their designers. Whether a garden is ancient or contemporary, she asks the same questions: How did it come to be? What did it mean to the people who built it? Why was it designed as it was?

"Gardens are similar to architecture," she suggests. "They reflect our dreams and aspirations." The designer should be able to elicit those aspirations from a client and then, McGuire proposes, "cater to their fantasies—because gardens are fantasy, basically." This is not as frivolous an exercise as it sounds, however. "Gardens are part of our cultural history and part of our psyches," she believes, "and if we understood more about that, we would understand a great deal more about designing them."

OEHME, VAN SWEDEN & ASSOCIATES

Great plumes wave above spiky cushions of grass, coarse leaves offset delicate ones, lustrous greens sparkle against grays and golds: This is the work of Oehme, van Sweden, & Associates; it is not for anyone who is timid about using plants.

After studying in the botanical gardens at Berlin and Delft, Wolfgang Oehme and James van Sweden brought their tastes for exuberant garden design to Washington, D. C., where relatively mild winters and long hot summers nurture a rich variety of both native and exotic plants. They began working on backyards in Georgetown and Baltimore, and although those spaces are only part of their practice today, many of their design principles have evolved in response to the spatial limitations of city gardens.

Oehme and van Sweden see their gardens as dynamic places, organized as a series of layered spaces that become progressively less architectural as they move away from the house. Variety is their essential goal, at one moment and over time, because variety enhances the richness and effective size of even the smallest spaces. Each Oehme and van Sweden garden is designed for four seasons, with special emphasis on a clear plan articulated with tones and textures that persist through the gray Washington winters. In January and February, as van Sweden describes, "we like our gardens to look like big dried arrangements full of flowers, leaves, and grasses." He also believes in lighting gardens, to enhance dramatic views throughout the year and to facilitate evening use during the warm summer months.

Plants play the leading role in Oehme and van Sweden's gardens. "We choose species that have value throughout the year—in leaf, flower, seeding habit and overall form—and we set them out in masses, leaving an open space just large enough to be useful." In planting small gardens, scale is a particularly important consideration, since too many large plants overwhelm and create excessive shade, and too many little ones look lost. Wolfgang

The curve of a flight of stone steps that weaves between tall stands of Miscanthus floridulus *and a sweet bay magnolia adds mystery to a small city garden.*

Spiky textures of yuccas and pines are softened by the lacy leaves of an Aralia spinosa, *its clusters of pink flowers echoed in the geraniums below.*

Tulips skirt the stems of a Magnolia virginiana. *Pots of geraniums—ivy-leaf, 'Martha Washington,' and the ordinary variety—will burgeon once tulips fade.*

Stiff clumps of yucca and the succulent stems of **Telephium 'Autumn Joy'** *(a Sedum relative) are balanced in a summer border by a loose mound of spodiopogon and feathery masses of lavender-flowered Scotch heathers. In cold weather these plants will hold their forms—the flowers will dry and the grasses will turn golden, creating a somewhat different garden picture that will carry its interesting colors and textures through winter.*

Oehme advocates using big plants, however, the largest that the garden can possibly hold. Mounds of pampas grass and plume poppies, coarse rosettes of yucca, hosta, and bergenia work well in confined spaces, he believes; they can accent or modulate space, provide strong focal points, and establish a bold sense of proportion.

From the 6-foot (1.8-meter) spikes of miscanthus to miniature mounds of fescue, grasses are among the most distinctive features in an Oehme and van Sweden design, and they illustrate many of the firm's basic goals. Most importantly, grasses are hardy and exceptionally easy to take care of. "Grasses stay in clumps and don't readily seed themselves," according to van Sweden. "They

change dramatically through the year; they move in the wind, making lovely sounds; they have soft colors and beautiful golden tones in the winter. They are reliable in terms of scale because their sizes are perfectly predictable; and in addition to all of that, they provide food and nesting material for birds."

Of all of Oehme and van Sweden's elements, it is the grasses that best reflect their underlying conviction that gardening is "the art of the ephemeral." James van Sweden describes often "having to explain to people that their gardens will never look the same, from day to day or from year to year." They shouldn't look the same, he and Oehme insist—and their gardens are their evidence in support of the argument.

RUSSELL PAGE

A planting of mixed shrubs in a garden north of Rome feels loose and careless, but is neatly structured nonetheless. Pinks and whites are carried from foreground to distance with modern and shrub roses, leading the eye up toward the stone house. Glossy evergreens and billowing mounds of yellows and glaucous greens add interest; the straight line of a clipped hedge introduces order, suggesting that a more formal section is nearby.

In 50 years of gardening around the world, Russell Page has had ample opportunity to develop a repertoire of design solutions and plant combinations, and he has expounded many of his ideas about gardening in *The Education of a Gardener*. In fact, everything that he designs is endowed with a certain style, yet there is no specific Russell Page stamp. Wherever his work takes him, he begins each garden anew, without preconceived ideas or set rules.

His gardens are as varied as they are widespread: he has designed a sculpture garden on the Mediterranean, cottage gardens in the English countryside, terraces on Italian hills, and a city garden in the middle of Manhattan. Page starts each garden on the site, by studying the existing features for inspiration. "For a theme of some kind, a basic idea is essential," Page writes, and in most cases, his ideas come from within the site. A rocky slope, a stand of mature trees, an old orchard, or an open lawn may be the starting point for his garden plan.

Choose the idea and express it emphatically, with simplicity and style, Page advises: "All the plan and planting should reiterate and reinforce the basic motif." Style is an elusive but essential element, and Page suggests that a garden designer in search of style must infuse his plan "with all the intensity or 'intelligence' that he can muster, so that the whole may have a quality peculiar to itself." Conviction is absolutely essential; the central idea must be strong, the elements bold, and everything that is extraneous should be eliminated.

Page works with ground modeling, water, and trees to shape simple plans that can be embellished with lavish planting. As for garden elements, he states his preferences freely in his book: "I like gardens with good bones and an affirmed underlying structure; I like well-made and well-marked paths, well-built walls, well-defined changes in level. I like pools and canals, paved sitting places and a good garden house in which to picnic or take a nap."

Above all, however, Russell Page likes plants. He is an Englishman, and his knowledge and choice of plants is based in a long tradition of practical gardening. He has supplemented his English palette with an extensive assortment of plants he has encountered in visits to gardens in many countries. His simplest plantings are richly detailed, with a variety of forms, textures, and colors; but the complexity of his arrangements of plants does not disrupt the clarity of the overall garden plan.

Trees outline a garden's structure, Page emphasizes, and when used simply, they can set the stage for more elaborate planting. Several small trees of the same type, for example, create "a frame within which you can plant as you like in detail without ever jeopardizing the harmony of the whole." Shrubs provide texture and shape, and Page advocates incorporating them in mixed plantings and even in perennial borders. Herbaceous plants should be displayed in generous sweeps, he believes, because "they are basically meadow flowers," and their arrangement should reflect their native habitat.

Page uses silver and gray foliage liberally, and he is particularly fond of white flowers—the double rugosa rose, rhododendrons, camellias, and hydrangeas. As a trained painter, he is a master of combinations and colors. He starts with a single plant—phlox, perhaps, or philadelphus—and weaves his composition around it. Each plant is related to its neighbor in color, texture, and form, assuring a pleasing overall effect.

Russell Page's gardens often include water, in a round or rectangular pool, typically, set flush in the ground and spouting a single vertical jet. He emphasizes that water sits most comfortably in low places, whether it is in a reflecting pool or a rivulet, and suggests that the form water takes should be designed to complement the surrounding planting. A garden luxuriously planted should have a simple water feature; where planting is restrained, water can be more ornamental.

Page readily admits, however, that in garden design, breaking the rules can be as effective as abiding by them. "Rules," he has said, "are good servants but not always good masters." Clear intentions are far more important when it comes to shaping gardens, according to Russell Page. Indeed, the clarity of his vision has resulted in some of this century's finest gardens.

Lavender cotton, Santolina chamaecyparissus, *and shrub roses against the dark greens of a sheared hedge and columnar evergreens.*

A white garden with roses, jasmine, hellebores, and gray Stachys olympica *leads to an allée underplanted with bergenia.*

In a wilder part of the garden, grass paths lined with rows of pink oxalis meander between beds with shrub roses.

A composition of soft grays, with an olive tree, santolina, stachys, and Helichrysum petiolatum, *in an evergreen frame.*

MICHAEL VAN VALKENBURGH

Smaller spaces provide an excellent medium for the exploration and expression of design ideas, according to landscape architect Michael Van Valkenburgh: their proportions can be precise, the details fine, and the palette of plants can be particularly choice. "The distinction of the successful modern garden lies in its attention to detail," he believes, "and that can be achieved most effectively at a small scale." Within the confines of smaller gardens, Van Valkenburgh experiments with ways to establish an illusion of spaciousness; and that effort is an important aspect of his design work.

Generally he begins by creating a series of subspaces within the framework of the larger garden. "Paradoxically, a garden can appear to be larger when it is divided into smaller areas than when it is completed by a single expansive design," he explains, adding that open space alone can be particularly dull in small gardens. He articulates the transitions between sub-spaces, often using architectural elements inspired by traditional garden structures and interpreted in contemporary forms and materials. The crisp lines of a pedimented arch mark the point where a path leaves the designed garden and enters the adjacent woods, stark white arches define a passageway, and clean trellises soften the edges between interior and exterior space. Occasionally, Van Valkenburgh scales down elements and incorporates the technique of false perspective to create depth: Paths narrow as they recede toward the garden's periphery, stepping stones become steadily smaller as they spill from terrace to lawn.

Mr. Van Valkenburgh's efforts to enlarge and enrich garden space is evident in his use of plants as well. Because trees are of relatively limited use in small gardens, he concentrates on deciduous and evergreen shrubs, perennials and ground covers, shaping space with drifts of mixed plants, proportioned as generously as the space will allow. Combinations of leaf textures and colors

View into a city garden channeled by a pair of slender steel arches and a row of arborvitae, Thuja occidentalis. *The second set of arches articulates a transition between different spaces.*

Within the garden, dwarf evergreens—Hinoki cypress, Chamaecyparis obtusa *'Nana Gracilis,' and white pine,* Pinus strobus *'Nana'—with PJM hybrid rhododendrons and spikes of Siberian iris.*

A wooden arch in a country garden was inspired by details from the Colonial house. Set in a hedge of hemlock, Tsuga canadensis, *the arch frames an axis from within the house and marks the point where the designed garden meets the adjacent woodland. Azaleas and feathery spires of astilbe line the approach to the arch; in the woods, dogwood blossoms repeat the white note.*

define and highlight different areas, and can be used to enhance the illusion of spaciousness. Coarse leaves in the foreground juxtaposed against finer ones in the distance, for instance, create an exaggerated sense of depth.

Seasonal changes and varied color schemes introduce variety and thereby increase a garden's effective size, Van Valkenburgh points out, which is why he values plants and planting plans that provide continuous change throughout the year. When one client expressed her desire for a garden full of magenta-colored flowers, he designed a scheme where everything from paving to planting created a complementary setting for the purplish-pink palette. "But it wasn't all magenta or constant magenta," he explains. "A straightforward translation of the client's favorite color into a monochromatic garden would have grown stale—for the client as well as for me. That sort of continuum is not desirable in a small space." He proposed that animation was more important, and that it was the

result of change. Thus deep pinks became the garden's leitmotif, alternated with vivid pinks in early spring and bright yellows in midsummer. "By working with a palette that included some variety, the magenta was much more welcome."

Colors and details should be integral to the overall design, Van Valkenburgh emphasizes, if the garden is to read as a unified place: "A good design is much more that a collection of brilliant objects." In fact, any one detail that draws attention with its exquisite refinement is likely to be an error, he suggests. A garden should be a harmonious place with its own special ambience: "It must grow from the spirit of its owner, the wonder and promise of its time, and the celebration of nature," according to Van Valkenburgh. The designer's responsibility is to respond to the physical and spiritual needs of the client, and that, he proposes, is why outstanding clients are fundamental to the creation of outstanding gardens.

CHAPTER SIX

GARDEN WISDOM

by Norman K. Johnson

GENERAL PLANNING
BASIC UNDERSTANDINGS
THE YOUNG GARDEN
REVISION AND RESTORATION

GENERAL PLANNING

The better part of garden wisdom has to do with patience. You simply cannot make a garden in a hurry. No matter how much money may be spent for full-grown plants, terraces, walls, pavings, furnishings, or ornaments, a garden still gains character with time and maturation. Unlike a piece of architecture or interior design, a garden is never really "finished." It constantly evolves; it is a living work of art. Nature may be helped along, but it cannot be rushed to completion.

Rarely do you make a garden all at once, since it takes many years to mature. A garden plan, then, is an outline for the future. Indeed, a well-made plan assures a place for everything. It guarantees that, five years later, a planting of perennials need not be removed to make room for a swimming pool, or that a seemingly innocent young tree does not shade one's roses as it matures.

Although the planning of a garden takes some time, its making can take a lifetime; days or weeks of preparation are small compared to years of satisfaction. Design is really a matter of creative problem solving, a workman-like procedure based on questioning, research, and objectivity. Using the chapters in this book will help you visualize the choices available to you, whether you have in mind a certain style, a favorite use, or a choice set of garden elements.

The initial problem is deciding what you want—for the present and the years to come. You must ask basic questions. What, for example, is the garden's purpose? Is it simply to enhance the look of a home, or is garden-making an intimate expression of a personality? Both are valid goals, but their attainment will follow separate procedures. The "looks" gardener is less concerned with horticultural treasures and time-consuming maintenance than with such useful things as terraces, privacy, and irrigation systems. The plantsman, on the other hand, does not expect to recoup a garden investment only through improved eye appeal. He also expects a certain satisfaction from constant creative labors.

Obviously, budget is an important consideration. How much garden can you truly afford, both in terms of time and money? Time, of course, is in the garden-maker's favor; with the aid of a good plan, the process of construction may continue over many years. Regardless of schedules, however, a budget must be set to ensure that garden-making efforts do not occur sporadically, but as an ongoing series of planned and regular accomplishments.

The final part of wisdom lies in knowing when and where to get help. The services of a landscape architect, horticulturist, nurseryman, or garden designer can be well worth the cost. These gardening professionals can answer questions, make suggestions, and outline procedures. Avoiding innocent but costly errors will more than equal the price of a consultation, while not preventing the individual gardener from keeping creative control over the garden plan.

Brick paving and rounded lines unify a Georgetown backyard: the convex line of the planting bed is echoed in a concave seat wall that sweeps behind a circular bed cut out to hold a small tree. Oehme, van Sweden & Associates, designers.

Plants and a stone path are enough to structure a woodland garden. Because dogwoods, azaleas, and andromeda are all understory species native to the forests of the northeastern United States, the composition has a natural unity. Ruth Levitan, designer.

BASIC UNDERSTANDINGS

Whether you are working alone or with professionals, the garden-planning process should begin with a measured plan. Indeed, this drawing forms the basis for all garden-making work. It documents what is to be done and helps you calculate the overall cost. Square footages of paving, turf, and planting beds, for example, can be roughly determined from the plan, as can the quantities of plants to be installed. With this information you can then create a budget and a schedule for the basic garden project.

To be of long-term use, of course, a plan must be precise. Accurate measurements are essential. Otherwise, the plan on paper will not suit the changing site. Although tax maps or survey maps may provide some basic measurements—lot dimensions and general placement of a house—they rarely locate driveways, walks, and trees. Also, these maps are frequently too small in scale to be of use in planning. However, by carefully transferring known dimensions to a one-quarter scale grid (1.50 in U.K. measure), you can easily obtain a workable base map. Other existing features can then be measured from a known point, such as a corner of the house, and plotted on the grid.

Plotting topography, however, is more difficult; unless a garden is fairly level, the services of a professional surveyor are useful, especially if you intend to modify the ground plan extensively. This survey can also verify locations of the house and other features. In cases of extremely sloping lots, you should consult a landscape architect before designing a drainage system or retaining walls.

Once existing features have been charted on the plan, the most pleasant part of design begins. On tracing paper overlays or photocopies of the plan, note such things as paving types and condition, desirable views, areas that will need screening to give privacy, and the pattern of sun and shade. Existing plants should also be labeled by type, size, and condition. To verify a plant name, compare a sample leaf or twig with a labeled nursery plant. For native or less common ornamental plants, it may be necessary to consult a local arborist or horticulturist. Sometimes these professionals will make a visit to identify existing plants. Whatever the procedure, it is important to know a plant precisely in order to determine its garden value. And as common names vary with location, you should also learn botanical names to better research each plant in horticultural books and other publications.

For all of its essential value, however, a

ROUGH TEST FOR SOIL QUALITY	
SOIL SURFACE	CHARACTER
Clay	Stiff and plastic; can be worked with the hands into shapes.
Clay-loam	Sticky; can be "shined" by rubbing a little in the hands.
Medium loam	Neither stiff and plastic nor gritty.
Sand	Gritty; will not stick to hands.
Sandy loam	Gritty; some will stick to fingers.
Silty loam	Feels silky or soapy in the hand.

Stakes and string are basic to the layout of any garden, from the simple grid of a vegetable plot to the sweeping lines of a border containing shrubs and herbaceous plants.

base plan can only be filled in once the soil has been analyzed. The character of garden soil is the most important aspect of a plant's success. Analysis shows where the soil may need help—in the form of sand, lime, compost, and fertilizer—and it can reveal potentially dangerous problems such as heavy metal concentrations and septic pollution. As soil types may vary on a single property, several samples should be taken to ensure a thorough understanding of the basic garden medium.

Once this background information has been collected and researched, the garden planning starts in earnest. The matter of use comes first, for if a garden doesn't suit the owners' way of life, it will never be successful. Consequently, a garden plan must be practical and affordable, and yet it must afford delight. In order to accomplish this, the garden-maker should compile a list of all those things that would make his or her perfect garden; this listing should be guided by imagination, style preferences, and dreams.

A typical lifestyle listing could include such things as a swimming pool, tennis court, rose garden, fountain, gazebo, and/or herbaceous border. Consider your favorite plants and pavings; activities such as outdoor dining, vegetable gardening, and children's play; and general amenities like privacy and shade.

Once this "wish" list is complete, a more objective list of basic garden needs—entrance walks, driveways, storage structures, and the like. Should visitors use the formal entrance? If so, is it easily accessible and clearly labeled for their use with walkways, plants, and lighting? Is the driveway wide enough for extra cars, or does there need to be a parking place especially for guests? Where do you put the barbecue, gardening equipment, bicycles, and trash cans? Are gas and electrical meters placed so that they can be serviced? Is mail delivered to the door or to a street-side box?

The making and revising of these lists will take some time, but this is time well spent. It allows you to consider many options; by thoroughly exploring these alter-

Above left: The star-like flowers of **Clematis** venosa var. violacea *and delicate golden-green leaves of a Sunburst locust,* Gleditsia triacanthos 'Sunburst,' *which both thrive in soil that is slightly alkaline. Clematis grow with their heads in the sun, their feet in the shady protection of other plants; their slender stems are susceptible to disease if broken.*

JUDGING SOIL BY EXISTING PLANTS	
PLANT	SOIL CHARACTER
Campanula (bellflowers)	Limey
Carduus (thistles)	Exhausted
Carex (sedges)	Boggy, poor
Digitalis purpurea (foxglove)	Sandy, dry
Juncus (rushes)	Boggy
Potentilla fragaria (wild strawberry)	Barren, dry
Rumex acetosella (sorrel)	Acid, dry
Stellaria media (starwort, chickweed)	Fertile
Ulex europaeus (furze)	Infertile
Urtica dioica (stinging nettle)	Fertile

natives, you can gradually compile a master list of gardening objectives.

The next step is to apply the plan to the ground. Working with a copy of the base plan, arrange and rearrange the garden's parts until they suit the site and your own sense of order and style. Armed with clipboard, pencils, tape measure, and a copy of the base plan, begin to experiment with the space. The alignment of walkways, terraces, and planting beds can be laid out with stakes and string, or with a garden hose; their dimensions can then be recorded on the paper plan.

Once the garden is designed on paper, establish priorities for the actual work. As a garden grows from the ground up, that is the place to start. Grading and soil preparation come first; this is followed by the planting of the shade trees, hedges, and slow-growing shrubs that will be the garden's "bones." After this is done, lay the garden's walks, terraces, and other pavings, and construct decks and arbors. Garden furnishings—tables, chairs, and benches—should then be purchased to complete the living space. Only when the garden's structure has been well established should you move to details such as smaller plants and flowers. Only then does the planning stage end and the garden begin to take on its future form.

THE YOUNG GARDEN

Mulch looks neat, conserves moisture, and discourages weeds on exposed soil—but wood can rob nitrogen as it decays, so fertilizer should be nitrogen-rich.

Making a new garden is an exciting proposition. You are not encumbered with the misplaced walks and terraces of former garden owners nor the woes inherited from someone else's planting. With the possible exception of some native trees and shrubs, nothing is overgrown or growing where it ought not be. The challenge is to establish the young garden quickly, leaving room for the full scheme to develop over time.

The first step, of course, is to prepare the plan and lay the groundwork. By putting down the gravel base of walkways, you will begin to see the promise of the garden's form. The same is true of terraces and other garden pavings. Even though their final surfaces may not be available immediately, no effort has been wasted. Gravel bases can be walked on for the interim; this will help compact the base, simplifying the installation of final finishes.

The early preparation of planting beds is also a good idea. It defines the pattern of the garden's planted framework and assures a healthy future for those plants. If planting must come later, beds can still be "dressed" with mulch or compost, or sown with annuals. These plants are perfect for a garden in the making: They grow and flower quickly, providing a finished look, and if they are grown from seed, the cost is minimal. Best of all, annuals are temporary. No plants will have to be removed to make room for permanent shrubs and flowers.

Edges are especially important to new gardens. Be it the edging of a walk, or boundaries between a lawn and planting bed, these lines of demarcation need to be distinct to emphasize the garden's sense of order. Unlike a well-established garden, where spaces are defined by heights and densities of plantings, walls, and fences, the newly made garden frequently appears to be a single, open space. Its structure is established, not by volume, but with lines and patterns that are laid upon the ground.

In order to preserve clean edges and thus maintain the garden's form, new-garden owners must give extra care to maintenance. Weeds are a special problem—both visually and horticulturally. They obscure the crispness of a garden's layout and compete for nutrients, which slows the growth of garden plants. Consequently, the makers of new gardens should invest in a cord trimmer or other edging tool to better keep the garden's edges well defined.

Permanent, in-ground mowing strips of brick, concrete pavers, or railroad ties are also useful in new gardens. They give instant definition to a lawn or planting bed; they protect young plants from possible mower damage; and they simplify edge maintenance by offering a guide for mower tires.

Another quick effect with long-term value is to use container plants as instant accents. Whether it be a pot of annuals at the front door or pairs of urns to frame an axis, container plants create a positive impression with minimal effort and investment. If plants and containers are selected with care, these plantings can also be retained as permanent garden features. The trick, of course, is to select a quality container; as only a few are needed (too many spoil the drama), they should be chosen for beauty and durability, as should the plants that they contain. Otherwise, the effect will be too timid to stand alone—and that defeats the purpose of providing an immediate feeling of abundance.

Lighting also adds drama to a newly made garden. A spotlight on a well-placed tree or shrub, for example, doubles its effectiveness by making the plant an accent after dark. And if you use a fixture with a generous amount of cord, the light can be relocated to emphasize a plant in bloom or to cast the shadows of winter branches against an otherwise blank wall.

With any quick-effect technique, the objective is to make the most of what has been done—not to camouflage those things that haven't been completed. A garden's voids should be designed to make them appear intentional, not overlooked. Mulches are a versatile solution. They give a finished look to empty garden spaces, and they improve the soil by retaining moisture and providing organic matter. If large sections of a garden must be left unplanted, several mulches may be used to give those barren spaces pattern, color, and texture. "Flower" beds, for example, could be carpeted with compost, while a future bed of shrubs could be dressed with straw or shredded bark.

Gravel can be used like a mulch—but never over plastic, not if the bed is ever to be planted. Plastic causes overheating of the soil and repels water, which can be disastrous for future plants. A six- to eight-page layer of newspaper, however, is an ideal base for any mulch. It helps deter the growth of weeds, and as it decomposes, the paper also adds organic matter to the soil.

Finely textured gravels are generally recommended for mulching as these can later be tilled into the soil to improve its drainage and texture. Although white marble chips are popular, they are far from perfect as a mulch. They frequently discolor to an unfortunate gray-green, and as they break down chemically they can adversely change the soil's pH factor by leaching calcium. Decomposed granite, pea gravel, and expanded shale, on the other hand, do not pose this danger; their darker coloration is less conspicuous and therefore better suited as a mulch.

It must be remembered, however, that mulches are a temporary garden feature; indeed, that is their value. They are a means of buying time—of giving patience purpose. Like all quick effects, they are a step along the road to garden satisfaction; they are part of the plan.

For a California hillside, a garden of native and drought-resistant plants is a "fit" alternative to the traditional lawn and flower borders. Native plants require less maintenance than exotics, for they have adapted to survive local growing conditions.

MAKING GARDENS OVER

Left: *A concrete walk from the street to the front door had been lodged between island beds and patches of lawn.* **Right:** *Eliminating the grass allowed the beds to flow across the path, giving more room for plants and improving the transition from public to private space.*

*E*very garden remake has a threefold plan of action: enhancement of existing features, elimination of hindrances, and suitable additions.

The matter of existing features comes first. As with any garden project, remakes should begin with an objective overview. Plantings, pavings, drainage systems, storage structures, and a garden's ornamental features all must be assessed in terms of current quality, location, and contribution to the garden as a whole. This assessment will take time, and it will depend on patient, careful observation.

Only by living with a garden—by making notes throughout a season or an entire

year—can you judge a garden's merits, find its flaws, and see its true potential. And these notes should be recorded on a measured plan. Areas of sun and shade, the pattern of water drainage, off-site views, and neighbors' trees that overhang the garden should all be recorded, as should the location of existing plants.

Whenever possible, of course, it's better to preserve a garden than to redesign it. There is a certain satisfaction in deciphering the garden's plan and carrying it forward. Preservation may take the form of pruning and thinning trees and shrubs, repointing masonry walls, repainting woodwork, and resetting dry-laid walks and

terraces. Indeed, the general setting in order of existing features may avoid the need for more extensive renovation.

Almost every old garden, however, comes with its "disasters"—broken pavings, leaky fishponds, tumbled-down garages, and decrepit barbecues. Too-narrow porches, steps, and driveways, bare spots under trees, and lights that do not work are other common failings of the aged garden. Then, there is the commonest of garden nuisances: overgrown foundation planting.

You must assess the value of existing features and decide what to keep and what to discard. One persuasive way of judging what to change is the question: "How much will it cost to keep, to change, or to remove a given garden feature?"

A dilapidated wall provides a useful case in point. Keeping the wall will not be cost-free: It will have to be repaired. Removing the wall will also incur expenses: demolition and removal of the rubble. For comparison, you should also calculate the cost of building a new wall of similar construction. Comparison of these costs will help you judge the value of the wall.

Similar assessments will suggest the generic worth of garden plants, pavings, structures, and amenities like fountains and pools. Ultimately, however, you must base decisions on personal conviction. This, of course, is the objective of redesigning—to reshape a garden as an intimate expression of one's personality and way of life.

When dealing with additions, the new design must follow basic principles of planning a new garden. You must set priorities and long-range goals; the attainment of those goals must observe a logical and systematic program. Results, however, tend to be much faster with a remake, thanks to the context of existing features. Yet this bonus has a drawback. Additions are less conspicuous when gardens are remade; even major improvements may seem undramatic if they truly fit into the total scheme of things.

For this reason, remakes should be carefully designed for optimum effect. The removal of foundation planting, for example, will be simpler and more impressive if it is all done at once; the addition of a parking court will have greater presence if it is accompanied by a new lighting scheme.

Although the cost of large-scale changes may seem more expensive than a series of minor alterations, the actual cost will likely be reduced, due to the concentration of effort. Lawn regrading, for example, could be done in concert with the excavation of a pool to maximize the process of earth-moving operations. Indeed, any project that requires the use of large equipment or by-the-hour labor will be more cost efficient if several projects can be done simultaneously.

Above: Clipped evergreens and a large aucuba gave half-hearted definition to a side entry. *Below:* A broader bed with a neatly defined edge creates a more inviting welcome. The small tree repeats the fullness of the aucuba; shade-loving impatiens, a hosta with white margins, and clumps of ferns fill in the ground plane; and a vine clambering over the railing carries the garden up to the edge of the porch.

SOURCES

FEATURED DESIGNERS

Arq. Luis Barragán
Gral. Fco. Ramirez No. 12
Col. Daniel Garza
Mexico, D.F. 22830

Mr. John Brookes
Clock House Denmans
Fontwell near Arundel
Sussex BN18 OSU
England

Sr. Roberto Burle Marx
Rio-394-70-24
Cardoso Jr. 15
Lananjeiros, Rio de Janeiro
Brazil

Ms. Pamela Burton
2324½ Michigan Avenue
Santa Monica, CA 90404

Mr. A.E. Bye
523 East Putnum Avenue
Greenwich, CT 06830

Mr. David Engel
Engel/GGP
204 West 27th Street
New York, NY 10001

Ms. Teresita Falcon
Mr. Juan Antonio Bueno
Falcon & Bueno
4061 Battersea Road
Coconut Grove, FL 33133

Ms. Barbara Fealy
4805 Southwest Chestnut
  Place
Beaverton, OR 97005

Innocenti & Webel
The Studio Box 260
Greenvale, NY 11548

Mr. Dan Kiley
East Farm
Charlotte, VT 05445

Ms. Lois Lister
145 Farnham Avenue
Toronto, Ontario MHV 1H7

Ms. Diane K. McGuire
209 Vol Walker Hall
School of Architecture
University of Arkansas
Fayetteville, AR 72701

Mr. Wolfgang Oehme
Mr. James van Sweden
Oehme, van Sweden &
  Associates
2813 N Street, NW
Washington, DC 20007

Mr. Russell Page
12 Cadogan Garden
London SW3
England

Mr. Michael Van Valkenburgh
23 Myrtle Avenue
Cambridge, MA 02138

LANDSCAPE DESIGN ASSOCIATIONS: UNITED STATES AND CANADA

ALBERTA ASSOCIATION OF
LANDSCAPE ARCHITECTS
P.O. Box 3395
Station D
Edmonton, Alberta T5L 4J2

AMERICAN SOCIETY OF
LANDSCAPE ARCHITECTS
1733 Connecticut Avenue,
  NW
Washington, DC 20009

ASSOCIATION DES
ARCHITECTS PAYSAGISTES
DU QUEBEC
4003 Boul DeCarie
Suite 227
Montréal, Québec H4A 3J8

ATLANTIC PROVINCES
ASSOCIATION OF
LANDSCAPE ARCHITECTS
c/o A. Bruce Martin
362 Saunders Street
Fredericton, New Brunswick
  E3B 1N9

BRITISH COLUMBIA
SOCIETY OF LANDSCAPE
ARCHITECTS
c/o The Registrar
115–2004 Mainland Street
Vancouver, British Columbia
  V6B 2T5

CANADIAN SOCIETY OF
LANDSCAPE ARCHITECTS
P.O. Box 3304
Station C
Ottawa, Ontario K1J 4J5

MANITOBA ASSOCIATION
OF LANDSCAPE
ARCHITECTS
c/o Department of Landscape
  Architects
Faculty of Architecture
123 Bison Building
Winnipeg, Manitoba R3T
  2N2

ONTARIO ASSOCIATION OF
LANDSCAPE ARCHITECTS
170 The Donway West
Suite 212
Don Mills, Ontario M3C 2G3

SASKATCHEWAN
ASSOCIATION OF
LANDSCAPE ARCHITECTS
c/o Mr. Douglas Clark
671 University Drive
Saskatoon, Saskatchewan
  S7N 0J1

LANDSCAPE DESIGN ASSOCIATIONS: UNITED KINGDOM

LANDSCAPE INSTITUTE
12 Carlton House Terrace
London SW1

SOCIETY OF LANDSCAPE
AND GARDEN DESIGNERS
Mr. James Seymour
22 Reigate Road
Ewell, Surrey KT17 1PS

RETAIL NURSERIES: UNITED STATES

ADAMS NURSERY
Box 606, Route 20
Westfield, MA 01085
(413) 562-3644, 736-0443

ARMSTRONG NURSERIES
Box 4060
Ontario, CA 91761
(714) 984-1211
fruit trees, roses

ARROWHEAD GARDENS
115 Boston Post Road
Wayland, MA 01778
(617) 358-7333

BACHMAN'S INC.
6010 Lyndale Avenue South
Minneapolis, MN 55423
(612) 861-7600

WARREN BALDSIEFEN
Box 88
Bellvale, NY 10912
(914) 986-4222
rhododendrons

BOUNTIFUL RIDGE
NURSERIES
Princess Anne, MD 21853
(301) 651-0400
*berry plants, ornamentals, fruit
and nut trees*

THE BOVEES NURSERY
1737 Southwest Coronado
Portland, OR 97219
(503) 244-9341
*uncommon rhododendron and
azalea species and hybrids*

BROOKS TREE FARM
9785 Portland Road NE
Salem, OR 97305
(503) 393-6300
*deciduous trees, shrubs and
conifers in small sizes*

BUNTING'S NURSERIES
Selbyville, DE 19975
(302) 436-8231
*berry plants, strawberries, fruit
and nut trees, ornamentals*

W. ATLEE BURPEE CO.
300 Park Avenue
Warminster, PA 18974
(215) 674-4900
*flower and vegetable seeds,
general nursery stock*

BUSSE GARDENS
Box 13, 635 East 7th Street
Cokato, MN 55321
(612) 286-2654
*rock plants, dwarf shrubs,
perennials, wildflowers*

CALIFORNIA NURSERY CO.
Box 2278
Fremont, CA 94536
(415) 797-3311
fruit and nut trees

CARLSON'S GARDENS
Box 305
South Salem, NY 10590
(914) 763-5958
rhododendrons, azaleas

CARROLL GARDENS
Box 310, 444 East Main Street
Westminster, MD 21157
(301) 848-5422
*dwarf evergreens, trees and
shrubs, perennials, roses,
herbs and ground covers*

COENOSIUM GARDENS
425 North 5th Street
Lehighton, PA 18235
(215) 377-1495
dwarf conifers, unusual trees

CORLISS BROS. NURSERY
AND GARDEN CENTER
31 Essex Road
Ipswich, MA 01938
(617) 356-5422

THE CUMMINS GARDEN
22 Robertsville Road
Marlboro, NJ 07446
(201) 536-2591
*rhododendrons, azaleas,
dwarf evergreens, companion
plants*

DAUBER'S NURSERIES
Rear 1705 North George
 Street
Box 1746
York, PA 17405
(717) 848-6088
uncommon trees and shrubs

DAYSTAR
Litchfield-Hallowell Road
RFD 2
Litchfield, ME 04350
(207) 724-3369
(formerly 'THE ROCK
 GARDEN')
*miniature roses, rock plants,
heaths, dwarf shrubs*

SAM DIBLE NURSERY
RFD 3, Box 86
Shelacta, PA 15774
(412) 726-5377
evergreens

HENRY FIELD SEED AND
NURSERY CO.
407 Sycamore Street
Shenandoah, IA 51602
(712) 246-2110
general nursery stock

FIORE ENTERPRISES
Route 22
Prairie View, IL 60069
(312) 634-3400
trees and shrubs

FLICKINGERS' NURSERY
Sagamore, PA 16250
(412) 783-6528
*evergreen seedlings and
Christmas tree plantings*

FOXBOROUGH NURSERY
3611 Miller Road
Street, MD 21154
(301) 836-7023
*uncommon trees, dwarf
evergreens*

GAME FOOD NURSERIES
Box V
Omro, WI 54963
(414) 685-2929
*wild rice and other marsh and
upland plants for gamebirds*

GARDENS OF THE BLUE
RIDGE
Box 10
Pineola, NC 28662
(704) 733-2417
*wildflowers, native trees,
shrubs*

D.S. GEORGE NURSERIES
2491 Penfield Road
Fairport, NY 14450
(716) 377-0731
clematis

GIRARD NURSERIES
Box 428
Geneva, OH 44041
(216) 466-2881
*azaleas, uncommon trees, pre-
bonsai, conifer seeds, dwarf
and unusual evergreens*

GREER GARDENS
1280 Goodpasture Island
 Road
Eugene, OR 97401
(503) 686-8266
*pre-bonsai, dwarf conifers,
Japanese maples, azaleas
and rhododendrons*

GURNEY SEED AND
NURSERY CO.
Yankton, SD 57078
(605) 665-4451
*flower, vegetable seeds,
perennials, trees and shrubs for
the Plains*

HASTINGS
434 Marietta Street NW
Box 4274
Atlanta, GA 30302-4274
(404) 524-8861
*vegetable seeds, fruit and nut
trees, kiwi*

HEARD GARDENS
5355 Merle Hay Road
Route No. A, Box 134
Des Moines, IA 50323
(515) 276-4533
*trees and shrubs, lilacs and
crab apples*

MARC HENNY NURSERY
10415 72nd Avenue NE
Brooks, OR 97305
(503) 792-3448
azaleas, daphnes, odoras

DILATUSH NURSERY
780 Route 130
Robbinsville, NJ 08691
(609) 585-5387
*uncommon trees and shrubs,
dwarf evergreens*

DUTCH MOUNTAIN
NURSERY
7984 North 48th Street,
   Route 1
Augusta, MI 49012
(616) 731-5232
shrubs, vines, trees

EASTERN SHORE NURSERIES
Box 743, Route 331
Easton, MD 21601
(301) 822-1320
landscape-size stock

EASTVILLE PLANTATION
Box 337
Bogart, GA 30622
(404) 769-5000
*shrubs, some ornamentals, fruit
trees*

EISLER NURSERIES
219 East Pearl Street, Box 70
Butler, PA 16001
(412) 287-5151
general stock, landscape size

EMLONG NURSERIES
2671 West Marquette Woods
   Road
Stevensville, MI 49127
(616) 429-3431
fruit trees, general nursery stock

FARMER SEED AND NURSERY
818 Northwest 4th Street
Faribault, MN 55021
(507) 334-6421
vegetable and flower seeds

EARL FERRIS NURSERY
811 4th Street, NE
Hampton, IA 50441
(515) 456-2563
*evergreens, shrubs, general
nursery stock*

THOMAS HENNY NURSERY
7811 Stratford Drive NE
Brooks, OR 97305
(503) 792-3376
*excellent selection of
rhododendrons*

C.M. HOBBS & SONS
9300 West Washington Street
Box 31227
Indianapolis, IN 46231
(317) 241-9253
general nursery stock

HOLLY HEATH NURSERY
Route 25A
Wading River, NY
(Mailing address:
Box 55A, Calverton, NY
   11933)
(516) 727-0859
*Glenn Dale and other azaleas,
holly, heather, dwarf plants*

HORTICA GARDENS
Box 308
Placerville, CA 95667
(916) 622-7089
*Japanese maples, conifers,
azaleas, pre-bonsai*

INDIAN RUN NURSERY
Allentown Road
Robbinsville, NJ 08691
(609) 259-2600
rhododendrons

INTER-STATE NURSERIES
Hamburg, IA 51644
(712) 382-2411
*fruit trees, perennials, general
nursery stock*

ISLAND GARDENS
701 Goodpasture Road
Eugene, OR 97401
(503) 343-4711
*Exbury azaleas,
rhododendrons*

JACKSON & PERKINS CO.
Box 83A
Medford, OR 97501
(503) 776-2400
*blubs, dwarf fruit trees, some
vegetables, roses*

JUNG SEED CO.
335 South High Street
Randolph, WI 53956
(414) 326-3121
general nursery stock

KEIL BROS.
220-15 Horace Harding
   Boulevard
Bayside, NY 11364
(212) 224-2020
*heaths and heathers, rock
garden and dwarf plants,
general nursery stock*

KELLY BROS. NURSERIES
Dansville, NY 14437
(716) 335-2211
*bulbs, fruit and nut trees,
general nursery stock*

JOSEPH J. KERN ROSE
NURSERY
Box 33
Jackson Street and Heisley
   Road
Mentor, OH 44060
(216) 255-8627
old, new, and rare roses

KIMBERLY BARN FLORAL AND
GARDEN CENTER
1221 East Kimberly Road
Davenport, IA 52807
(319) 386-1300
general nursery stock

RUDOLPH KLUIS NURSERY
Box 116
Ryan Road
Marlboro, NJ 07746
(201) 462-4694
unusual shrubs, dwarf conifers

KRIDER NURSERIES
Box 29
Middlebury, IN 46540
(219) 825-5714
general ornamentals, fruit trees

MICHAEL A. AND JANET L.
KRISTICK
RD 1, Mockingbird Road
Wellsville, PA 17365
(717) 292-2962
*Japanese maples, dwarf
conifers*

LAFAYETTE HOME NURSERY
Box 1A, RR #1, Route 17
LaFayette, IL 61449
(309) 995-3311
trees and shrubs

LAMB NURSERIES
East 101 Sharp Avenue
Spokane, WA 99202
(509) 328-7956
*hardy succulents, perennials,
ground covers, rock garden
plants, dwarf shrubs*

H.L. LARSON
3656 Bridgeport Way West
Tacoma, WA 98466
(206) 564-1488
*seeds of unusual
rhododendrons*

A.M. LEONARD, INC.
6665 Spiker Road
Piqua, OH 45356
(513) 773-2694
gardening and pruning tools

LIGHT'S LANDSCAPE
NURSERYMEN
9153 East D Avenue
Richland, MI 49083
(616) 629-9761
*extensive selection of trees and
shrubs*

LITTLEFIELD-WYMAN
NURSERIES
227 Centre Avenue
   (Route 123)
Abington, MA 02351
(617) 878-1800
*general nursery stock, trees,
shrubs, evergreens*

LOUISIANA NURSERY
Route 7, Box 43
Opelousas, LA 70570
(318) 948-3696
fruit trees, perennials, uncommon ornamental trees and shrubs, assortment of magnolias

MATSU-MOMIJI NURSERY
Box 11414
410 Borbeck Street
Philadelphia, PA 10111
(215) 722-6286
Japanese black pines, Japanese maple cultivars

MAY NURSERY CO.
Box 1312
Yakima, WA 98907
(509) 453-8219
fruit and nut trees

EARL MAY SEED AND
NURSERY CO.
Shenandoah, IA 51603
(712) 246-1020
general nursery stock

MCKAY NURSERY CO.
254 Jefferson Street
Waterloo, WI 53594
(414) 478-2121
general nursery stock, specimen-size trees and shrubs

MELLINGER'S
2310 West South Range Road
North Lima, OH 44452
(216) 549-9861
tree seeds, bonsai containers, wide variety of small-size trees and shrubs

J.E. MILLER NURSERIES
Canandaigua, NY 14424
In New York State: (800) 462-9601,
outside: (800) 828-9630
ornamental trees and shrubs, berry plants, fruit trees (including some old varieties)

MUSSER FORESTS
Box 340
Indiana, PA 15701
(412) 465-5686
conifers for Christmas tree plantings

NEOSHO NURSERIES
Box 550
Neosho, MO 64850
(417) 451-1212
general nursery stock, roses, fruit trees and perennials

NUCCIO'S NURSERIES
3555 Chaney Trail
Box H
Altadena, CA 91001
(213) 794-3383
azaleas and large camellia listings

OLIVER NURSERIES
1159 Bronson Road
Fairfield, CT 06430
(203) 259-5609
uncommon trees, pre-bonsai plants, rhododendrons, dwarf conifers, and rock garden plants

PANFIELD NURSERIES
322 Southdown Road
Huntington, NY 11743
(516) 427-0112
Wholesale branch at Ceram
Road
Mt. Sinai, NY 11766
(516) 473-9170
tress and shrubs, perennials, native plants

GEORGE W. PARK SEED CO.
Greenwood, SC 29647
(803) 374-3341
vegetable and flower seeds: retail, wholesale; nursery stock: retail only

PETERS AND WILSON
NURSERY
East Millbrae Avenue and
Rollins Road
Millbrae, CA 94030
(415) 697-5373
fruit trees, ornamental trees and shrubs

PLUMFIELD'S GARDEN
CENTER
Box 410
735 West 23rd Street
Fremont, NE 68025
(402) 721-3520
general nursery stock

POWELL'S GARDENS
Route 2, Box 86
Princeton, NC 27569
(919) 936-4421
rock plants, perennials, dwarf evergreens

ORLANDO S. PRIDE
NURSERIES
145 Weckerly Road
Butler, PA 16001
(412) 283-0962
rhododendrons, hollies, azaleas

ROSEDALE NURSERIES
Saw Mill River Parkway
Hawthorne, NY 10532
(914) 769-1300
general nursery stock

ROSES OF YESTERDAY AND
TODAY
802 Brown's Valley Road
Watsonville, CA 95076
(408) 724-3537

SALTER TREE FARM
Route 2, Box 1332
Madison, FL 32340
(904) 973-6312
trees and shrubs (including native azaleas) of the South

SCARFF'S NURSERY
Route 1
New Carlisle, OH 45344
(513) 845-3130
general nursery stock

SEVEN DEES NURSERY
16519 Southeast Stark
Portland, OR 97233
(503) 255-9225

PUTNEY NURSERY
Putney, VT 05346
(802) 387-5577
wildflowers, ornamental trees and shrubs, perennials, ferns

RAYNER BROS.
Box 1617
Salisbury, MD 21801
(301) 742-1594
strawberries, other berry plants, fruit and nut trees

CLYDE ROBIN
Box 2091
Castro Valley, CA 94546
(415) 581-3468
small ornamental trees and shrubs, pre-bonsai, uncommon conifers, tree and wildflower seeds, native California plants

THE SHOP IN THE SIERRAS
Box 1
Midpines, Ca 95345
(209) 966-3867
western native trees and shrubs

SILVER FALLS NURSERY AND
CHRISTMAS TREE FARM
Silver Falls Highway
Star Route, Box 84
Silverton, OR 97381
(503) 873-4945
wide selection of shrubs, trees, conifers and western native plants

FRANCIS M. SINCLAIR
RFD 1, Newmarket Road
Exeter, NH 03833
(603) 772-2362
native trees and shrubs,
wildflowers

SISKIYOU RARE PLANT
NURSERY
2825 Cummings Road
Medford, OR 97501
(503) 772-6846
rare alpine plants and dwarf
shrubs

JOEL W. SPINGARN
1535 Forest Avenue
Baldwin, NY 11510
(516) 623-7810
large variety of dwarf conifers,
Japanese maples, rock garden
rhododendrons

SPRAINBROOK NURSERY
448 Underhill Road
Scarsdale, NY 10583
(914) 723-2382
general nursery stock

SPRING HILL NURSERIES
Elm Street
Tipp City, OH 45371
(513) 667-2491
perennials, ground covers,
vines, general nursery stock

SPRUCE BROOK NURSERY
Route 118, Box 925
Litchfield, CT 06759
(203) 482-5229
general nursery stock

STAR ROSES (CONRAD-PYLE
CO.)
West Grove, PA 19390
(215) 869-2426
Roses, shrubs and trees

STARK BROS. NURSERIES
Louisiana, MO 63353
(314) 754-5511
ornamental shrubs and trees,
fruit trees

STERN'S NURSERIES
607 Washington Street
Geneva, NY 14456
(315) 789-7371
general nursery stock

SYLVAN NURSERY
1028 Horseneck Road
South Westport, MA 02790
(617) 636-4573
heaths, seashore plants,
heathers

TALL TIMBER
4520 Lariat Drive
Castle Rock, CO 80104
(303) 688-3664
pre-bonsai and other conifers

THOMASVILLE NURSERIES
Box 7
Thomasville, GA 31792
(912) 226-5568
daylilies, liriopes, azaleas,
roses

TILLOTSON'S ROSES
992 Brown's Valley Road
Watsonville, CA 95076
(408) 724-3537
modern and old-fashioned
roses

WILLIAM TRICKER, INC.
74 Allendale Road
Saddle River, NJ 07458
(201) 327-0337
7125 Tanglewood Drive
Independence, OH 44131
(216) 524-3491
waterlilies and bog plants

VALLEY NURSERY
Box 4845
Helena, MT 59601
(406) 442-8460
cold climate trees and shrubs

MARTIN VIETTE NURSERIES
Route 25A (Northern
  Boulevard)
Muttontown, NY 11732
(516) 922-5530
extensive range of perennials
and wildflowers

WATNONG NURSERY
The Don Smiths
Morris Plains, NJ 07950
(201) 539-0312
dwarf evergreens, rare trees
and shrubs

WAYNESBORO NURSERIES
Route 664, Box 987
Waynesboro, VA 22980
(703) 942-4141
berry plants, fruit trees, general
nursery stock

WAYSIDE GARDENS
Hodges, SC 29695
(803) 374-3359 and (800)
  845-1124
extensive selection of vines,
perennials, shrubs

WESTON NURSERIES
East Main Street (Route 135)
Box 186
Hopkinton, MA 01748
(617) 435-3414
From Greater Boston: 235-
  3431
rock garden plants, perennials,
general nursery stock

WHITE FLOWER FARM
Route 63
Litchfield, CT 06759
(203) 567-0801
bulbs, uncommon trees and
shrubs, perennials

WINTERTHUR PLANT SHOP
Winterthur Museum and
  Gardens
Winterthur, DE 19735
(302) 656-8591
uncommon shrubs and trees

WOODLANDERS
1128 Colleton Avenue
Aiken, SC 29801
(803) 648-7522
plants native to the southern
Piedmont and coastal plain

YERBA BUENA NURSERY
19500 Skyline Boulevard
Woodside, CA 94062
(415) 851-1668
native plants of California

RETAIL NURSERIES: CANADA

ALBERTA NURSERIES AND
SEEDS, LTD.
Box 20
Bowden, AL T0M 0K0
(403) 224-3362
vegetable and flower seeds,
ornamental and fruit trees

ALBERTA NURSERY TRADES
ASSOCIATION
10215 176th Street
Edmonton, Alberta T5S 1M1

ALPENGLOW GARDENS
13328 King George Highway
North Surrey, British Columbia
  V3T 2T6
(604) 581-8733
rare alpines, dwarf conifers,
flowering shrubs

ATLANTIC PROVINCES
NURSERY TRADES
ASSOCIATION
Terra Nova Landscaping
130 Bluewater Road
Bedford, Nova Scotia
  B4A 1G7

BEAVERLODGE NURSERY LTD.
Box 127
Beaverlodge, Alberta
  T0H 0C0
(403) 354-2195
hardy plants suitable for
northern gardens

BRITISH COLUMBIA
NURSERY TRADE
ASSOCIATION
Suite #101A-15290 103A
  Avenue
Surrey, British Columbia
  V3R 7A2

JOHN CONNON
NURSERIES
Waterdown, Ontario
L0R 2H0
(414) 354-2195
general nursery stock

WILLIAM DAM SEEDS
Highway 8
West Flamborough, Ontario
  L0R 2K0
(416) 628-6641
*untreated vegetable and flower
seeds; Canadian and
European varieties*

H.M. EDDIE AND SONS
4100 SW Marine Drive
Vancouver, British Columbia
  V7V 1N6
(604) 261-3188
roses, general nursery stock

FLOWERS CANADA
219 Silver Creek Parkway
  North
Unit 29
Guelph, Ontario N1H 7K4

FLOWERS CANADA
251 Clark Street
Sherbrooke, Québec J1J 2N6

LANDSCAPE CANADA
1293 Matheson Boulevard
Mississauga, Ontario
  L4W 1R1

MANITOBA NURSERY AND
LANDSCAPE ASSOCIATION
104 Parkside Drive
Winnipeg, Manitoba R3J 3P8

NURSERY SOD GROWERS'
ASSOCIATION OF ONTARIO
Carlisle, Ontario L0R 1H0

RICHTERS
Goodwood, Ontario L0C 1A0
(416) 640-6677
*herb seeds, esp. basil,
gingseng seed*

SASKATCHEWAN NURSERY
TRADES ASSOCIATION
c/o Harrison's Garden Centre
Box 460
Carnduff, Saskatchewan
  S0C 0S0

SHERIDAN NURSERIES
700 Evans Avenue
Etobicoke, Ontario M9C 1A1
(416) 621-9111
Greenhedges
650 Montée de Liésse
Montréal, Québec H4T 1N8
(514) 744-2451
Glenpark
2827 Yonge Street
Toronto, Ontario M4M 2J4
(416) 481-6429
*perennials, roses, general
nursery stock*

WOODLAND NURSERIES
2151 Camilla Road
Mississauga, Ontario L5A 2K1
(416) 277-2961
rhododendrons, lilacs, azaleas

RETAIL NURSERIES:
UNITED KINGDOM

DAVID AUSTIN ROSES
Bowling Green Lane
Albrighton, near
  Wolverhampton
Salop
roses

WALTER BLOM AND SON
LTD.
Coomberlands Nurseries
Leavesden, Watford, Herts.
bulbs

BETH CHATTO GARDENS
White Barn House, Elmstead
  Market
near Colchester, Essex
unusual plants

T.R. HAYES AND SONS LTD.
Lakeland Nurseries
Ambleside, Cumbria
alpines, conifers

HIGHFIELD NURSERIES
Western Forestry Co. Ltd.
Whitminster, Gloucs.
shrubs, fruit trees

HILLIER NURSERIES
(WINCHESTER) LTD.
Ampfield House, Ampfield
Romsey, Hants.
shrubs

W.E.T. INGVERSEN LTD.
Birch Farm Nursery, Gravetye
East Grinstead, Sussex
alpines

JOHN MATTOCK LTD.
Nuneham Courtenay, Oxford
roses

NOTCUTTS GARDEN
Woodbridge, Suffolk
ornamental trees, shrubs

SCOTTS NURSERIES
Merriot, Somerset
general stock

WATERERS GARDEN CENTRE
The Nurseries, Bagshot,
  Surrey
water plants

PUBLIC GARDENS:
UNITED STATES

ARBORETUM OF THE
BARNES FOUNDATION
57 Lapsley Lane
Merion, PA 19006
*woody perennials of the
northern hemisphere*

ARNOLD ARBORETUM
The Arborway
Jamaica Plain, MA 02130
*comprehensive collection of
north temperate zone woody
plants*

BALBOA PARK
San Diego, CA 92101
palm arboretum, desert garden

BELLINGRATH GARDENS
Route 1
Box 60
Theodore, AL 36582

BILTMORE HOUSE AND
GARDENS
1 Biltmore Plaza
Asheville, NC 28803
*fruit trees, floral borders,
greenhouses, conservatory*

BROOKGREEN GARDENS
A Society for Southeastern
  Flora and Fauna
Murrell's Inlet, SC 29576
avenues of massive oaks, zoo

THE BROOKLYN BOTANIC
GARDEN
1000 Washington Avenue
Brooklyn, NY 11225
*remarkable Japanese gardens
and flowering cherry tree
collection*

BUSCH GARDENS
300 East Busch Boulevard
Tampa, FL 33162
*massed flower plantings,
tropical setting, wildlife
sanctuary*

CALLAWAY GARDENS
Pine Mountain, GA 31822
*thirteen lakes surrounded by
woodlands, azalea trail*

CASA AMESTI
c/o Monterey History of Art
   Association
Monterey, CA 93940
*formal Italianate gardens with
California touches*

CHANCE GARDENS
319 East Sneed Street
Centralia, MO 65240
*Oriental influences, wide
variety of flowers and shrubs*

CHESTERWOOD
c/o Administrator
P.O. Box 248
Stockbridge, MA 01262
*petunias, maidenhair ferns, fruit
trees*

CLFIVEDEN
c/o Administrator
6401 Germantown Avenue
Philadelphia, PA 19144
*Georgian-style homes,
azaleas, rhododendrons*

THE CLOISTERS
Fort Tryon Park
New York, NY 10040
*three authentic cloister gardens
harmonize with medieval
tapestries*

COLONIAL WILLIAMSBURG
P.O. Box B
Williamsburg, VA 23185
*characteristic plants of colonial
Virginia, 17th-century Dutch
school*

CYPRESS GARDENS
c/o Department of Leisure
   Services
Hampton Park
Charleston, SC 29403
*ornamentals, cypress-lined
waters, boat rides*

CYPRESS GARDENS
P.O. Box 1
Cypress Gardens, FL 33880
*exotic and native trees, 80-foot
ferns, boat rides*

DECATUR HOUSE
c/o Administrator
748 Jackson Place NW
Washington, DC 20006
*serene elm-shaded garden,
azaleas*

DESCANSO GARDENS
1418 Descanso Drive
La Canada, CA 91011
camellia-lined forest walks

DUKE GARDENS
c/o Duke Gardens
   Foundation, Inc.
Somerville, NJ 08876
*eleven exemplary gardens
under glass*

SARAH P. DUKE GARDENS
Duke University
Durham, NC 27706
*pine forests, formal and
informal gardens*

DUMBARTON OAKS
1703 32nd Street NW
Washington, DC 20007
*intricately landscaped
succession of room gardens*

AN EIGHTEENTH CENTURY
GARDEN
Independence National
   Historic Park
313 Walnut Street
Philadelphia, PA 19106
*intimate garden featuring
colorful display of annuals*

THE ELMS
Belleview Avenue
Newport, RI 02840
impressive sculpture gardens

FAIRCHILD TROPICAL
GARDEN
10901 Old Cutler Road
Miami, FL 33156
*paradisical growth of palms,
woody flowering plants*

FILOLI CENTER
Canada Road
Woodside, CA 94062
*harmonious blendings of formal
and naturalistic gardens*

FOUR ARTS GARDEN
Four Arts Plaza
Royal Palm Way
Palm Beach, FL 33480
*varied collection of tropical
plants, twelve theme gardens*

GARDEN IN THE WOODS
Hemenway Road
Framingham, MA 01701
*fifteen acres of wild flora
indigenous to the U.S.*

ISABELLA STEWART
GARDNER MUSEUM
280 Fenway
Boston, MA 02115
*formal gardens reminiscent of
Renaissance palazzo*

GREEN ANIMALS
c/o Preservation Society of
   Newport County
118 Mill Street
Newport, RI 02840
*foremost U.S. collection of
topiary shrub art*

GUNSTON HALL
Gunston Hall Plantation
Lorton, VA 22079
*18th-century colonial Virginia-
style garden*

HAMPTON NATIONAL
HISTORIC SITE
535 Hampton Lane
Towson, MD 21204
*formal garden with stately
native and exotic trees*

HERSHEY ROSE GARDENS
AND ARBORETUM
Hershey, PA 17033
*over 1,200 colorful varieties of
award-winning roses*

HUNTINGTON BOTANICAL
GARDENS
1151 Oxford Road
San Marino, CA 91108
*outstanding desert collection,
famous Shakespeare garden*

KINGWOOD CENTER
900 Park Avenue W
Mansfield, OH 44906
*formal gardens, bird sanctuary,
giant conifers*

LONGWOOD GARDENS
Kennett Square, PA 19348
*impressive fountains, rich
variety of flowering plants*

GARDEN OF LOS ANGELES
STATE AND COUNTY
ARBORETUM
301 North Baldwyn
Arcadia, CA 91006
*historical sections and
continental areas, orchids, vast
lagon*

LYNDHURST
c/o Administrator
635 South Broadway
Tarrytown, NY 10591
*native and exotic trees, fruit
trees, rockeries*

MAGNOLIA PLANTATION
AND GARDENS
Route 4
Charleston, SC 29407
*lake garden in plantation
setting, azaleas and camellias*

MIDDLETON PLACE
Route 4
Charleston, SC 29407
*oldest landscaped garden in
U.S., period gardens in water
setting*

MISSOURI BOTANICAL
GARDENS
4344 Shaw Avenue
St. Louis, MO 63110
*elaborate display of tropical
plants under geodesic dome*

MOHONK MOUNTAIN
HOUSE GARDENS
Mohonk Lake
New Paltz, NY 12561
*Victorian and naturalistic
garden styles, picturesque
nature walk*

MONTICELLO GARDENS
Charleston, SC 29401
*numerous tree varieties
including evergreens, poplars,
beeches; former home of
Thomas Jefferson*

MORRIS ARBORETUM
University of Pennsylvania
9414 Meadowbrook Avenue
Philadelphia, PA 19118
*ornamental plants of the Far
East, English landscape style*

NATIONAL ARBORETUM
United States National
  Arboretum
24th and R Streets NE
Washington, DC 20002
*National Herb Garden,
Historic Rose Garden, azaleas*

NAUMKEAG
Box 115
Stockbridge, MA 01262
*graceful transitions between
numerous theme gardens*

NEMOURS
c/o The Nemours Foundation
Reservations Office
P.O. Box 109
Wilmington, DE 19899
*fountain garden, acre-long
swimming pool, French 17th-
century design*

NEW YORK BOTANICAL
GARDEN
Bronx, NY 10458
*outstanding rock garden,
Haupt Conservatory*

NORTH CAROLINA
BOTANICAL GARDEN
University of North Carolina
Chapel Hill, Totten Center
  457 A
Chapel Hill, NC 27514
*famous outdoor display of
carnivorous plants*

OATLANDS
c/o Administrator
Route 2, Box 352
Leesburg, VA 22075
*formal gardens, magnolia
trees, bowling green*

ORTON PLANTATION
GARDENS
Winnabow, NC 28479
*former rice plantation
converted into lagoon setting*

OLD WESTBURY GARDENS
P.O. Box 420
Old Westbury, Long Island,
  NY 11568
*romantic pleasure gardens,
late 19th-century Victorian style*

PLANTATION GARDENS
Koloa, Kauai, HI 96756
*tropical setting yields exotic
flowers and unusual desert
plants*

PLANTING FIELDS
ARBORETUM
P.O. Box 58
Oyster Bay, Long Island, NY
  11771
*comprehensive ornamental
shrub collection, azaleas,
rhododendrons*

RENISCH ROSE GARDEN
AND DORAN ROCK
GARDEN
430 West 10th Street
Gage Park
Topeka, KS 66604
*300 rose varieties, Rock
Garden Lake*

REYNOLDA GARDENS
Wake Forest University
100 Reynolda Village
Winston-Salem, NC 27106
*conservatory, greenhouses,
woodland environment*

ROCK CITY GARDENS
1400 Patten Road
Lookout Mountain, TN 37350
*natural gardens in lovely
woodland setting*

GROUNDS OF STATE
CAPITOL AT SACRAMENTO
Between 10th and 15th
  Streets
Capitol Park
Sacramento, CA 95184
*outstanding ornamental
arboretum*

SAN DIEGO ZOOLOGICAL
GARDENS
P.O. Box 551
San Diego, CA 92112
*extensive collection of
succulents, cacti, erythrina;
over 300 species of palms*

SANTA BARBARA BOTANIC
GARDEN
1212 Mission Canyon Road
Santa Barbara, CA 93105
native California plants

MARIE SELBY TROPICAL
GARDENS
800 South Palm Avenue
Sarasota, FL 33577
*epiphytes, Spanish moss,
special collection of gesneriads*

SHADOWS-ON-THE-TECHE
c/o Administrator
P.O. Box 254
New Iberia, LA 70560
*stately oaks adorned with
Spanish moss*

SHERWOOD GARDENS
Baltimore, MD 21233
famous Dutch tulips

STERLING FOREST GARDENS
RR1 Sterling Lake Road
Tuxedo, NY 10987
*series of lakes and dazzling
theme gardens*

STRYBING ARBORETUM
AND BOTANICAL GARDENS
Golden Gate Park
9th Avenue and Lincoln Way
San Francisco, CA 94122
*over 5,000 labeled species,
succulent and conifer garden,
Moon-Viewing Garden,
demonstration gardens*

TRYON PALACE
RESTORATION
613 Pollack Street
New Bern, NC 28560
*swirling parterres and
serpentine hedges, English
landscape school*

TULSA MUNICIPAL ROSE
GARDEN
Woodward Park
1370 East 24th Place
Tulsa, OK 74120
*rose collection of 9,000
varieties*

UNIVERSITY OF CALIFORNIA
BOTANICAL GARDENS
University of California at
  Berkeley
Centennial Drive
Berkeley, CA 94720
*cacti, azaleas, orchids,
rhododendrons*

UNIVERSITY OF CALIFORNIA
SANTA CRUZ ARBORETUM
c/o Crown College
Santa Cruz, CA 95064
*fine collection of Australian and
South African plants*

VIZCAYA
3251 South Miami Avenue
Miami, FL 33129
*authentic Italian Renaissance-
style gardens*

ANNA SCRIPPS WHITCOMB
CONSERVATORY
Belle Isle Park
Detroit, MI 48207
*remarkable collection of fruit
and flower-bearing plants,
cactus collection*

WINTERTHUR MUSEUM
Reservations Office
Winterthur, DE 19735
*pinetum of rare conifers,
Spanish and Siberian
wildflowers*

WOODROW WILSON
HOUSE
c/o Administrator
2340 S Street NW
Washington, DC 20008
*fine example of early 20th-
century formal garden, former
home of 28th President*

WOODLAWN PLANTATION
c/o Administrator
Mount Vernon, VA 22121
*nature trails, naturalistic
English-style, Frank Lloyd
Wright home*

PUBLIC GARDENS: UNITED KINGDOM

BICTON GARDENS
Bicton, Devon

BLICKLING HALL
Blickling, Norfolk

BRANKLYN GARDENS
Perth, Perthshire

GREAT DIXTER
Northiam, Sussex

HASCOMBE COURT
Winkworth, Surrey

HATFIELD HOUSE
Hatfield, Herts.

HIDCOTE MANOR GARDEN
Mickleton, Gloucs.

KEW GARDENS
Kew, Greater London

LEVENS HALL
Levens, Cumbria

SAVILL & VALLEY GARDENS
Windsor, Berks.

SISSINGHURST CASTLE
GARDENS
Sissinghurst, Kent

SPRINGFIELD GARDEN
Spalding, Lincs.

STOURHEAD GARDEN
Stourhead, Wilts.

TRESCO ABBEY
Tresco, Scilly Isles

WISLEY GARDENS (R.H.S.)
Wisley, Surrey

PUBLIC GARDENS: CANADA

BUTCHARD GARDENS
Victoria, British Columbia

EDWARDS GARDENS
Toronto, Ontario

HUMBER ARBORETUM
Rexdale, Ontario
native trees and wildflowers

MONTRÉAL BOTANICAL
GARDEN
Montréal, Québec
succulents, ferns, alpine flowers

THE NIAGARA PARK
COMMISSION SCHOOL OF
HORTICULTURE
Niagara Falls, Ontario
regional and exotic trees

QUEEN ELIZABETH
GARDENS
Vancouver, British Columbia

ROYAL BOTANICAL
GARDENS
Hamilton, Ontario
many flower varieties

BIBLIOGRAPHY

UNITED STATES AND CANADA

Adams, William Howard. *The French Garden 1500-1800*. New York: George Braziller, 1979.

Ambasz, Emilio. *The Architecture of Luis Barragán*. New York: The Museum of Modern Art, 1976.

Bardi, P.M. *The Tropical Gardens of Burle Marx*. New York: Reinhold Publishing Corp., 1964.

Brookes, John. *The Small Garden*. New York: Macmillan Publishing Co., Inc., 1978.

Church, Thomas D., with Grace Hall and Michael Laurie. *Gardens are for People*, 2nd ed. New York: McGraw-Hill, 1983.

Cowell, F.R. *The Garden as a Fine Art*. New York: Houghton Mifflin, 1978.

Diekelman, John and Robert Schuster. *Natural Landscaping*. New York: McGraw-Hill, 1982.

Engel, David. *Japanese Gardens for Today*. Rutland, VT: Charles Tuttle, 1959.

Engel, David with Masanobu Kudo and Kiyoshi Seike. *A Japanese Touch for your Garden*. Tokyo: Kodansha International, 1980.

Fairbrother, Nan. *The Nature of Landscape Design*. New York: Alfred A. Knopf, 1974.

Gothein, Marie-Louise. *A History of Garden Art*. New York: Hacker Art Books, 1979.

Harvey, John. *Medieval Gardens*. Beavertown, OR: Timber Press, 1981.

Hayakawa, Masao. *The Garden Art of Japan*. New York: John Weatherhill, Ltd., 1973.

Jaskemski, Wilhelmina F. *The Gardens of Pompeii*. New Rochelle, NY: Caratzaz, 1979.

Jellicoe, Geoffrey and Susan. *The Landscape of Man*. New York: Van Nostrand Reinhold Company, Inc., 1982.

Johnson, Hugh, *The Principles of Gardening*. New York: Simon and Schuster, 1979.

Keswick, Maggie. *The Chinese Garden*. New York: Rizzoli, 1978.

Leighton, Ann. *American Gardens in the Eighteenth Century "For Use or Delight."* New York: Houghton Mifflin, 1976.

————. *Early American Gardens "For Meate or Medicine."* New York: Houghton Mifflin, 1970.

Morris, Edwin T. *The Gardens of China*. New York: Charles Scribner's Sons, 1983.

Newton, Norman T. *Design on the Land*. Cambridge, MA: Belknap Press of Harvard University, 1971.

Page, Russell. *The Education of a Gardener*. New York: Random House, 1983.

Perry, Frances. *The Water Garden*. New York: Van Nostrand Reinhold Company, Inc., 1981.

Prest, John. *The Garden of Eden: The Botanic Garden and the Re-Creation of Paradise*. New Haven, CT: Yale University Press, 1981.

Repton, Humphrey. *Fragments of the Theory and Practice of Landscape Gardening*. New York: Garland Publishing, 1982.

Schaarschmidt-Richter. *Japanese Gardens*. New York: William Morrow & Company, Inc., 1979.

Simonds, John O. *Earthscape: A Manual of Environmental Planning*. New York: McGraw-Hill, 1978.

————. *Landscape Architecture*. New York: McGraw-Hill, 1982.

Stoksand, Marilyn and Jerry Stannard. *Gardens of the Middle Ages*. Spencer Museum of Art, Lawrence, KS: University of Kansas Press, 1983.

Thacker, Christopher. *The History of Gardens*. Berkeley, CA: University of California Press, 1979.

Verey, Rosemary. *The Scented Garden*. New York: Van Nostrand Reinhold Company, Inc., 1981.

Watkin, David. *The English Vision*. New York: Harper & Row, 1982.

Wiebenson, Dora. *The Picturesque Garden in France*. Princeton, NJ: Princeton University Press, 1978.

UNITED KINGDOM

Boland, Maureen and Bridget. *Old Wives Lore For Gardeners*. London: Bodley Head, 1976.

Brookes, John. *Room Outside*. Harmondsworth: Penguin Books, 1969.

Chatto, Beth. *The Damp Garden*. London: Dent, 1982.

————. *The Dry Garden*. London: Dent, 1981.

Conran, Shirley, *The Magic Garden*. London: Macdonald, 1983.

Ellacombe, Canon. *In a Gloucestershire Garden*. London: Century, 1982.

Fleming, Laurence and Alan Gore. *The English Garden*. London: Michael Joseph, 1979.

Foster, Raymond. *Trees and Shrubs In Garden Design.* Newton Abbot, Devon: David & Charles, 1982.

Fox, Robin Lane. *Better Gardening.* London: Croom Helm, 1982.

Genders, Roy. *The Cottage Garden.* London: Pelham Books, Ltd., 1983.

Grey-Wilson, Christopher and Victoria Matthews. *Gardening On Walls.* London: Collins, 1983.

Harvey, John. *Medieval Gardens.* London: Batsford, 1983.

Hay, Roy. *Reader's Digest Encyclopeadia of Garden Plants and Flowers.* London: Reader's Digest, 1975.

————. *Reader's Digest Gardening Year.* London: Reader's Digest, 1976.

Hellyer, Arthur. *Illustrated Encyclopedia of Gardening.* London: Collingridge, 1982.

Hepper, Nigel. *Kew—Gardens For Science and Pleasure.* Norwich: HMSO, 1982.

Hobhouse, Penelope. *Gertrude Jekyll On Gardening.* London: Breslich & Foss, 1983.

————. *The Smaller Garden.* London: Collins, 1981.

Itoh, Teiji. *Space and Illusion in the Japanese Garden.* Weatherhill/Tankoska, 1973.

Jekyll, Gertrude. *Children and Gardens.* Woodbridge, Suffolk: Antique Collectors Club, 1982.

————. *Colour Schemes For the Flower Garden.* Woodbridge, Suffolk: Antique Collectors Club, 1982.

————. *Garden Ornament.* Woodbridge, Suffolk: Antique Collectors Club, 1982.

————. *A Gardener's Testament.* Woodbridge, Suffolk: Antique Collectors Club, 1982.

————. *Home and Garden.* Woodbridge, Suffolk: Antique Collectors Club, 1982.

————. *Roses For English Gardens.* Woodbridge, Suffolk: Antique Collectors Club, 1982.

Lees-Milne, Alvilde, and Verey, Rosemary. *The Englishman's Garden.* London: Allen Lane, 1983.

————. *The Englishwoman's Garden.* London: Chatto & Windus, 1980.

Lloyd, Christopher. *The Adventurous Gardener.* London: Allen Lane, 1983.

Lyte, Charles. *Sir Joseph Banks.* Newton Abbot, Devon: David & Charles, 1980.

Page, Russell. *Education of a Gardener.* London: Collins, 1971.

Painter, Gillian and Power, Elaine. *A Garden of Old Fashioned and Unusual Herbs.* London: Hodder & Stoughton, 1982.

Paterson, Allen. *History of the Rose.* London: Collins, 1983.

Phillips, C.E. Lucas and Barber, Peter. *Ornamental Shrubs.* London: Cassel, 1981.

Rose, Graham. *The Low Maintenance Garden.* Leicester: Windward, 1983.

Rothschild, Miriam and Clive Farrel. *The Butterfly Gardener.* London: Michael Joseph, 1983.

ROYAL HORTICULTURAL SOCIETY PUBLICATIONS: Bechtel, Helmut, Phillip Cribb and Edmund Launert. *The Manual of Cultivated Orchid Species.* Blandford Press, 1983.

Crowe, Dame Sylvia. *Garden Design.* Packard Press, 1983.

Dressler, Robert L. *The Orchids.* Harvard Press, 1983.

Green Pages: A Guide to Nurseries and Garden Centres in Great Britain. Granada Press, 1983.

Hinde, Thomas. *Stately Gardens of Great Britain.* Ebury Press, 1983.

Massingham, Betty, *Century of Gardeners.* Faber, 1983.

Rittershauser, B. & W., *Popular Orchids.* Rittershauser, 1983.

Sheehan, Tom and Marion. *Orchid Genera Illustrated.* Berkshire: Van Nostrand Reinhold, 1983.

Shigemori, Kanto. *The Japanese Courtyard Garden.* Oxford: Phaidon Press Ltd., 1983.

Sackville-West, Vita. *The Garden Book.* London: Michael Joseph, 1968.

Sanecki, Kay. *The Fragrant Garden.* London: Batsford, 1981.

Saville, Diana. *Walled Gardens.* London: Batsford, 1982.

Scott-James, Anne. *The Cottage Garden.* London: Allen Lane, 1981.

————. *Sissinghurst.* London: Michael Joseph, 1975.

Strong, Roy. *The Renaissance Garden In England.* London: Thames & Hudson, 1979.

Synge, Patrick. *Lillies.* London: Batsford, 1980.

Thomas, Graham Stuart. *Old Shrub Roses.* London: Dent, 1979.

————. *Perennial Garden Plants.* London: Dent, 1982.

————. *Trees In the Landscape.* London: Chatto & Windus, 1983.

INDEX

PICTURE CREDITS

Kate Bader: p. 86

Luis Barragan/Raul Ferrera: p. 170, 171

Pamela Burton: p. 176, 177 (l,r)

Karen Bussolini: p. 51, 54, 59, 68, 88, 98 (t,b), 99, 100 (bl), 106 (tl,bl), 110, 112 (t), 117 (r), 125 (br), 129 (tr), 157 (cr), 159 (t), 201, 202, 204, 206

A. E. Bye: p. 178 (l,r); 179 (l,r)

Gerald Carr: p. 39 (t,b)

Langdon Clay: p. 12–13, 35, 56, 62 (bl)

Susan Cohen: p. 38 (t,bl,br)

Ken Druse: p. 26

John E. Elsley: p. 40 (l,r), 156 (b), 157 (tc,cl), 208 (l,r), 209 (t,b)

Engel/GGP: p. 180, 181 (l,r)

Falcon & Bueno: p. 169, 182 (l,c,r), 183 (l,r)

Derek Fell: p. 11, 34, 37, 41, 42 (t,b), 43, 47, 48–49, 50, 53 (r), 55, 57 (tl,tr,bl,br), 58 (l,r), 62 (tl,tr,br), 70, 71 (tl,tc,tr), 73 (tr,br), 74, 75, 76, 77 (l,r), 78, 81 (bl,bc), 87 (bl), 90 (l,c,), 91, 92, 93 (tl,tr,br), 94 (b), 95, 96, 97 (t), 100 (tl,tr,br), 101, 103, 107, 109 (tl,tr), 111 (tl,tr), 113 (all), 114 (t,c,r), 115, 117 (l), 119 (bl,br), 124, 125 (tr), 126 (bl), 127, 129 (b), 131, 132, 133, 134 (bl,br), 135 (tl,tc), 136, 137 (t,b), 138, 139 (l,c,r), 140 (c,b), 141 (tl,tr,cr,bl,br), 142 (t,br), 143 (tl,tr), 144 (b), 145 (t,bl), 146–147, 147 (t), 148 (t), 149 (tl,tr,cl,bl), 151, 152 (l), 153 (t,c), 156 (c), 157 (tl,cc,bl,br), 159 (b), 163 (b), 186, 203 (r)

Richard Fish: p. 22 (bl,br), 23, 122 (br), 123

Felice Frankel: p. 147 (b), 153 (b)

Garden Design (magazine)/Panda: p. 190, 191 (t,b)

Courtesy of the Greek National Tourist Organization: p. 18, 19 (tl,tr)

Tom Haar: p. 24, 126 (br)

Jerry Harpur: p. 32, 33, 49 (r), 52, 61, 64, 65 (tr), 69, 72, 73 (bl), 79 (b), 85 (r), 87 (r), 97 (b), 108, 128, 129 (tl), 135 (tr), 144 (t), 145 (br), 150 (l,r), 152 (c), 155 (r), 194 (c), 203 (l)

Courtesy of the Frances Loeb Library, Graduate School of Design, Harvard University: p. 20 (t,b), 21, 28

Norman K. Johnson: p. 60, 63, 82, 118 (b), 121 (tr,br), 142 (bl), 143 (br), 174 (t,b), 175 (tl,tr,b)

Dana Levy: p. 66–67, 67 (br), 84 (bl), 134 (tr), 140 (t), 141 (cl)

Christopher Little: p. 30, 31, 104–105, 158

William B. Logan: p. 149 (cr)

Mark Lowe: p. 83, 89, 163 (t)

Michael McKinley: p. 45 (l,r), 53 (l), 65 (tl), 67 (tr), 79 (t), 84–85, 90 (r), 93 (bl), 106 (cl), 116, 119 (t), 120–121, 137 (c), 150 (c), 154, 155 (l), 157 (tr), 162, 167, 194 (l,c), 195

Courtesy of the Metropolitan Museum of Art: p. 16–17

The Nelson-Atkins Museum of Art, Kansas City, Missouri (Gift of the Herman R. and Helen Sutherland Foundation Fund): p. 25

Courtesy of the Philadelphia Museum of Art: p. 15

Nicholas Quennell: p. 29

Marlene Salon: p. 184, 185 (l,r)

Städelsches Kunstinstitute, Frankfurt am Main: p. 27

Curtice Taylor: p. 44 (t,b), 87 (tl), 196, 197 (tl,tr,bl,br)

Michael Van Valkenburgh: p. 156 (t), 164, 198 (l,r), 199

Phil Vinson: p. 187

Alan Ward: p. 161, 188, 189 (tl,tr,bl,br), 192 (tl,tr,b), 193

E. Wemple and Associates: p. 125 (l)

Josephine Zeitlin: p. 80 (l,r), 81 (br), 109 (br), 111 (b), 112 (b), 118 (t), 122 (br), 134 (tl), 148 (b), 148 (br), 152 (r), 157 (bc), 172 (l,r), 173 (t,b), 205, 207

KEY TO ILLUSTRATION CODES:
tl: top left; *tc*: top center; *tr*: top right;
cl: center left; *cc*: center center; *cr*: center right;
bl: bottom left; *bc*: bottom center; *br*: bottom right;
t: top; *c*: center; *b*: bottom; *l*: left; *r*: right